PRAISE FOR... RICH IS A STATE OF MIND

"This has been a wonderful education ... a must ... for everyone who does not have a sound investment program."
— Samy Chong, CEO, (

D0865184

"To me, *Rich is a State of Mind* means somethi
This is why the book is so powerful. Take from
and your family today, then come back to it down the road when your
circumstances need a new perspective. I use *Rich is a State of Mind* in
my practice because I believe in the financial planning process.
—Andrew B. Mayhew, cfp®, Mayhew Wealth Management

"This book teaches, not preaches, about the beauty of combining dreaming
and planning. It teaches about personal evolution, changing life circumstances and the practicality of financial planning. In short, it teaches you
how to not just plan your finances; it teaches you to live your life."
— Michelle Kowalchuck, HR.com

"This book will succeed in getting younger clients thinking about their
financial goals and what they must do to reach them. It also shows how
families can have discussions about money with their offspring in a
conversational and non-threatening manner. This book would be a must-
read for your clients' children as a way to educate them about financial
planning and goal setting."
— Deanne Gage, Advisor.ca

"Too often financial planning involves a delusional definition of wealth
defined by a dollar and cents figure. That is not the case with this book.
Rich is a State of Mind helps us to define wealth on our terms and using
that basis to begin creating a blueprint for our financial future"
—Philip Hauser, cfp®, Sterling Mutuals Inc.

"An engaging and easy-going look at planning one's financial future.
It combines information, strategy, philosophy and a touch of soul.
I highly recommend it."
— David B. Posen, M.D., author of *Always Change a Losing Game*

"This book is a great teaching tool for Financial Planners and a great
learning tool for clients. I recommend this book to everyone, and 'insist'
that they read the book before I decide to move forward with them.
— Michael W. Rice, Consultant, Investors Group

"The "story" format makes this an engaging read — not your typical "how-
to" financial book. *Rich is a State of Mind* turns an otherwise onerous subject (planning and arranging one's financial affairs) into an appealing and
understandable activity, using clear, straight forward explanations. Suitable
for all, from the "I know nothing's" to the "financially well-educated".
—Mark W. Winter, Family Investment Planning Inc.

PRAISE FOR... RICH IS A STATE OF MIND

"Rich is a State of Mind is a magical story on financial planning written from the perspective of a person whose priority is to live a full life. Most financial books provide "how to." This book shows how financial planning is a means to an end, not the end itself. This book is ideal reading for a client prior to meeting with their financial planner to prepare them for deeper discussions about their future."
— DAVID HANKALA, Insurance Agent, Sun Life Financial Inc.

"Rich is a State of Mind is a well-rounded exegesis of proven financial planning principles that, when applied, will get you a long way to accomplishing your goals. "
— STEPHEN GADSDEN, MSN.ca

"Rich is a State of Mind is a must read for everyone. Not only does this book help you realize your personal and financial potential, it also explains how to accomplish it.
— SNIGDHA MALIK, Branch Manager, Advent Financial Group

"While many chapters outline basic financial concepts, from risk management to wills, a considerable amount of space is dedicated to work-life balance, quality of life, and personal motivation issues. It's these concepts that set the book apart from others in this genre."
— KIRA VERMOND, *FORUM Magazine*

"Avoiding the dry language of finance texts, this book combines simple strategies with personal philosophy to engage and inform readers. Canadians will discover how creating a practical plan will benefit them for years to come."
— *Canadian Manager Magazine*

"If I can learn to understand compound interest, RRSPs, and seeing the parallels between financial planning and a hockey game—another subject I know nothing about—almost any reader can. And probably many potential readers should."
— E.E. CRAN, *Saint John Telegraph-Journal*

"Rich is a State of Mind is a gift that every financial advisor should be using to educate their clients about the fundamental tried and true principals of creating wealth. This book should be in every financial advisor's marketing toolbox.
—SIMON REILLY, President, Leading Advisor Inc.

RICH
is a state of mind

Building Wealth and Happiness — A Blueprint

by Robert M. Gignac

Live Richly!
Robert Gignac

This work has been carefully researched and verified for accuracy; however,
due to the complexity of the subject matter and the continual changes
occurring in the subject matter, the authors cannot be held responsible for
errors or omissions, or consequences of any actions resulting from information in this book. Examples discussed are intended as general guidelines
only. Fictional names and characters bearing any resemblance to real
persons or events is purely coincidental. The reader is urged to seek the
services of a competent and experienced professional should further
guidance in financial planning or income tax planning be required.

Library and Archives Canada Cataloguing in Publication

Gignac, Robert M.
   Rich is a state of mind : building wealth and happiness : a blueprint /
Robert M. Gignac. — Rev. and updated

Includes bibliographical references.
ISBN 978-0-9731849-1-4

   1. Finance, Personal—Canada. 2. Investments—Canada. 3. Estate planning—
Canada. I. Title.

HG179.G54 2009   332.024'01   C2008-906653-7

First Printing—August 2011
Second Printing—January 2013

Editor: *Catherine A. Leek, GreenOnionPublishing.com*
Page Design, Composition & Print Production: *WeMakeBooks.ca*
Cover Design: *John Lee/Scott Ion*
Cover Image: *Grant V. Faint/Getty Images*

Printed and bound in Canada

To Nadine,
for always reminding me
what "Rich" truly means

—RMG

TABLE OF CONTENTS

CHAPTER 7:
Who Else Would You Pay // 61

Making the decision to save is an easy concept for James and
Joyce, but learning to pay themselves first and sticking to the plan
may be easier said than done.

CHAPTER 8:
The Money Factory // 77

Explaining RRSPs as a money factory is a novel approach and
leads to further discussions of CPP, RRIFs, and annuities.

CHAPTER 9:
The Three Guarantees // 98

Revealing the influences on your wealth creation involves two of
the guarantees—inflation and taxation—which leads to discussions of interest, Canadian dividends and capital gains.

CHAPTER 10:
Getting a Bigger Stick // 113

Using leverage to make up for not starting to invest earlier in life
is an exciting prospect to James and Joyce until Richard and John
introduce some real life complications.

CHAPTER 11:
To RRSP or Not to RRSP? // 131

Continuing to explore the idea of leverage, the group compares
good and bad debt, discards the myths of leverage and discovers
the advantages of using RRSPs and leverage together.

CHAPTER 12:
Risky Business // 152

Risk—crisis or opportunity? Discover it is a combination of both
as the group discusses market timing, investor psychology and
the risk of outliving your savings.

CHAPTER 13:
Investment Allocation // 185

Discussing Asset Allocation, Diversification and Dollar Cost
Averaging answers James and Joyce's question of where to put the
money they are saving.

CHAPTER 14:
Creating the Game Plan // 211

> James and Joyce pull all the pieces together in a Game Plan and
> see that the strategy must be flexible enough to change with the
> situation—like the three periods in a hockey game.

CHAPTER 15:
Where There's a Will // 234

> Discussing the last few pieces of the puzzle without Richard is
> difficult at first, but the smaller group soon gets around to wills,
> insurance, powers of attorney and living wills.

CHAPTER 16:
The Legacy Lives On // 251

> John fulfills the promise he made to Richard in his final hours;
> James and Joyce are the fulfillment of Richard's promise to himself.

Epilogue: *Selecting a* Financial Planner // 262
A final word from John to help point you in the right direction to get
started with your financial blueprint.

Appendix A: *Resources for Financial Planning* // 267

Appendix B: *The TFSA—Tax Free Savings Account* // 269

ACKNOWLEDGEMENTS

While my name gets to be on the cover, there are many others who have played an integral role in getting this book to print. A simple 'thank you' wouldn't seem to be enough reward for the help provided, so perhaps seeing your names in print will be. A big 'thank you' to: Jane O'Donnell (for endless reading and feedback), Cathy Leek (for patience and editorial guidance), the staff at Heidy Lawrance & Associates (for layout and design), Scott Ion (for graphics and website), and to my 'draft' readers—Rick Denley, Janet Willan, Lucy Lovric, Sharron Parsons, John Yatabe and Carol Clarke—your early feedback was great encouragement.

My final thought belongs to Robert & Mary Gignac (also known as: Mom & Dad) — thank you for teaching me the value of money (even as I ignored the teaching from time to time…), your encouragement and love mean more to me than you know. Thank you!

—*RMG*

PREFACE

Why this book?

It's a valid question. In these dynamic and volatile times, it seems everyone wants the answer to the question, "What should I be doing about my personal finances?"

I had the same question over fifteen years ago and was fortunate to encounter a financial planner that not only helped me discover the answer, but also encouraged me to continue asking questions. To his dismay at times, I haven't stopped asking them.

"Creating a successful financial future is really just the repetitive application of basic principles." It was a comment I heard made a long time ago, which still applies today.

When I asked a couple of financial advisors for their thoughts about a book, they were adamant that I write from the perspective of the client instead of the planner. Good advice. As I've only ever been a client, and have no desire to be a planner, it's the only perspective from which I can write.

What I hope I have created is an entertaining book, providing the reader with solid, practical ideas to create a personal financial 'game plan' without all of the technical financial jargon. Yes, there are some graphs and charts, but they are intended only to illustrate, not intimidate. It's the dialogue that provides the lessons.

I hope you find it useful in helping to create your own successful financial future.

The Last Day
in the Life

There was never yet an uninteresting life. Such a thing is an impossibility. Inside of the dullest exterior there is a drama, a comedy, and a tragedy.
Mark Twain

"John, it's been a fascinating ride."

It was difficult to hear the raspy voice. A translucent plastic mask concealed the lower portion of a stubble-covered face, interfering with the attempts to speak. The gentle whisper of flowing oxygen reminded me to concentrate. "You will honour the promise right?"

"Yes, but I don't think …"

"Don't think—just do …"

Those were the last words uttered by Richard Jarvis, who after vocalizing them simply laid his head back on the hospital pillow—then all hell broke loose. Buzzers, alarms, 'code blue,' medical personnel buzzing about the room, my hasty and physically encouraged exit into the hallway. It didn't do much for my state of mind to know they were probably fighting a losing battle in that room. Richard had been in a dangerous position since he fell off a horse yesterday. The doctors had told me that closed head injuries are very dangerous and unpredictable. I had been here at his bedside since I got the call—that's what friends do for each other. I was both mildly amused and honoured to be listed as Richard's 'next of kin.'

"Mr. Linden—I'm very sorry." I rose and was facing a young intern, who stood uneasily before me. "There wasn't much we could do. You can go in if you like, please take all the time you need." I mouthed a silent thank you, but the words just wouldn't come out. I turned toward the open door.

The room was strangely silent, no machines beating their electronic rhythm. I looked at Richard lying there, as if asleep. Serene. Quiet. It might be seen as poetic justice that his passing was as understated as his life appeared to be—at first glance.

Richard Jarvis, born September 17, 1948, the middle of three children to David and Beth Jarvis, grew up in what might be called a 'post-war era' Canadian childhood. It wasn't until much later that the term 'boomer generation' was applied to this particular period. His home consisted of a stay-at-home mother, a blue-collar father, and a decidedly suburban middle-class upbringing. An average student in school, average athlete, average popularity among his peers, average height, average weight—in fact, the word 'average' seems like a good adjective to describe Richard's childhood.

Fortunately, as the people he cared about will soon find out, there was nothing average about the way he lived his adult life. Fun loving and adventure seeking, Richard approached life with enthusiasm.

We met almost 25 years ago—almost immediately after I opened my office. John Linden—Financial Planning. In fact, I think Richard would have been client number seven if I had actually assigned things like client numbers back then. I didn't have it all figured out on day one. Our advisor/client relationship grew into friendship over the years—regardless of where Richard happened to be in his life, or where I happened to be in mine; I could count on letters or post cards, phone calls and most recently e-mail.

I remember asking Richard about the rationale behind the choices he made in life. I always got the same three-word answer: "for the experience." He always said his goal was to create a rich, diverse collection of experiences. I'd say he obtained it, and then some.

Richard told me the first significant experience in his life occurred the day he kissed Patricia Evans in May 1967. Theirs was a whirlwind courtship, leading to their marriage in October. Ten months later, the second and far more significant event occurred. Both Patricia and their unborn child passed away due to complications during childbirth. Not surprisingly, he plunged into a deep depression, which unfortunately estranged him from his parents and siblings. It was a situation that was never fully resolved and certainly won't be now.

His urge to discover and experience life exploded in the mud and rain, on a piece of land known as Yasgur's Farm in Bethel, New York, on a weekend in August during the summer of 1969. It was perhaps 'the' seminal event for his generation and it was to profoundly change his life. The Woodstock

Music and Art Fair preached freedom, sharing, and the distrust of anyone over the age of 30.

Richard left Woodstock fundamentally changed, viewing life as something to be lived with passion and abandon—as there were in fact no guarantees. He felt a need to make an impact on the lives of others and he set out to acquire 'experiences' and try a variety of occupations.

Two months later, he was lying face down in the mud of a Vietnamese rice paddy, shooting with a camera instead of a gun. He became adept at capturing the human side of an otherwise inhuman endeavour. He managed to escape physically unscathed and upon his return vowed that he would experience Canada on a firsthand basis, as an antidote to the madness he had immersed himself in for 12 months. He moved from province to province, working his way across Canada, one province every year.

In 1981 he decided to settle back into his hometown, near his family, with the intent of rebuilding the severed family bonds, and to continue with his quest to make a difference in the lives of those around him. He taught photography at the community college, and was highly respected for his ability and style.

Richard even ventured into the restaurant business, owning and operating Dick's Diner—which he claimed was as happy a period in his life as any he had ever had. His decision to sell the diner coincided with the infamous stock market crash of 1987, the same market into which he had invested approximately $100,000 only 23 days before the market tanked. A cause for panic and depression in many, he viewed it merely as a learning experience—something to be gained not regretted.

He then undertook the project that made him the most proud. He purchased a small wooded lot outside of town and proceeded to build his own log cabin—from designing the building, cutting the timbers, acting as general contractor, to completing the final finishing touches. It was a warm, friendly place to relax, kick back and enjoy nature. Many of our best conversations took place under the canopy of pines on the sweeping front porch.

An impressive list of experiences to be sure, but they are just snapshots. The majority of his experiences and accomplishments went unnoticed by his family. The episode of depression aside, Richard was considered a loner by nature. He didn't see the need for maintaining close contact with people with whom he had little in common, especially when those same people didn't show the slightest interest in him. They in turn felt little need to keep in contact with someone who chose to live on the fringe of society.

But Richard didn't really live on the fringe—besides, what constitutes fringe these days? In fact, he was just an average guy who chose to live life on his own terms. In the narrow upbringing of his family, anyone who didn't work 50 weeks a year, marry by age 25, own a house in the suburbs and aspire to be middle class, middle management was someone who lived on the fringe.

I was suddenly aware of another presence in the room. The duty nurse went about her job with a quiet precision, making the final notes on Richard's chart, marking the time of death. The passing of another human being had been recorded. I left the room quietly, just steps ahead of her, and as she turned out the light in room 418—the real story was about to begin …

The Word
Gets Out

A man's family sets him apart from all other living creatures. Only man stands with his children from first to last, from birth to death, and to the grave.
Robert Nathan

The crisp stylish script etched on the glass doors of the office read "Bradley Jarvis Enterprises." It didn't tell you exactly what they did, but it certainly gave you the impression they were important.

Richard had never told me very much about Brad, other than he was a successful businessman, owned his own company, liked to be considered important, and always felt he should have really been somebody.

I stepped up to the reception desk, and in my best corporate voice stated, "May I see Brad Jarvis please?" I slid a business card toward her.

"I'm sorry, do you have an appointment?" was the brusque, official sounding reply, from the attractive brunette manning an oversized desk.

"Unfortunately, I don't."

"Mr. Jarvis doesn't see anyone without an appointment I'm afraid, Mr. Linden, but I would be happy to set one up for you. Let me see when he has some free time."

"Unfortunately Lisa, death rarely calls ahead for an appointment." I've always liked this line and it never failed to elicit the reaction that I knew was coming.

"Excuse me? What do you mean by death?" I certainly had her attention now.

"I'm here to see Mr. Jarvis about his brother Richard. He passed away this morning. It's not something I wanted to do over the phone."

"Are you sure you're in the right place? I've worked for Mr. Jarvis for almost a year now, I've certainly never heard a brother mentioned."

Apparently Richard was right—they weren't close—but even in families that I know that weren't close, they at least acknowledged each other's existence. I flipped open my portfolio and started to read, "Bradley Jarvis, born August 22nd, 1946, married to Samantha, father of Alan and Joyce, owner of Bradley Jarvis Enterprises located at 27 Strathmore Avenue, Suite 410, lives at 2108 Pineneedle Drive," I looked up from the page.

"You're in the right place," she said picking up the phone. Moments later I heard, "I know, yes I know … you asked not to be disturbed. There is a gentleman here, Mr. John Linden, who really does need to see you immediately. Yes, … now. "

Lisa hung up the phone with the sheepish look of a child who had just been scolded for disobeying. Brad appeared from the hallway behind Lisa's desk.

"Mr. Linden, is it?"

I stood to greet him, and extended a hand, which to my surprise wasn't met with mutual consent.

"Yes, John Linden, I'm a friend of Richard's—is there someplace we can talk in private—this is quite personal." Brad gave me the once-over, and apparently meeting his approval, we retreated to a side office off the lobby.

> **Unfortunately, death rarely calls ahead for an appointment.**

"I'm sorry Brad, we've never met and I'm not sure where to begin. I've never had to do this before."

"Ok,—let's start with why you are here." He leaned back on the table, extending his palms up in a sweeping gesture that at least seemed more welcoming than his opening approach. I guessed there would be no easy way around this.

"Richard passed away this morning at 10:34 a.m." I searched his face for some reaction—shock, dismay, or any suitable emotion. Finding none, I decided to continue. "He had asked me to tell his immediate family in person, not over the phone, that's why I'm here." I still can't say that I saw much emotion, but it was obvious he was searching for something, but unsure of what to say. I figured that I'd just stay quiet until he spoke.

"This certainly isn't what I expected to hear Mr. Linden." I wasn't sure if I should take that as a bad sign or not. "But I have to ask, how do you fit into this picture?"

"I am, well was, Richard's best friend, or at least a trusted one. We've known each other over 25 years. A long time ago we agreed to carry out each other's wishes in the event of this happening. I can't really say I thought I'd be doing it at this point in time. It hasn't sunk in yet for me either." A look of genuine concern swept over him as I finished speaking.

"How?"

"Basically, a head injury, brain swelling, after falling off a horse yesterday." The medical terms were escaping me at the moment; I was hoping that he wouldn't ask.

"I suppose that we'll need to make some arrangements of some sort unless you were entrusted with that as well." I couldn't get a good read on Brad, but I certainly sensed wishful thinking that I be the one—not him.

"I think there is a lot that you don't know about your brother. He was quite the planner, very well organized. He had arranged for all of this several years ago. I've already checked with the funeral home. The service will be on Friday at 11:00 a.m.—I trust you'll be there and you'll let Samantha, Alan and Joyce know." He seemed surprised that I knew the whole family without referring to any other material. "I need to go see Mary now. I know this comes as quite a shock Brad—I'm not sure I comprehend it yet. If you have any questions, you can contact me anytime, please don't hesitate to call."

Always treat all people with respect and politeness.

I extended a business card toward Brad—a plain card perhaps, but it had all of my relevant contact information. He took the card, examined it, and spun it around in both hands, as if trying to determine why I was really here.

"I'm sure we'll be talking before Friday," was the efficient businesslike reply. "Thank you for coming in person, I respect people who honour the commitments they have made." Brad extended a hand and with a firm handshake that signalled the end of our conversation we stepped back into the lobby.

"Thank you Lisa, have a nice day," I said as I exited via the etched glass doors. During our friendship I had learned many things from Richard; one was to treat people with respect and politeness.

Richard had never been very expressive when talking about his family, but it was obvious that he had a special place in his heart for Mary, his younger sister. That was going to make this much tougher than telling Brad, who seemed to take it with an almost businesslike, unemotional manner.

Late afternoon on an otherwise beautiful summer day found me pulling into the driveway of Daryl and Mary Thomas located at 171 Maple Street. It was approximately seven years ago they had moved into the home where Mary, Richard and Brad had grown up. Their father had passed away five years previously. When Mary and Daryl offered to move in to help her mom, it was a great fit. Unfortunately it lasted only 18 months before Beth passed away peacefully in her sleep. In the 25 plus years that I'd known Richard it was the only time that I'd seen him express any undue emotion. Beth's funeral was the last time Richard, Brad and Mary were all in the same place at the same time.

Mary was wrist deep in garden soil. Not wanting to sneak up on her, I called out "Hello Mary" from a distance as I approached.

"Oh, Hello. Can I help you?"

"Mary, my name is John Linden; I'm a friend of Richard's."

"Linden? Richard has mentioned you before; something about financial stuff, right?"

"While I am his financial advisor, I'd like to be thought of more as his friend, which makes what I'm about to say very difficult." Mary stood up quickly, dropping her garden implements—it was obvious she realized I wasn't here on a social call. "Richard passed away this morning at 10:34 a.m., I'm very sorry Mary. Many years ago Richard and I made a pact that we would notify each other's families personally. I've just come from Brad's office."

Unlike the cool, businesslike approach of her brother, tears streamed down Mary's face while she stood in disbelief on the manicured lawn. "How?" she mumbled.

"Injuries sustained from falling off a horse yesterday. He hit his head and they couldn't control the swelling. His request was that no life support be undertaken. I was with him this morning when it happened. I'm not sure what to say, this must come as a terrible shock."

"Richard must have thought very highly of you if he asked you to undertake this, which means that you probably know that we haven't been the closest family. Let's go sit in the backyard, there is more shade there." We walked in silence toward the backyard, in the middle of which was a majestic oak tree, the one Richard fell out of and broke his collarbone on his 18th birthday.

I was offered a seat on the cedar deck. As I sat surveying the immaculately kept lawn and gardens, I could almost envision a young Richard racing around the backyard, leaving havoc and laughter in his wake.

"So tell me about yourself John, you must have been close to Richard."

I told Mary the story of how we met almost 25 years ago and how our business relationship had grown into a close friendship.

"I imagine there might be a lot that you don't know about your brother Mary. He was quite a planner, extremely well organized; he had arrangements made to cover this eventuality several years ago. I've already checked with the funeral home and the service will be on Friday at 11:00 a.m.—I trust you'll be there and you'll let Daryl and your son, James, know. I know this comes as a major shock. If you have any questions, you can contact me anytime; please don't hesitate to call me." I extended my card to Mary. She slipped an arm around my shoulder, squeezing gently. "Thank you for coming John. We'll see you on Friday."

As I backed out of the driveway, the sun was still streaming through the trees, and I was beat. Sometimes you are prepared for what life throws at you—sometimes it catches you blindside. Today was the latter. My cell phone showed 17 new messages. Today was only Tuesday; I had much to accomplish before Friday.

> **He was quite a planner, extremely well organized; he had arrangements made to cover this final eventuality several years ago.**

Saying Goodbye
to a Friend

A man may die, nations may rise and fall, but an idea lives on. Ideas have endurance without death.
John F. Kennedy

Friday morning dawned with glorious sunshine and a cloudless blue sky. If you had to bid farewell to someone, it was better done on a day like today than under the sombre grey skies that seem to dominate funerals in the literature Richard enjoyed.

Stoddard Funeral Home and Chapel was the chosen location. I didn't choose it, Richard had. As with much of his life, all the details had been exceptionally well planned and paid for in advance; he could be pretty retentive that way. It certainly left me in a position not to have to be responsible for making too many decisions on his behalf once he was gone. Brad and Mary and their respective spouses were in the front hall as I came through the door.

"John, nice to see you again!" with the requisite pat on the back. Somehow I had been transformed into a friend and companion in the span of 72 hours. I wasn't sure how to take the change in attitude, but to accept it for what it was—a show of flash over substance. Mary's greeting was much more subtle, quiet and subdued and, to be honest, felt warmer and more genuine.

"Have you seen all of the flowers?" Mary whispered to me as she led me to the side, away from Brad. "Who are all these people?"

"Richard was very popular, well respected by those he came in contact with, and by his friends. You seem very surprised?"

"I … I … I just can't believe this, we always figured that Richard was more of the loner type."

Two people were quickly making their way across the room, heading directly for me. They looked enough alike to be brother and sister, but were cousins. Born less than a year apart, they were the 'next generation' as Richard liked to call them.

James Thomas and Joyce Jarvis, 22 and 21 respectively, were two of the brightest, most energetic 'kids' I'd met in a long time. We had first met in a park about a year ago—it was Richard's idea—and we had spent a lazy afternoon eating Richard's culinary creations and talking about the future.

"Hi John" spoken almost in unison, their voices both emotional and questioning at the same time. It drew a puzzled look from Brad, as James shook my hand firmly. Joyce chose a slight one-armed hug instead. It was obvious that Richard's entire family fell into the 'non-hugger' category of emotional display.

"Can you believe how many people are here?" Joyce asked.

"Mom and Dad can't believe this either," James added. "But I guess you aren't surprised."

"Yes and no. Not surprised by who's here. I'm still coming to grips with the fact that we are here at all." They quietly nodded their agreement. I was trying to maintain my best businesslike composure; the reality of what was about to transpire was just starting to hit me.

"We won't let our project die, will we?" James whispered with a hint of desperation in his voice.

"No, of course not!" Joyce whispered back.

"Yes, we will finish the project, no ifs, ands or buts, but there are things we need to talk about. For now, however, you'll have to excuse me—I need to attend to a couple of things. If we don't get to talk later today, come to my office on Tuesday—bring lunch—ok?"

Before I could comprehend what was really happening I was standing at the lectern at the front of the room to address the people gathered there. A healthy crowd to be sure—a cross section of old and young, business types and general folk. A tribute to the impact Richard had on the people around him. It was as good a time as any to start.

"I want to thank you for coming today; Richard would have been quite amused, and embarrassed by this outpouring of emotion. I'm not sure how to begin to say goodbye to someone who had such an impact not only on my life, but obviously also on those in this room. We are all here because he touched us in some manner, through his spirit, his laughter, but perhaps most of all by his ability to teach and encourage us. Richard had the ability to show us that there is more to life than we see and that we are capable of more than we can imagine. As you know, Richard considered himself to be a repository of useless information, well read, and the addition of the Internet to his arsenal of information sources made him hard to keep up with. Trends, demographics, inventions, business news, entertainment—Richard seemed to be on top of it all. Still, he always found the time for a casual chat on the front porch of the cabin. 'Learn to ask better questions John, better questions will get you better answers, better answers will increase your knowledge, increase your knowledge and you can go anywhere.' I have heard him speak these words many times, to many people. If you are hearing them for the first time today, take heed, you have just been given a lesson from a master.

"I was there, swatting at an army of mosquitoes, in the middle of five acres of white pine when he took a stick and drew a picture in the dirt of his idea for the ideal cabin. Not just the cabin, but also that he planned to build it himself, with the trees surrounding us. I can remember asking him many times during that project, 'Why are you doing this?' Invariably, like clockwork, the reply would issue forth, 'for the experience!' Followed of course by the trademark laugh that endeared him to us all.

The best reason to try something—*for the experience!*

"His laugh and his spirit are what I'll miss the most, and while I am not sure what the future brings, for now, it will simply be another experience for you, Richard. Given that, I guess it is really not goodbye, but only a 'we'll see you later …' Until then, my friend."

I had pretty much held my composure, but then the cracks started to show. I've never been prone to emotional displays, not that I dislike them, they just aren't part of me. I stood there with tears in my eyes, and then I retook my seat and listened as others got up to speak. There was a common theme that flowed through everyone—Richard had taught them to look at the world and the people around them differently, to see more than was there, and to do something with what you saw.

There was a lawyer who got up to talk about business Richard sent his way when he first opened his practice and clients were hard to come by. The owner of the local newsstand, where Richard purchased his magazines and newspapers, spoke of how Richard always took the time to ask him how he was doing, to get to know him, never just tossing the coins on the counter for the paper as countless others did.

Brad, Mary and I had decided there would be a small reception after the service, and everyone who wanted to join in was welcome to descend upon Bailey's—a quaint pub-style watering hole that was a favourite of Richard's.

Judging by the volume of the conversation, and the bustling of the servers, everyone was having a good time.

Brad and Mary spent most of their time with their spouses, seemingly in awe of what was unfolding around them. I think they were astounded to realize that Richard talked about them to other people, but they really knew little about Richard. I hoped, somewhat selfishly, they would realize what they had missed out on. It was a situation rectified in the last 12 months with the 'next generation,' but I'm getting ahead of myself.

Keep your eyes and ears open, you'll be surprised where learning can come from.

As the crowd dwindled, I spotted James and Joyce sitting across the room, talking with Alan, Joyce's brother, and Alex. They waved me over. I had only met Alan once, recently married to wife Alex, the parents of one-year-old Tamara. The entire marriage and parenthood scenario was new to both of them. I extended my hand as Alan rose, "Hi Alan, John Linden, nice to see you again."

"Nice to see you too. You said some nice things about Richard today. I wish I had the opportunity to spend time with him, I'm sure I could have learned something."

"Keep your eyes and ears open Alan, you'll be surprised where learning can come from ..." A tap on the shoulder distracted me; it was Brad with Mary standing to his left.

"Hi Brad, how are you holding up?"

"Good, thanks. Can we tear you away for a moment?"

The three of us walked over to a table laden with remnants of the afternoon's socializing. Mary was looking tentatively at me, so I aimed my comment in Brad's direction, "So, what's up?"

"Did Richard have a will?"

"You're kidding, right?"

"So you've learned nothing about our brother in the past three days Brad?" I was actually a little taken aback by the tone of Mary's voice.

"I wasn't trying to be rude John, and yes sis, I have learned a thing or three about Richard in the past three days. I was just trying to find out if John knows anything about it that he can share with us."

"Yes, Richard had a will. I have a copy of it in my files. The young lawyer who spoke this morning was the one who drafted it. It's current and valid, and, aside from some paperwork issues that remain to be taken care of, it is ready to be read and executed."

"When will that happen?"

"Brad! Have you no shame?" Mary turned and hit Brad with a stare that I'm glad wasn't directed at me. "We had a service today where the message clearly was about giving to others. Maybe you should have paid more attention—you'd be better for it."

"Don't go getting all emotional on us, Mary. I'm as sorry as you are that we are even having this discussion, but when it comes to death and dying, it's basically a business issue. Affairs have to be put in order, there are tasks to accomplish."

"A business issue?" The volume of Mary's voice attracted a couple of glances from those in close proximity. "Tasks to accomplish? Richard wasn't a business; he wasn't an item in the corporation you run. He was our brother. I feel confident that Richard entrusted John to take care of this for us— because he probably felt that we wouldn't have been bothered to do it ourselves." Mary was fighting back tears as she finished, and I jumped to her rescue.

"Ok. This has been an extremely emotional day, in fact, an emotional week. Today is Friday, let's take the weekend to spend time with our families, maybe reflect a little on everything that we've learned this week. We can meet on Monday, either by phone or at my office, whatever works best for everyone."

"I don't think the kids need to be involved do they?"

"Actually Mary they do, that was part of Richard's plan."

"Look, I have a full schedule on Monday, I'm out of town on Tuesday and Wednesday, we have everyone here now. Why can't we just do this today?" Brad was sitting on the edge of the table across from me.

"It's ok with me, if it is with everyone else. Mary?"

"Sure," with an exasperated sigh. "I'd hate to be an interruption in the Monday schedule."

Brad waved to the table where Alan, Alex, James and Joyce were having a rather animated discussion. They picked up their drinks and joined us.

"What's up, Dad?" in unison from Alan and Joyce. It must be a family trait.

"John has some information that he needs to share with us and I figured that since we're all here, there's no time like the present. Go ahead John."

I surveyed the faces of those around the table, and I felt like Richard had given me insights into everyone there. "As you have all learned in the past several days, we have all lost a special person. As you also know, Richard and I have been close friends for many years and he entrusted me with executing his plans in the event that we even had to have this discussion. Richard planned his life with a great deal of care and as such has a valid and executable will. All of you are requested to be at the reading of same. The location will be his cabin; the date will be Friday, September 14th at noon. I'll be sending each of you a registered letter to that effect just as a formality and a reminder, but please make whatever plans you need to in order to be there. Is everyone ok with that?"

I scanned the faces again, all of them looking at me. The looks that I was getting seemed to indicate that I had gotten the message across. As I expected, Brad took the lead.

"I'm left with the impression that Richard was a very diligent planner and very detail oriented, so I have to ask, is there any significance to the date, September 14th?"

I had to smile; maybe Brad was starting to get it after all.

"In fact there is—not so much with the date, but the timing. September 14th is 49 days from today. His notes to me were that the reading was to be held 49 days from the date of the funeral."

"What is so significant about 49 days?"

"Well, funny you should ask Joyce, because for yourself, James, Alan and Alex this will probably be a short history lesson. A long time ago, there was this guy named Max Yasgur who owned a farm in upstate New York …"

"Please don't tell me this is a Woodstock reference!" Brad seemed annoyed at the prospect.

"In fact it is, Brad. Richard felt that being at Woodstock was a pivotal moment for him. The last song that he heard before he left that weekend was "49 Bye-Byes" by Crosby, Stills, Nash and Young. It was a favourite of his and it

> **Discover what is important to you and then stick to your convictions.**

seems fitting that 49 days after the funeral the will should be read. He felt that would be an appropriate period of time to say goodbye. So, that's pretty much all I have to say for right now, unless there are any questions."

"How cool is that? Richard really did understand what was important to him, and he stuck to his convictions."

"Yes he did, James; it's a good lesson too."

I stood up to take my leave, shook the hands of the men, and gave a 'Jarvis Hug' to each of the women.

"Richard would have asked that we enjoy the weekend, don't dwell on what we lost, but on what we've gained, and how much there is still to learn. Ok?"

I caught the eyes of James and Joyce over my shoulder as I turned toward the door—I could tell from the look in their eyes that they got it.

3

The Genesis of
the Project

It takes half your life before you discover life is a do-it-yourself project.
Napoleon Hill

I don't actually remember the date, but I do remember it was a splendid early autumn day, just about noon—Richard had asked me to meet with him in Fleury Park overlooking the river. He said he had a big favour to ask. Big favour? The last time I did a big favour for Richard we both ended up at Woodstock '99.

Richard certainly wasn't hard to spot in the park—a grown man wearing a fluorescent yellow T-shirt usually isn't. He tossed me a Diet Coke from the cooler bag beside the bench and I noticed there was something resembling a picnic basket next to it. More than a little curious, I asked, "So what's up? You've invited me to a picnic?"

"I have a favour to ask of you John, remember?"

"Shoot."

"Remember our discussion some months back about James and Joyce?"

It had taken me a second, and then I clued in. We were sitting on the porch at his cabin and he was telling me that his two youngest relatives, his nephew James and niece Joyce, had recently contacted him. Impressed with their phone discussion he invited them out to see him at his cabin. Richard was intrigued by how they had even found their way to contact him—it was through a fluke opening of a trunk in Mary's attic. James had always been curious about their family and opening the trunk only raised more questions. One of the first items he pulled out of the trunk was a picture of Brad,

Mary and Richard sitting on an old tire swing hanging from the oak tree in the backyard of 171 Maple, where James now lived with his parents. He immediately recognized his Mom and Uncle Brad, but the other person was a mystery.

Curious to learn more, but not wanting to go directly to his parents, he went to the person with whom he had discussed his curiosity before, his cousin, Joyce. Joyce Jarvis, one year younger than James, a university student working on a business degree—she was equally intrigued by what James had found. It prompted her to do some of her own snooping through her dad's stored boxes and she turned up a letter with a phone number. Bingo! They had a point of contact.

Diligence paid off, and after a month of calling every couple of days, James and Joyce finally made contact with Richard. It was a rambling, lively conversation. To their surprise, Richard knew far more about them than they had suspected or counted on. Questions were flying back and forth when Richard said, "This phone stuff is nice, but why don't the two of you come out for a visit next Saturday?" Rapid agreement was obtained and the visit was set.

Richard had related that on the appointed day, Joyce pulled up in a Blue Onyx Pearl Lexus LS460 which he felt had to be his brother Brad's. They joined him on the sweeping porch, where Richard was sitting in the middle of the three rocking chairs, a fixture of the place. It was Richard's favourite place to relax, read and ponder the events of the day.

"Don't be afraid, I won't bite. Promise." Richard said with an amused smile.

Joyce was the first one up the flagstone walk and she greeted Richard with what I would come to call the 'Jarvis Hug.' Really a half-hug, half-handshake. It was an awkward greeting to be certain, but it seemed the entire family used it. James had used a more businesslike handshake approach.

"Yes, I remember, I remember you being very impressed with them."

"Indeed. I'm impressed. So much so that I've invited them here today to join us for a picnic. I'd like you to meet them. I've also got an idea."

The sly grin and glimmer in his eye meant that he had more than an idea. In the 25 years I'd known Richard I'd rarely known him to approach me with anything other than a well-developed plan, well-researched, critically thought out, and almost ready to implement.

"An idea, huh? This I have to hear—just what are you thinking?" Before he could answer, two blonde-haired streaks came to a screeching stop on the bike path about 30 feet away. Joyce was the first off her bike, a huge smile and she punched James playfully. Both were out of breath.

"See, wimp boy, never underestimate the female; once again I kick your sorry butt in a bike race."

"Yeah, yeah, you won that one, don't expect to win the race back—you can take that to the bank."

Competitive and good sports, I had yet to be officially introduced, but I already knew I'd like them. They walked their bikes over and dropped them gently on the grass. James extended a hand, "Nice to meet you Mr. Linden, I'm James Thomas. Uncle Richard has told us lots about you." I shot a quick, puzzled glance at Richard who just smiled and shrugged his shoulders.

"Well ok then, you should know that your Uncle Richard is prone to slightly exaggerate the truth, and before we go any further, I am 'John.' As for 'Uncle Richard' over there—you can call him whatever you please."

Richard, who was in the process of smoothing out a checkerboard blanket for what I was assuming was lunch, smiled at that suggestion and quickly responded with, "Richard would be just fine, thank you very much!" followed by his trademark laugh.

What is Rich? Can you answer the question?

We spent the next hour stuffing ourselves with food selections from the picnic basket, which seemed to have no end. Seems he really had learned a thing or two about food while running Dick's Diner.

Richard was laughing as he tossed me a bag of Oreo cookies—while I had Diet Coke as a personal vice, Richard had a weakness for Oreos and was in the process of trying to fit four into his mouth—a dare I had offered up—when Joyce calmly asked, "So Richard, are you rich?"

"Shut up! What kind of question is that?" exclaimed James.

Richard, to my surprise, didn't choke on the cookies he had stuffed in his mouth. He merely held up one finger in the classic 'give me a minute' gesture, chewed thoughtfully, took a long sip of coffee from his thermos and remarked, "Why do you ask, Joyce?"

"I'm sorry! I didn't mean to offend you. It's just that, it's—oh, forget it."

"Joyce, I'm certainly not offended, just curious. Besides, what does rich mean? Depending on your definition I could be very rich, rich, not so rich, perhaps even poor. Does it matter to you?"

"No. It really doesn't matter at all; I don't even care if you are or if you aren't, really. I guess I'm just confused that's all."

"I'll say you're confused. Richard I apologize on behalf of my dimwitted cousin, I'm sure …"

"No apologies, either on Joyce's behalf, or your own—especially when they aren't required. Let's see if we can get to the bottom of Joyce's confusion, shall we?"

Joyce seemed to regain her composure, as she continued, "It's just, well, I talked to Mom and Dad about our visit to the cabin and they asked what you were working at now—like you had no job. Then I thought about it and you have this great place, but you don't seem to have a job or haven't talked about one—and the only people I know who don't have jobs are either retired or rich, and since you are too young to be retired, then I guess I figured, well, you know."

"I admire the logic Joyce, and your fearlessness in asking the question. You'll come to discover that the inability to ask a question, either because you don't have one, or because you are unwilling to ask the one you have, can have major implications in life. But to answer the basics to your question—I don't know, and no, I don't have a job," he punctuated the word job. "At least not what either of your parents would consider a job."

Richard then explained to James and Joyce what I had come to admire him for; it was his problem solving business acumen that was prized. He simply called it common sense, but it was a way of looking at problems and issues that other people didn't or couldn't see. He claimed to have developed this talent after years of looking through a lens at a single object, but being able to keep the bigger picture in focus. It was a unique ability—to help people solve problems, and to teach other people how they could solve their own in the future—and that was what Richard did for a living. A full-time occupation? No, but it could be if he wanted it to. A rewarding one? Definitely. James and Joyce seemed intrigued by it all. Joyce from the business aspect since she had just finished her second year in a business program and had taken on a role in the accounting department of Bradley Jarvis Enterprises as her fall work term. James from the idea of not being tied to a full-time job, something that at the ripe old age of 22 he had come to see as a sign of submitting to 'the system' as he called it. It was perhaps one of the only ways that the two cousins were opposite in opinion.

> The inability to ask a question, either because you don't have one or because you are unwilling to ask, can have major implications in life.

"You know Joyce, you probably don't realize it, but your question has opened a huge avenue of thought, even larger than the one that brought us here today."

Joyce and James looked puzzled, first at each other, then at me. I had to admit, I probably looked a little puzzled myself. Richard and I had not managed to get around to discussing why we were here and his 'idea' before they arrived. I decided to venture forth, "Richard, aside from the fine grub and conversation, why *are* we all here today?"

"Friends, Romans, Countrymen, lend me your ears …"

"Argh! Not Shakespeare. Et tu Richard?" James rolled over as if stabbed in the back.

"Didn't I tell you these kids were bright John?"

"Kids!" a mutual exclamation.

"Look, I'm 53 years old, you're in your early 20s, like it or not you are kids. But trust me, I won't be treating you like kids unless you deserve to be—fair enough?"

"Well …" a mutually less-than enthusiastic reply.

"I asked John to come here today because I have a business proposal to make. The fact that you asked me if I was rich has only solidified my resolve to pursue it, but I'd like your help—all of you."

"Great. Let's do it, I'm in." James sat back up from his Shakespearean mock death pose.

"Should we perhaps not find out how deep the pool is before we dive in headfirst James? If enthusiasm was a university course, you'd still be there," Joyce arched an eyebrow as she finished.

"Richard, I've known you the longest of the bunch, which means I know that you have already thought this through. You know what you want from us, you know we're probably willing to buy in, but we do need to know something first—what are we buying into?"

"The question about 'rich' has been on my mind quite a bit lately, with many recurring themes—What is rich? Who is rich? How do you get rich? Can anyone get rich? Why do we want to be rich? Is rich a dollar value? Maybe rich is simply a state of mind? I believe I've learned a few things about the topic in my day, and from what I haven't learned I certainly have some opinions.

"What I am proposing is that we attempt to create a blueprint about wealth and finance, using the best of all our abilities. We have John, an excellent financial planner, capable of bridging theory and concepts. James provides us with a sense of passion and enthusiasm. Joyce brings a methodical approach based on her education. Me? I bring some actual life experiences and a desire to help people become more than they think they can be, or at least see that it is possible even if they choose not to pursue it. So, whaddya think?"

"A blueprint about finance? I'm not sure I understand what you mean Richard."

"You know, a blueprint, for building something, similar to this." With that Richard withdrew a long silver tube, from within which he removed several sheets of rolled up paper, quite weathered and dog-eared. "These are the original blueprints for the cabin, well, some of them at least. I like the concept of blueprints because at this level you get to see the structure, the pieces, the layout and you don't get bogged down in the mundane details."

> **A financial blueprint: clearly defined structure, assembly of all the pieces, defining your plan to create your financial future, but no fine details.**

James and Joyce were spreading the papers about, they seemed intrigued by the concept that the blueprints represented.

"So this is what the cabin was originally supposed to look like?"

"Yep. Some changes were made, obviously, some after the fact, some during construction. That again is why I like the blueprint concept—they are suggestions, recommendations, even guidelines if you will, for the structure I was building. They provide a great framework, but they don't bog you down in the details such as what brand of nails do I use? What colour are the walls going to be? Which type of shingle is going on the roof? My thoughts for this financial blueprint are very similar. It should clearly define what the structure looks like, how all the pieces fit together, what your plan or approach to creating your financial future should be, but not get bogged down in the details. Too many people set out to define their financial future and they immediately start obsessing over which stock, bond, or mutual fund to select, when the most important question is almost always—'What are you trying to accomplish?'"

Silence. From the puzzled looks we were all exchanging, I think we were a little confused by it all. Except for Richard of course, I could tell from his posture that he was enjoying this immensely, and he wasn't about to help us out. He was waiting for us to make the first move. Now was as good a time as any.

"So Richard, combined in all four of us you see the potential for creating a blueprint on wealth and finance when prior to this point in time, we have had zero experience in writing?"

"Right!"

"Right?" three incredulous replies.

"This will be a great experience, something we can play with and to be honest, I just might have an ulterior motive." The grin on his face certainly indicated to me that he did.

"Ah ha! The ulterior motive, now we are getting to the real crux of the idea. Stand back kids, you're about to discover that the why is often more important than the how."

"I'm glad to see that you've learned a thing or two over these 25 years, John," the grin was still there.

"Yeah, right. So cut the suspense—what's the why?"

"You're looking at two of them right here."

"Us?" the usual unison reply. "Why us?"

"Because I think you will listen, because I know you can learn, but mostly because it is time to give something back to our family. If we don't accomplish what we set out to, we won't have lost anything other than some time, and we'll all get to know each other better in the process. Not to mention that I'm sure we'll have some fun along the way. So? Whaddya think?"

"Cool. I'm in." James was first.

"Me too!" Joyce was second.

Three sets of eyes were on me, especially those of a close friend who was asking for a favour.

"Me three. I'm in!"

"So where do we begin Richard?" Joyce seemed eager to start.

"Oh sure, I have to be the spirit behind this project as well as the brains? I guess we're in big trouble team. But since you have asked I do have a suggestion. Why don't we meet on Thursday evening at 7 o'clock, John's office—dinner is on me. We'll see if we can toss around enough ideas to discover if we might be able to produce something useful. If we can't, we'll move on, and we all get dinner out of the process. Fair enough?"

The three of us looked at each other and shrugged our shoulders in unison. Joyce assumed the spokesperson role, "Fair enough."

Richard then pulled two of my business cards from the picnic basket and offered them to James and Joyce. "We start on Thursday evening—here's our first homework assignment."

"Homework? I'm not in school because of homework. You're kidding right?"

"I said this would be fun, I didn't say it wouldn't require any work. Besides, this is an easy one. Assignment number one—think about the following—What is rich? This will be a great jumping off point." Richard reached into the basket and pulled out four 5"×7" cards printed on both sides.

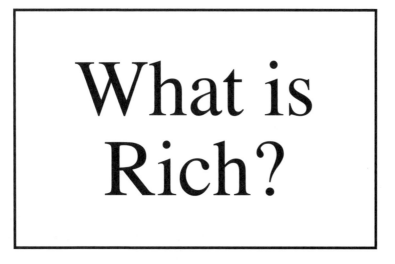

What is Rich?

"What do you mean—'What is Rich?' What about rich?"

"Anything you like James, bring a definition if possible, maybe some examples of what rich is or what rich means to you. Perhaps why people care or don't care about being rich."

"There are people who don't care about being rich?"

"Sure, lots of them, but that is because it means different things to different people. But that's a discussion for next time."

"But what about …"

"No buts, just give the topic some thought—no rules, no right or wrong. Just think about it. I have some things to attend to now, you'll have to excuse me," and he reached around the large picnic basket for a pair of roller blades that had been hidden from view. I never had asked him how he got there. We watched as he swapped his sneakers for blades, and we all stared in amusement as a middle-aged man in a fluorescent yellow T-shirt carrying a picnic basket in his left hand and cooler bag over his right shoulder bladed down the bike path and out of sight.

We were all silent for several minutes. Perhaps it was the events of the day, perhaps it was just the sunshine beating down, and we all seemed reflective and lost in our own thoughts. It was an interesting question— 'What is Rich?' It could mean just about anything.

4

What Does
Rich Mean?

Be studious in your profession, and you will be learned. Be industrious and frugal, and you will be rich.
Benjamin Franklin

Rain.

We could do without the rain. It had been raining for the past five days, almost non-stop and everyone had seen pretty much enough of it. I was watching drops snake their way down the floor-to-ceiling windows of my office, staring absentmindedly at the traffic crawling its way along outside. My thoughts of nothing were interrupted by the first of seven tones coming from the brass clock on the credenza behind my desk. The sixth tone had just sounded when Richard strode through my office door.

"Evening John, beautiful day isn't it?" Only Richard could see the beauty in five consecutive days of rain.

"Evening Richard. Yes, beautiful day if you're a duck."

"Don't be so cynical, last month you complained when it was over 30 degrees for seven days running, what do you want in your life, balance? Remember, one must live in the moment and enjoy what you have, as Joni Mitchell sang, 'you don't know what you've got 'til it's gone.'"

Richard swung a picnic basket onto the table by the window where I had been sitting. "No sign of the kids yet?"

"Not yet, weather probably. Traffic is a mess. Just look out there."

"Punctuality John, weather is no excuse for lack of punctuality," he was busy removing sandwiches, napkins, utensils, containers of salad and rolls. It looked like we were in for another feast. Finally he removed a large bag of Oreo cookies, opened it and popped one in his mouth. "Life can be short and unpredictable John, sometimes you should eat dessert first. As for the kids, you snooze, you lose. Let's dig in."

I created a heaping plate, but before I could take my first bite, Joyce's head popped into the doorway.

"Whew. I'm glad to see you guys; I thought I would never get here in this rain. Sorry I'm late," she was covered head to foot in a green nylon rain suit, carrying a waterproof backpack.

"Nice day for a ride?"

"Yes actually, got me here faster than driving if you can stand the dampness," she hung her dripping suit on the coat rack along with Richard's jacket. "You know, this rich concept is pretty fascinating. I had never really thought about it before, I was surprised to …"

"Hold that thought Joyce," Richard interrupted, "there are rules if you will. First we eat, then we work; second, we'll discuss the concept of time when your cousin gets here."

Joyce seemed taken aback to have her enthusiasm squashed, but didn't appear to be too offended by it. "Ok, eating it is," as she joined in with us at the table. We were all discussing the rain, as everyone seemed to these days, and we had been at it for about 25 minutes when I could hear a shuffling sound in the hallway.

"John? Richard? Anyone?" then suddenly James was in the doorway looking both dishevelled and bewildered. "Man, I'm glad to find you guys. I forgot John's card, I couldn't remember exactly where the office was, and I had to rely on my memory from last week. If I hadn't seen Joyce's bike locked up out front, I'd still be out there wandering in the rain."

"So glad you could join us James," Richard's tone was quite condescending, and carried the message across that he wasn't amused by his late arrival.

"Sorry Richard. Sorry John." he seemed to get the point.

"Grab some food James, the first rule is that we don't start working until we've eaten." Apparently Joyce was a natural born leader and wanted to get going. James didn't need any prompting; he piled a plate with abandon and joined in.

Twenty minutes later, Richard got up and made his way toward the wall opposite the windows. Several years ago in a stroke of self-determined genius, I had installed an entire wall of whiteboard—it offered a great place for creative doodling and for mapping out financial concepts for my clients. Grabbing a marker from the holder, Richard wrote the following:

1) Food, then work
2) Punctuality
3) What is Rich?

"Let me share some thoughts on how I like to work. First, I don't like to work hungry; I find it hard to think when you want to eat. Second, time is very important. I'm a fan of Ben Franklin, who so aptly said "time is money." If we are going to do this, we need to make a commitment to it and being punctual is how we honour each other in the process. I'll make the assumption that I won't have to bring it up again?"

James and Joyce looked at each other, then me. I didn't need to say anything; I had learned my lesson on time from Richard years ago.

"Got it," in unison.

"Ok, let's start. So what is rich? James?"

I could see where Richard was going with this. He already knew that Joyce was ready to talk; he wanted to see if James was equally committed to the process, and had done any preparation.

"Rich? Well, rich is having a lot of money."

"How much?"

"A lot. Like a million dollars."

"So a million dollars is a lot?"

"Isn't it? It sounds like it to me."

"Ok, so money makes you rich?"

"No, buying stuff with it, things you can use."

"Examples?"

"Cars. A house. Computers. Clothes. Stuff like that."

"Stuff? So, people with a lot of stuff are rich?"

"Sure, I guess."

"Your mom and dad have a lot of stuff, they have a house, two cars, a computer, furniture, clothes, appliances, etc. Are they rich?"

"No."

"So, define the word rich for me."

"Rich is having all the money or stuff you'd ever want or need. I think that is it."

"Any dissenting opinions? Joyce?"

While Richard and James had been volleying back and forth, I watched as Joyce had removed an orange spiral notebook from her backpack and I could see from where I was sitting that she had taped the card Richard had given us last week onto the top of the first page. The remainder of the page was covered in a neat stylish script.

"Well, the dictionary definition of rich would be as follows: Having abundant possessions and especially material wealth; having a high value or quality; magnificently impressive; vivid and deep in colour; synonyms are wealthy, affluent or opulent."

"Nice work keener!" James was slumping down in his seat.

"Yes. A nice technical definition Joyce, but what does it mean to you personally? How does it feel?"

"How does it feel? What do you mean by that?"

"Words are nice, they help us define things, categorize things, but to get to the true meaning of something you have to look at how it makes you feel."

"Yes, but aren't we getting ahead of ourselves?" I interjected.

"Ok John, how do you see rich?"

"I like Joyce's definition, but I know what you're getting at, we need to get under the surface of the definition, at what is beyond the face value."

"Exactly!"

"We can't look at it in terms of just money, but you can't ignore it either. What about family, friends and relationships?"

"Go on."

"For everyone it is going to be different, some don't desire material things, they want to be rich with time and the ability to spend that time with the people they love. Others want to travel to exotic locations they've only read about in magazines. I know a few who would be content to simply sit back and watch their money grow and never spend any."

The shift in the discussion seemed to be confusing James and Joyce, or that was certainly the expression they had on their faces. I was pretty sure that in their peer group they hadn't spent much time in theoretical discussions of the type that Richard and I thrived on. So while we were right at home here, I was afraid we might be losing them.

"I saw a definition of rich that talked about having more than enough to satisfy normal needs or desires," Joyce was flipping through her notebook as she talked. "Wealthy seemed to indicate the possession of property or valuable things, while affluent seemed to suggest ever increasing property and wealth, but they only talked about the money side or accumulation of things."

"Because that is all that is important Joyce," James was still slumped, not looking particularly interested.

"Ok James, I have an offer for you. I'll give you a cheque for one million dollars but it comes with a little string attached—your mom and dad are removed from your life forever. You're now rich, at least by your earlier definition, you have the million dollars you wanted. Money is the most important thing after all isn't it?"

"Nice try Richard, you can't write me a cheque for a million dollars."

"You really don't know if I can or if I can't—do you? We started this process a week ago when Joyce asked if I was rich. I never did say."

Richard had turned his chair around and straddled it facing the table. I could tell that he was beginning to enjoy this. Even James was getting re-engaged. I found it interesting what the mere mention of a million dollars could do for someone's attitude.

"Would you do it? Trade your relationship with your parents for a million dollars?"

"No."

"Why not?"

"Because they're my parents, that's why."

"But they aren't money. You said money was the most important thing, money makes you rich."

"This is stupid Richard, nobody would do that."

"Some might James, that's all I'm suggesting. Money makes people behave in strange and mysterious ways. It can be as powerful as a drug for some, and seem absolutely useless to others. John, you see this all the time, right?"

> I found it interesting what the mere mention of a million dollars could do for someone's attitude.

"All the time. One of the first questions I ask any prospective client is how they feel about money, what it means to them and what they know about it. For many it might be the first time anyone has asked them to think about money in that fashion. These feelings are important because they allow me to determine if there is any bias or prejudice about money, hidden fears, that sort of thing."

"So we are afraid of money?"

"Not so much afraid of money James, but afraid of what money means to us, the concept of money, of how money makes us act, and afraid that those who have more money than we do, don't deserve it as much as we would."

"John touched on an interesting topic a second ago—prejudice and fear about money. What did you mean John?"

"Money is perhaps the source of more anxiety than any other thing on earth. Wars have been fought over it. People have been killed for it. Most people worry about it. Others steal it. Money implies status, it determines where you can live, what brand of car you drive, where and what you eat for dinner, in fact even if you will be able to eat dinner, the clothes you wear and the people you associate with. That only begins to scratch the surface of why money is so complex."

> **Money makes people behave in strange and mysterious ways.**

"Most of my friends don't have any interest in money at all."

"There are two issues to that James. First, they probably don't need to at this point in their lives. If they are living at home like you are, money isn't an issue. The big things in life are taken care of for them, and since you make some money, you have almost complete control over all your income, which is mostly discretionary spending. Once you are out on your own, money will take on a much larger role. Second, they're lying to you. People who say that money doesn't interest them are typically the ones most afraid of the topic and they hope it will go away before they have to deal with it. You'll just have to trust me on that one."

Joyce, picking up on Richard's earlier use of the board, rose and wrote the following question beside his earlier note:

Why would people be afraid of money?

"Money inspires fear. We are afraid that we don't have enough, therefore we aren't successful. But conversely if we accumulate too much, people's opinions of us, and their demands on us, will change for the negative."

"People are afraid that having a lot of money is bad?"

"Not that it *is* bad James," he was certainly re-engaged in the conversation now, "but that people will perceive them as bad, unworthy, or undeserving. What did they do to deserve it? How did they *really* get it? Money is a taboo subject to the vast majority of people. Sex or politics is fine, but when it comes to money—mind your own business."

With that, Joyce was already writing in her notebook. She finished and looked at James who was looking back at her. "What?" she asked. James didn't say anything. She reached into her backpack, removed a second spiral notebook and slid it across the table along with a pen. "Now write that down will you? You might just learn something."

"Thanks cuz," a smile, perhaps more of a smirk, accompanied the reply. I was getting the impression that we had just witnessed part of an ongoing dynamic of their relationship. "Just put it on my tab, you know I'm good for it."

Richard rose to his feet, went over to the board and wrote:

Cash, Credit & Money

On the way back to his chair he remarked, "For future reference—carry on John."

"As I was saying, the concept of money inspires a great deal of self-doubt and guilt. We all feel we should be able to figure all this money stuff out, we should know how to deal with it, make some, save some, and when we can't or when we are overwhelmed, we shut down, drop the topic and hope it goes away. My personal opinion is that there are two major contributing factors to this problem—first, what we are taught by our own families and, second, what we are not taught by our school system."

> **Being children during the depression of the 1930s heavily influenced that generation.**

"That's right John. I think families can be a problem," Richard leaned back in his chair. "But not for ours, at least not anymore."

Joyce was puzzled. She alternated looks at Richard and me. She finally directed her questions to me, "Why are our families the problem? Don't families help each other?"

"They do Joyce, families help each other, but there are limits. Your family can't teach you what it doesn't already know. Let's take all of us as examples of this issue. My parents were typical of their generation, like your grandparents. Being children during the depression of the 1930s heavily influenced them. The biggest issue with money they had growing up was that so few had any. I can explain to you what they taught me about money in one sentence." I stood, moved over to the board.

Don't spend more than you earn!

"That's it?" in unison, in mock disbelief.

"That's it. You Richard?"

Richard rose and I tossed him the marker and he wrote beneath my writing:

Do not borrow money—Debt is bad
Save money for a Rainy Day

"You have to understand that before the late 1970s, early 1980s, the concepts of money and wealth creation were seen as some sort of right for the well-to-do. The rest of us didn't seem to have what it took to do much with money. People worked hard, saved a little where they could, they bought what they needed and that was pretty much it.

"Getting back to families—we were never really taught about money, our parents couldn't teach us what they didn't know. This model worked for them, so that's what they taught to us. And I'll assume for the moment that this is what your parents have taught you. Since so few people are ever taught about money in a clear and direct way, we end up operating with either confusing, contradictory or incomplete information. But the information is there, readily available, all we have to do is go get it."

"John and I have shared what we learned at home, it's your turn now, lead on James."

"I can't say that I got anything much different than that. Mom and dad are big on the saving for a rainy day part. They stressed that from the moment I got my first allowance. I remember them taking me to the bank to open my first savings account. I do know that they are concerned about money, at least that's the impression I get, but they never talk to me about it."

"Me too, but maybe it's different with dad owning his own company. I'm not saying that it's more important, but he always talks about finding ways to make more money. Mom rarely mentions money at all, except when her Visa bill is due, I guess I got the same lessons, except for the 'debt is bad' part. Mom and dad seem to be big fans of credit cards."

"You mentioned something about the school system earlier, John. Can I blame them for my lack of knowledge?" James had a huge grin on his face. "I'd love to be able to tell my mom that one."

"Sorry James. You can't blame the school system for your lack of knowledge but it is certainly an issue. For example, you are in second year university Joyce, give me a list of the courses you took last semester."

"Accounting, marketing, economics, organizational behaviour, French and sociology."

"That's an impressive workload, but why am I not surprised they aren't offering you any classes in personal finance? They are teaching you everything you need to know about how to keep track of the well-being of a company, but not how to do the same thing on a personal level. Just an observation."

"And a good one John, I think it highlights one of the issues that we were discussing earlier. Money is a very personal issue; traditionally schools leave it to be figured out at home. At home nobody seems prepared to face it or teach it. A classic catch-22. I suspect that my parents saved their financial discussions for their personal private moments, behind closed doors. I'd even hazard to guess that your parents will be surprised, dismayed, offended, shocked, or perhaps even afraid—choose your adjective—to know that you were here discussing the topic, am I right?"

> Money is a very personal issue. Traditionally schools leave it for home; at home nobody is prepared to face or teach it. A classic catch-22.

James and Joyce looked sheepishly at each other, then back at us. Richard told me he didn't think they would tell their parents about the meeting—seems he was quite an acute observer of human nature.

"That's ok. It's ok to tell them. It's ok to keep it to yourself. Money does tend to be that personal. I was thinking of childhood memories the other day and I was thinking about this meeting and came to the conclusion that I have zero memories of any discussion about money."

"But what does any of this have to do with being rich? I don't get it. All we've talked about is where we learned stuff, our parents, lessons, we haven't talked about how to make money at all."

"You're right, we haven't James. To your dismay, we probably won't tonight either. Not because it's not worth discussing, but because—it's getting late and we're running out of time. But I promise you, we will. Can you accept that?" James nodded.

"I think this has been a great start."

"A great start? But we haven't done anything. All we've done is talk." James' furrowed brow expressed his confusion.

"Yes, talking, sharing ideas, this is important stuff James. We'll come back to these feelings about money and the ideas we've shared again and again. This process is a repetitive thing, isn't it John?"

"Certainly. When I meet with clients and prospective clients, certain themes will come up over and over. We'll talk about an investment strategy or opportunity, six months will pass, they'll ask about it again, we'll discuss it again, a year will pass, the topic will come up again, then finally we might implement some variation of it, months after that. Why does it take so long? Sometimes they didn't understand it the first time. Perhaps I didn't explain it well enough. Perhaps they did understand and weren't ready. In any case, it is the continual re-examination of issues and topics, until the person is ready to receive the information and move forward."

"It's like school I guess," Joyce hesitated. "Sometimes a topic is presented that makes no sense, you see it again, it makes no sense, your friend sits down and explains it to you and wham! Everything falls into place and you wonder how you didn't get it the first time."

"Precisely my point Joyce, and Richard's as well. Learning is a process, a process of sharing, not just Richard and I lecturing you. When it comes to personal finance and money, people don't want to be lectured to, at least that is what I have learned. The best learning comes out of sharing information and having fun in the process. That is what I think this is all about."

"Ok, ok, feelings, sharing, I'll try to get a handle on that, but I have a question for you Richard."

"Fire away James."

"What is your definition of rich? You never did say."

Silence. The room was quiet, and I knew that was an indication that Richard was thinking about his answer. He wasn't one to simply blurt out the first thing that came to his mind and he didn't seem to mind that the three of us were all watching him. I don't know how long we sat in silence, I'm sure it wasn't much more than 15 seconds, but silence always seems longer than it really is. Without any further comment, he went over to the whiteboard and wrote:

Freedom

After doing so, and without saying anything, he returned to his chair and sat down, looking at us and grinning.

> **The best learning comes out of sharing information and having fun in the process.**

"That's it?"

"What more do you need James?"

"That is pretty cool, I like it." Joyce was writing it in her book.

"Freedom from what?" James asked.

"Not freedom from, although it could be looked at that way. Rich for me would simply be described as freedom. Freedom to not worry about personal finances, but it's not about some arbitrary amount of money. When I was taking pictures in Vietnam in the early 70s I met a peasant farmer who was raising a family of five in a one room, tin-sided hut, earning his living on a rice-paddy, making what might have been the equivalent of $100 a year. He considered himself to be wealthy; his sole concern was for the education of his children because he wanted more for them than he could provide. He explained to me how he felt wealthy. For him, being rich was the freedom to live the kind of life that was meaningful for him, to be surrounded by family and friends, not to worry about money and what it could or couldn't buy. I could hardly believe my ears, this wisdom was coming from someone living in a region where bombs dropped in from the sky on a daily basis. He seemed amused by my western notion of money, and the fear and anxiety it created. I remember his last words to me about the subject—it doesn't matter how much money you have, if you're worried about it, you aren't rich. That's why I think that being rich equates to freedom.

It doesn't matter how much money you have, if you're worried about it, you aren't rich.

"I guess that is why I have always been amused by people who expect money to make them happy. Money won't make you happy, even though the vast majority of people figure it will. Actually, they don't figure that it will, they 'expect' it to. After all, all the messages we are inundated with are intended to make us believe that money will make us happy. I'll offer up this small piece of wisdom for you to think about.

"If money is supposed to make us happy, why is nobody smiling? Here, take a look at these," Richard removed some bills from his wallet and passed them out to us, "and yes, I would like them back, thank you very much."

"The faces all look pretty serious, you're right. I guess I never thought about it that way." James had collected all of the bills and passed them back to Richard.

"Wouldn't you think if this stuff was supposed to make us happy they'd at least put better pictures on it? Something that might inspire us to make more of it, or at least amuse us with the amount that we did have? Perhaps, like this?" Richard removed another bill, from his shirt pocket this time, and passed it around.

Once the chuckling subsided, Richard continued. "So, as I was saying, I think this has been a great start, we've been talking for almost two hours and we've generated a few more questions—I call that success."

I'm pretty sure that James and Joyce were probably a little bewildered by that statement. For them, discussions were probably supposed to answer questions, not generate them. Richard felt that the only way to learn was to generate questions and he was very good at it.

"I think we'll wrap up for this evening, the rain has let up, the traffic has gone, should be easy to get home. How are we feeling?"

Silence. The kids were looking at each other for direction. I knew Richard would let the question sit in silence for a long time. I decided to save them the agony.

"Interesting. I think it has been very interesting. But I can't speak for everyone." I figured I would give them an easy opening.

"Confused mostly, I guess. I'm not sure what we are supposed to be doing here. Last week we talked about some sort of blueprint for creating wealth, tonight we hardly talked about that at all. All we talked about were families or abstract things. Is that part of it?"

"Yes James. It's a part, I might not have this all figured out, but what I think Richard and John are trying to do, and I could be wrong, is that you can't get to Point B on the map unless you already know you are at Point A. That's why John talked about bias and prejudices toward money, he wanted to see how we feel about all of this and what we already knew before we got here."

"Exactly the point. This meeting wasn't about the creation of the blue-print, and I hope everyone wasn't expecting to have it complete on day one. Even Rome wasn't built in a day. This was to find out if we have enough interest, ideas, desire or knowledge to pursue such a task. As for the surface of the concept we've only made a tiny scratch, but it's a good one. One I'd like to pursue, but I don't want to be the only one. I won't drag you along with me. Whaddya think gang?"

"I'm still game," Joyce was drawing a copy of the whiteboard in her notebook, "I think this could be a learning experience, and I'm not afraid to learn something new, you James?"

"Hmmm. Ok I guess. I'm just not so clear about the process, we spent a lot of time talking, but not much in creating anything."

"Ideas James, we're creating ideas. Joyce has the right thought in writing them down."

"Always the student, that's our Joyce in a nutshell."

"You'd do well to emulate a little, James."

"But I don't like school Richard, I never have. Probably because my mother was a teacher."

"You don't have to be in school to be a student. That is perhaps what you should take away from this evening. I wasn't much of a student either; I barely made it through high-school. There is a lot to learn here, and we are just scratching the surface, does that make you feel any better? There are no grades, no report cards, no grading on the bell curve, nothing to be afraid of."

"Ok. I can live with that," it was only the second time this evening that I'd seen an actual smile on his face.

"You John?"

"Hey, I'm in, where do we go from here?"

You don't have to be in school to be a student.

"I think we go here," with that he pulled out another set of four 5"× 7" cards. He handed one to each of us. The last one he kept for himself and spun it around in his hands.

"What is the goal?" James seemed dismayed once again. "What is the goal of what?"

"Try not to think so literally James. It is not 'what is the goal of what?' Simply, 'what is the goal?' The definition of what, if any at all, is up to you. This should make for an interesting discussion."

"What date? What time?" I was surprised to see Joyce tapping on a BlackBerry®—she certainly appeared keen.

What is the Goal?

"Three weeks today—that will give us time to think about today, time to think about 'the goal.' Same time, same place, if John is willing."

"Yes," I replied laughing, "thank you for asking."

"Three weeks it is!"

"Let's go then, we'll get out of Mr. Linden's hair for the time being. I'll drop you both off if you'd like, we'll just toss Joyce's bike in the truck if that's ok?"

"Great!" in unison.

In a flash, Richard had packed all his material into the picnic basket; Joyce's backpack was slung over one shoulder as she removed her now dry rain suit from the coat rack. James tagged along behind with his new note-book under one arm. I received an almost simultaneous "See you John!" from the three of them, then they disappeared down the hall, leaving me in silence.

I sat for a moment, looking at the whiteboard and the questions that were listed there. I wasn't quite sure where we were headed on this journey, but the thoughts listed there were as good a place as any to start. As I flipped the switch and plunged the office into darkness, I was already looking forward to our next meeting.

5

What Is The Goal?

People are not lazy. They simply have impotent goals—that is, goals that do not inspire them.
Anthony Robbins

Crisp.

It seems that every season has its own special descriptor; for this time of year it would be crisp. Fall was just beginning to take over from summer, the leaves were starting to turn, evening temperatures were dropping, daylight fading a little earlier every day.

I was pretty intrigued by the topic 'What is the goal?' that Richard had given us at the last session. It also caused me to dust off my personal goal sheet, one I probably hadn't reviewed in a year or so. I was surprised, pleasantly so, to see that while I had not accomplished everything on the list, I had made some significant progress in several areas. Other items were no longer relevant. I was distracted by two quick raps on the door behind me. It was James and Joyce, both with large grins on their faces.

"Knock, knock John, can we come in?"

"Is he here yet?" James was scanning the room, as if Richard might be hiding somewhere behind a door, or under the table.

"Nope. No sign of him yet. He'll be impressed. Come on in."

"I learned my lesson last time. Punctuality."

"I hope that wasn't the only thing you learned?"

"No. More interesting stuff happened, but we'll talk about that later. Aren't we supposed to eat before we work, I'm starving?"

I had to laugh, one meeting and Richard had seemed to turn the next generation into little disciples—well, perhaps that was an overstatement.

Certainly, it appeared he had an effect on them in the short time they had become acquainted.

"Those would be the rules, so let's eat." I would never accuse Richard of eavesdropping, but he somehow always managed to pick the exact right time to make his entrance. The now familiar picnic basket was swung onto the table, he flipped open the lid and announced, "Dig in all, dinner is served!"

We spent the next 30 minutes fulfilling the first rule of 'the project'— eat then work. A rapid-fire discussion of who had done what since our last session ensued; Joyce was both excited and disappointed with her work term at Bradley Jarvis. James had been doing some odd jobs and had picked up some work as a bike courier. Richard intimated that he'd be heading to Ottawa in the next week to do some work with an unnamed technology company. And me? I had been busy meeting with both existing and prospective clients. The first sign of fall brings everyone out of their mental summer vacation and is a great time to review plans and set up properly for the year-end financial planning cycle.

During a lull in the conversation, Richard had observed the board: What is the Goal? He seemed to take this as a good sign to start the discussion.

"Ok team, what is the goal? Anyone care to offer up a definition?"

"Pick me, pick me!"

"Ok James. What is the goal?"

James dropped his yellow notebook onto the table, flipped it open and taped to the top of the page was the green 5"× 7" index card from the last meeting. I considered the friendly rivalry between the two cousins was certainly behind this change in behaviour, but I'm sure that Richard's influence played some part as well. There were notes beneath it. I hoped that Richard was taking note of this.

"Goal, as defined by the dictionary, would be as follows: Goal, Function: Noun. The end toward which effort is directed, the terminal point in a race."

"Nice work keener!" Joyce had a huge grin on her face.

"Again, a nice technical definition, but …"

"But how does it make me feel?"

"Precisely, how does it make you feel?"

"Can I say that I'm not sure?"

"Sure."

"I think I understand the definition, goals are something you pursue, are working towards, but I'm not sure how I'm supposed to feel about them. How does it apply to my daily life? Is everything I do and attempt a goal?"

"In a manner of speaking—yes. You knew you had to be here tonight at 7:00. You made arrangements to be here, you found a way to get here, you looked up a definition, you gave it some thought. So in fact, you set some goals in order to be here. That's a good start James."

"Don't they usually mean something bigger than that? More than just getting to a meeting such as this?"

"Yes. But Joyce, to someone who may have previously had no goals at all, the setting and executing of something simple like that is an accomplishment. I'm not picking on you James; I'm only offering it up as an example. First you start small and work your way up. Would you like to offer any thoughts John?"

"Goals are important. They are like roadmaps which help us get from point A to point B, and they can act as mileposts along the way to ensure we are staying on course and on target."

"So I can claim that my going to a party this Saturday night is a goal?" James held up a high-five to Joyce, who just looked at him with a disappointed glance.

"No, not exactly. Joyce's point was a valid one; goals are usually a little bigger than that James. However, that action can be part of a larger goal. For example, your goal might be to develop a close circle of friends that you associate with and confide in. By going to the party on Saturday, you are building these friendships, interacting with those people and working on your larger goal."

> **Goals are like roadmaps which help us get from point A to point B, and they can act as mileposts along the way.**

"That doesn't seem so hard then, setting goals should be pretty easy. I set them for school and getting my assignments done. I also set them at work for projects that I have."

"True, but there can be a subtle difference and it will make all the difference in the world if you can master it."

"What's that?"

"Most people either have no goals at all or they stop setting them once they leave school. Your reference to goals in terms of assignments was correct, but look at them as smaller items—they are more like tasks, due dates, time targets, all very important. But let's pull back one level, we need to look at the bigger picture."

I had photocopied the year old goal sheet that I retrieved from my files; it was handwritten and had creases in it—it didn't make for great photocopies. However, I knew it would make the point. I passed copies to everyone and asked them to take a look. As I expected, Richard was the first to comment.

```
      GOALS - JOHN LINDEN

  - EXERCISE MINIMUM OF ONCE/WEEK
  - ADD 2 NEW CLIENTS PER MONTH
  - READ 1 NEW BOOK PER MONTH
  - GET PILOTS LICENCE
  - ATTAIN NET WORTH OF TWO MILLION DOLLARS
  - TAKE 3 WEEKS VACATION PER YEAR
  - CONTINUE TO BUILD/DEVELOP FRIENDSHIPS
  - PURCHASE NEW CAR
  - UPGRADE OFFICE COMPUTER
  - WRITE 2 ARTICLES FOR C.F.P. MAGAZINE
  - CALL MOM/DAD AT LEAST ONCE/MONTH
```

"Impressive John, I'm assuming the ones with lines drawn through are your completed goals?"

"Either they've been completed or they were dropped as no longer relevant at this time. I've redone them with relevant additions here." I handed out a second sheet, freshly created, printed today with the completed items removed.

"You wanted to be a pilot?" Joyce was comparing the handwritten and the typed versions.

"I did, I have for a long time. But at this point, it doesn't work for me as a goal anymore. Things do change."

"A net worth of two million dollars—that's my definition of rich."

"It might be James, remember from our last meeting that everyone's definition will be different."

"So why would people not set goals? That doesn't seem to make any sense. That would mean they wouldn't want to accomplish anything—no?" James asked.

"Not exactly," Richard jumped in before I could respond. "What we are trying to say is that by writing them down and developing a series of short-, mid- and long-term goals you've already taken the first step toward accomplishing them. Many people fear that once they write them down that they are stuck with them, as if they've carved them in stone. Somehow it eludes them that goals are flexible and change with the passage of time or with the completion of other items on the list. Even changes in technology create new or revised goals. Ten years ago I didn't have a digital satellite receiver in my long-range goals—they hadn't been developed yet. I had mine installed last month. Things change."

> **Goals are flexible and change with the passage of time or with the completion of other items on your list.**

"Short-term? Mid-term? Long-term? Schmong-term? How many goals do we actually need? Why all these terms? Can't you just have goals and leave them at that?"

"The idea, James, is to make the process more manageable and easier to focus on. Short-term goals are things you focus on in the present, perhaps a three to 12-month window. I realize when you are 22 that a 12-month period of time seems like an eternity—but it's not. Saving for a new bike you have your eye on, Joyce focusing on a 4.0 GPA for next semester, my wanting to speak to all of my clients personally before Christmas. These are all short-term goals. Consider making a goal for saving money—starting at $20 a week, or $100 per month would be a great short-term goal.

"Your mid-term goals move your horizon out a little further, things you focus on in a two to five year timeframe. For Joyce, graduating from university, for me building my business to the point where I can hire another administrative assistant, for Richard, well … Richard?"

"Mid-range, as I prefer that term, for me would be things like planning an around the world cruise vacation, bringing in some younger talent to help run my business, looking for a property to purchase in Alaska for fly-fishing vacations, but I suspect that none of these will be complete in the next three years. That doesn't make them any less important."

Richard's comments seemed to leave James and Joyce in wide-eyed wonderment. Perhaps they had never heard their parents and friends talk of plans and goals of that nature. Perhaps it was that Richard simply rhymed them off with a matter-of-fact tone that told you these were things he was going to do, not merely things he wished he might be able to do. Goals are things you *plan* on accomplishing.

I continued, "Finally, long-term goals can go out as far as five, ten, 15 even 20 years or more. In the case of people your age, that isn't too long a window to look at. The sky is the limit here for you in terms of long range planning. People plan their retirements as long-range goals, raising families, travel, building trusts to help worthy causes. I prefer to see people dream a little bit at this level, be creative, the pictures will become clearer as the process starts and as your time frame changes. Most people never bother to take the time to put a pen on paper and begin. If you do much reading about goal setting, you'll no doubt encounter a famous study about the Harvard class of 1954. Some say it's a myth, others a fact, in reality it's a good lesson. As part of their class exercise, they were asked who among them had written down on a piece of paper the things/goals they hoped to accomplish in their lives. Of the respondents, only 2% had taken the time or had the inclination to specifically and clearly record their goals in writing. Twenty years later, in order to validate the study, the same group of people were contacted. Those individuals who were in the 2%, who had clearly defined, written goals, had amassed more wealth than the remaining 98% combined! Probably just a coincidence, right John?"

"The thing that I find interesting about goals is how few people have them well defined. When I meet with a prospective client, one of the first things I am interested in is what their goals are, where do they want to be one, five, ten or 20 years down the road. Of course, the timing is all relative to the age of the people I meet with, but there is no limitation on the setting of goals at any age in life. Your parents have—or should have—goals. I know that your grandparents had goals as well. Keep in mind that there is much more to life than just financial goals; don't let anyone suggest those are the only type. That said, for many people they will be combined together because their other goals may require a specific income or asset accumulation in order to accomplish them."

"Like being rich?" James was grinning.

"Rich is not a goal." His grin suddenly disappeared. "Because rich is not definable and will mean something different to all of us. If you asked 20 people, I'm sure you'd get more than 20 different definitions of what it means, even if all you asked for was a dollar value. There are people for whom $250,000 would be rich beyond belief, others for whom 20 times that amount wouldn't even qualify. It's all very subjective. That doesn't mean you can't make rich a goal, all you have to do is be able to define it."

That said, I walked over to the white board and wrote the following in a vertical line, leaving some space between each one.

S—Specific
M—Measurable
A—Achievable
R—Realistic
T—Time Based

"I don't lay claim to inventing this process, but it's not a bad way to look at goals—that to be a well-defined goal requires it to be SMART if you will." It made me feel good to see all of them, including Richard, writing in their respective books.

"S is for Specific. If you want a goal to be a good one it has to be specific. I want to be rich. I want a lot of money. These aren't goals, they're simply statements. How much? Define it. People don't want to do that because they're afraid that others will pass judgment. You want too much. You don't want enough. Why do you want that? It's a psychological thing. When you deal with finance as I do, I try to explain to people that you can't do math on *big*, *lots* or *more*. You want to have more money? Great. More than what? Not all goals are financial; your most important goals in life probably won't be. You'll have goals for family matters, friends, travel, learning and perhaps your own physical and spiritual development. Anything that matters to you, that you want to achieve. Does that make sense?" Nods from all.

"M is for Measurable. Now before you bring it up, there are some things that are just not measurable, or no definitive measurement is available. You could in that case substitute the word 'assessable.' Let's assume your goal is to accumulate a million dollars in assets. Measurement would be your yardstick. If all you have is money in the bank, measurement is easy; your bank statement will show you that. If you have a mix of bank accounts, mutual funds, stocks, bonds, a house, and pieces of collectable art—it's more difficult. Getting a relevant measure then is more subjective. Things such as art or real estate can fluctuate or be based on emotional aspects. Just keep in mind that measuring is how we determine if we are making progress toward a goal.

> **To have well-defined goals, requires them to be SMART.**

"A is for Achievable. People will not pursue a goal for very long if it is not credible and there is no hope of achieving it. We'll see how this fits in a moment. We can amaze ourselves at how often or regularly we can learn new things in a short period of time. Some people like to substitute 'aggressive' for 'achievable'—that's fine with me. Aggressive goals require you to stretch, stretching is good, but setting yourself up for failure is not. The fear of failure is a major reason why people fail to set goals in the first place.

"R is for Realistic. There has to be a sense of realism to the goals that are being set or you are setting yourself up to fail. Getting back to our one million dollar example that could be a very realistic goal for you and that will become obvious when we discuss actions in the future. But, if we say that the timeframe is only three years—it becomes much less realistic, which leads to the last letter.

"T is for Time-based. You can have goals that are open ended, but they can be difficult to quantify. T answers the question—by when? If you choose not to apply a timeframe then we can say that the goal is less serious, applying a timeframe makes it a goal and not simply a wish."

I was expecting at least some glassy-eyed feedback from James and Joyce, but I didn't see any. They both seemed to be in tune with what I had to say. Richard rose and joined me at the board, grabbed a pen from the holder and started drawing:

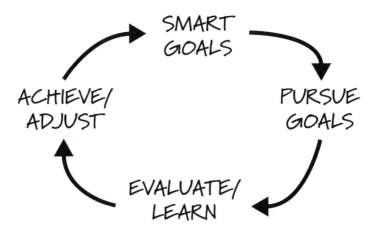

"John gave you the words, I'll draw you a picture instead. The process is a flow; the first step is to set the goals using the SMART criteria. Second, we go off and pursue them, doing whatever activities need to be done to make them a reality. At some point we take a break, visit what we have accomplished and map it against what we set as our goals. What did we learn? How are we doing? Once we know where we are, we can cross off what we have accomplished or make adjustments to goals if required. We then generate new ones to either replace the completed goals or to augment the remaining goals and the cycle starts all over again. With apologies in advance to the legal team at Disney, this just might be called the 'Circle of Life,' in a manner of speaking."

"Ok, I get this, well—I think I get this," James was looking puzzled, not glassy-eyed, just puzzled. "But to reiterate Joyce's earlier point—why don't more people do this John?"

"My personal bias is that people don't understand that there is no such thing as a right or wrong goal. The fear of failure keeps them from writing them down. They feel if they tell someone what their goals are and they don't attain them, then somehow they have failed. It's not a failure to attempt to do something and not achieve it; the failure comes in not making the attempt in the first place. When I opened my practice 25 years ago I didn't immediately start writing down all my goals, it took me some time to develop the habit. Once I realized that you only get out of anything what you put into it, I determined I needed to apply myself more and I needed to measure what I was doing. Once I got the hang of it, the more I was willing to work on it, the easier it became. If you want to keep things focused and this is new to you, create your goal list and put it in a prominent location, somewhere you will see it every day. Also keep in mind that it takes some effort, just because you create goals on paper doesn't mean you'll accomplish them all. But don't kid yourself—it takes work. Too many people associate the word 'work' with the word 'hard' and, to be frank, that is what stops people from beginning the process. Achieving goals can be an extremely fun and rewarding process, not to mention financially valuable."

> It's not a failure to attempt to do something and not achieve it; the failure comes in not making the attempt in the first place.

There was a momentary pause in which we were all silent. James and Joyce had a fair amount of new information tossed at them, and while they seemed to be coping with it well, both were making notes in their respective books, James drawing pictures, Joyce writing words. Richard broke the silence.

"Just because we've been using financial examples don't let that fool you into thinking that all goals have to be financial—some of your most important life goals won't be. But to make sure we get to apply some of what we've learned this evening let's try this exercise. Our goal, pardon the pun, for the next meeting is to create a list of five new goals for ourselves. Any topic or subject, they don't have to be financial, but let's see what we come up with. We'll share them with each other at the next session.

"But that's not all, we have something else to consider as well," Richard produced another four 5"× 7" cards. Again it was another question for us to consider.

"Speaking of our next meeting, when should we meet?" Joyce certainly appeared keen—this was good. I was hoping James would feel the same way.

"What date? What time?" At the last meeting I was surprised to see Joyce with a BlackBerry®, this time James had a small pocket calendar in his hands—not as technical as his cousin, but he was certainly making an effort.

What is the 8th Wonder of the World?

"How about Saturday, October 28th? Just about three weeks from today. That will give us time to think about our goals and some time to ponder the wonders of the world. Given it's a Saturday, let's try something different. Why don't we start at 7:30?"

"In the morning?" I'm sure that my facial expression showed certain dismay at the thought of starting that early. Richard was quite aware that I'm not a morning person.

"Is that a problem John?" Richard smiled.

"I guess that all depends on the night before," James was moving his shoulders in a circular, dancing motion.

"You can't learn anything while you're sleeping," I was a little surprised that Joyce was taking the opportunity to pick on us. That was Richard's job.

"Excellent point Joyce. Besides, if we start early, we finish early—and you can always take an afternoon nap."

"Well … ok," James and I added almost in unison, but sounding much less than convinced.

"Same place? I like having your whiteboard to scribble on. Assuming of course that it's ok with you John?"

"Sure, since I'll be up anyway," I replied laughing.

Richard quickly packed his material into the picnic basket; Joyce's backpack was slung over one shoulder; James tucked his notebook under one arm. A simultaneous "See you John!" from the three of them, then they disappeared down the hallway together, leaving me in silence. I was looking at the diagram Richard had drawn, thinking about how things run in cycles, and how time continued to move forward. As I flipped the light switch and darkened my office—I was wondering what would be next.

6

World of Wonders

All human power is a compound of time and patience.
Honore de Balzac

Fog.

I was pondering the fog as I drove into the office. Fog tends to shroud everything, putting a softer edge on the world, obscuring the imperfections from view. I guess that was one of the reasons I liked fog, except when it came to driving. Traffic was light, as it should be for this day and time. We had decided to meet on a Saturday at our previous meeting to try a different day; it was for the experience after all.

I had spent some time the past few days surfing around the Internet, looking at wonders of the ancient world, modern world, medical world, and many other things that people called wonders. This search was in order to answer the question for today's session, although I was pretty sure that what Richard had in mind had little to do with the wonders of the world that most people talked about.

A single tone from my clock indicated that it was quarter past the hour, the hour of 7:00 a.m. to be exact. I was caught off-guard when I turned to see both James and Joyce in the doorway.

"Hope you don't mind that I dragged James in, he was trying to be mysterious, hanging around your doorway in the fog."

"No," laughing, "but I didn't see you, when did you get here?"

"About ten minutes ago, I flew down by bike, the streets are empty at this time of day—I felt like I was cycling up the Champs-Elysees during the final stage of the Tour de France. Very energizing."

"A goal? Could that be a goal James?"

"Maybe. Maybe not. You'll have to wait and see."

"Either way, nice to see you thinking about them."

"Very nice, I'm always glad to see people thinking. You always have the opportunity to refine it later. You could even change your goal to be winning the race if that was important to you James."

I'm never sure how Richard does this magical appear and disappear act, but he seldom fails to show up at anything other than the exact right time to flow directly into a conversation. This morning was no exception.

"Good morning all, sorry I'm late."

I stole a glance at my clock; it was now 7:27 a.m.

"Late? Three minutes early isn't exactly late in my book."

"Just remember John, the person with the idea should never show up last, that's all."

Richard was already on his way over to the table to deposit breakfast. He was carrying a large takeout tray from his favourite diner.

"Dig in all. I've got a Diet Coke for John, coffee for me. I believe you prefer tea Joyce. Hot chocolate for James. In addition to a selection of stuff that we probably shouldn't eat for breakfast but was much too appetizing to pass up."

A box emerged from the bag and Richard opened it to reveal donuts, muffins and pastries—probably enough to feed eight. Not surprisingly he brought out a bag of Oreo cookies too. He was nothing if not consistent in his attempt to keep us well fuelled for the project.

> **The person with the idea should never show up last.**

We spent ten minutes or so discussing the events of the past week, the partial advance of winter into our general direction. The chit-chat at a lull, Richard strode to the whiteboard and wrote the following:

1) Completion of "The Project"
2) Meet 1 new person per month
3) Create personal Web site
4) Charitable Donations—Dec 1st
5) Learn to ride a horse

When he finished, he turned to us, "Who's next?"

Joyce popped out of her chair, literally bounced to the board to write the following:

1) Successful completion of work term at Bradley Jarvis
2) Singing lessons this winter
3) Maintain 3.5 GPA next semester
4) Cut back on junk food
5) Stay physically active all winter

"Ok. So the fifth one is a requirement after this morning and the fourth kicks in first thing tomorrow. I didn't know we were having this for breakfast today."

"No problem—James, you're next."

James, unlike Joyce, merely ambled to the board and wrote:

1) Complete Tour de France
2) Save enough to buy a car
3) Maintain/Expand circle of friends
4) Open an RRSP
5) ?????

Before I was asked, I moved to the board, James flipped me his pen and I wrote beside his list:

1) Complete client reviews by Dec 1st
2) Generate two new clients per month
3) Plan vacation getaway—for spring
4) Talk to parents—at least bi-weekly
5) Find a place to take piano lessons

"Nice job all, well done. This is a great start—as suggested last time, setting the goals is the first step to accomplishing them. I don't want to get into critiquing them, to see if they pass the SMART test. So for now, let's just give ourselves a hand for accomplishing the task and let's move ahead. We'll get back to them at a relevant point in the future. So what are we *wondering* about today?"

"Wondering why you gave us that question Richard, that's what I'm still wondering about." James was sipping on his hot chocolate as he finished his comment.

"Well, I'm not wondering why you asked that, I'm wondering what you expected us to bring back. I mean this is just scratching the surface." Joyce pulled out a stack of pages, at least an inch thick and deposited them on the table, "Wonders of the ancient world, the sports world, modern world, technological world—you name it."

"Ok, so read my mind Joyce, give me some wonders."

"Easy. In no apparent order they are—Pyramids of Egypt, Pharaohs of Alexandria, Hanging Gardens of Babylon, The Temple of Artemis, Statue of Zeus, Mausoleum at Halicarnassus, and The Colossus of Rhodes. Thank you. Please hold your applause!"

"Excellent work Joyce. But those are wonders of the ancient world and we live in the present. With the possible exception of the great pyramids, we can't visit any of these; they've disappeared from our world. Anyone want to offer up something more recent?"

Joyce didn't hide her disappointment well. I was pretty sure that she was accustomed to being not only correct in her scholarly efforts, but also praised for them. I decided to jump in and see what I could offer.

"Ok, these aren't any better I fear, but they are more current." I flipped open my journal to read, "How about the Taj Mahal, Great Wall of China, Easter Island Statues, Eiffel Tower, Mayan City of Tikal, Chartres Cathedral and the Space Shuttle. Thank you. Please hold your applause!" I smiled at Joyce, who returned a half-hearted smile.

"Ok John, more modern, I'll grant you that, but mostly architectural. So how do we think any of those apply to anything we have talked about so far on the project?" Richard was mindlessly tossing the marker from hand to hand. "That isn't to take anything away from either list, everything mentioned so far has in fact been a wonder, both past and present. Now I'm looking for relevant. James?"

James was sitting silently in his seat. I could see the card from the last session taped to the top of the page in his notebook. Written beneath was simply one line, not a list. He stared at the line, at us, back at the line. Encouragement was necessary.

"It's ok James, no right, no wrong, remember?"

"Ok, I saw all this stuff that John and Joyce mentioned, and plenty of other things too, but I couldn't make any sense of how they might be relevant to our concept of creating a financial blueprint. Almost everything I saw had lists of seven, then I was flipping through a book and I found this—some guy name Baron de Rothschild mentioned it as the eighth wonder—compound interest. Thank you. You're too kind. Please hold your applause!"

For 8:12 a.m. on a Saturday morning, at least we were all giving our best shot at being funny. James looked at Richard with some puzzlement; he was desperately awaiting some type of confirmation for his lone item.

Richard broke into a huge grin, spun around to the board and wrote in large letters:

Compound Interest!

"Bingo. Congratulations James. The eighth wonder of the world is none other than compound interest."

"But what exactly is compound interest?"

"Ok, let's start there. Compounding is what happens when you put money away and that money earns interest. Let's say that it takes a year for your money to earn 10% interest. So if you started with $100 and earned 10% then after a year you would have $110. Now here is where compounding comes in. That $110 that you now have invested is going to earn you interest. You are earning interest on the $100 you placed in your investment plus you are earning 10% on the $10 that you earned from last year. So instead of earning $10 in interest on the second year you actually earn $11. This $11 is added to your investment bringing the total of your investment up to $121.

"Now here is where it really starts to get good, you continue to earn interest on both your initial amount and on all the interest you have earned. It doesn't take long before your interest is worth more than the initial amount you put in to start. Few people truly recognize the power of compound interest and even fewer take advantage of it. After today, you and Joyce won't be in that group.

> The eighth wonder of the world is none other than compound interest.

"I'm going to make you a special limited time offer, available just for the two of you. Here's the deal, I'll offer you a signed cheque for one million dollars right now—Richard pulled a folded cheque from his shirt pocket—or instead, I'll write you a cheque in 30 days for the value of the total amount of one penny doubled every day for 30 days. The clock is ticking; the first one to speak up gets their choice."

James and Joyce looked quickly at each other. I could sense that both were doing some mental calculations, afraid to guess wrong, but not wanting to be last either. Finally James broke the silence, shouting "Give me the million today!"

"Ok," Richard nodded, wrote out, signed and passed what looked like a very real cheque to James. "Here you go James, you have one million dollars at your disposal. Be sure to invest it wisely. Might you have been happier waiting that short 30 days? I'm holding Joyce's cheque right here." He reached back into the same pocket and withdrew a second folded cheque. "Just for fun let's see how this plays out, shall we?" Richard then turned and wrote the following:

Day	Amount	Day	Amount	Day	Amount
1	.01	6	.32	11	10.24
2	.02	7	.64	12	20.48
3	.04	8	1.28	13	40.96
4	.08	9	2.56	14	81.92
5	.16	10	5.12	15	163.84

"We're halfway there, how do you feel James?"

"Pretty good. One million dollars for me, a hundred and sixty dollars for Joyce. Sorry about that Joyce."

"Hey, you win some, you lose some," I could almost see the beginning of a slight grin; perhaps she got further in her calculations than James had and she knew where this was headed?

"Well, there were a few things I learned farming out west during the 70s James. It was important then, and it still applies now. To paraphrase, don't count your pennies, before they are done accumulating." Richard turned back to the board and completed the chart:

Don't count your pennies, before they are done accumulating.

Day	Amount	Day	Amount	Day	Amount
16	327.68	21	10,485.76	26	335,544.32
17	655.36	22	20,971.52	27	671,088.64
18	1,320.72	23	41,943.04	28	1,342,177.28
19	2,621.44	24	83,886.08	29	2,684,354.56
20	5,242.88	25	167,772.16	30	5,368,709.12

"So, tell me what you are thinking now James," Richard passed the other cheque to Joyce.

"Is this some sort of math trick?" James seemed indignant at the thought that he might have been cheated.

"No math tricks, merely the power of compounding James. Look at what happens in the last ten days, from $5,200 to $5.3 million in just ten days. Why? We started doubling larger and larger numbers. So what are the five most important days on the chart?"

"The last five, look at what happens to the numbers." Joyce was looking at the cheque in her hands; it was for an unbelievable sum of money.

"Actually, it was the first five days, right?"

"Why James?"

"If you didn't start with the first five days then you wouldn't even get to the last five days. That's why you had us focus on goals at the last meeting. Right?"

"Why is that James?"

"Because once we create goals and write them down, we are on our way to achieving them. But if we don't start, then we'll never get anywhere. In this example, if we had never set the goal for 30 days of compounding, we'd have never started."

"Bravo! I'm very impressed. But don't let this example get you down James. First, the cheques aren't real, but I did want you to see what the numbers looked like—sorry! Second, the concept of doubling money daily, while a nice mathematical example, doesn't do justice to the real world of financial affairs. For that we have to look at realistic time horizons and realistic rates of return. That's why we have John. Let's hear it for John Linden!"

"Thank you Richard," as I rose, Richard flipped me the pen he had been using. I decided to start with a basic example that I felt had great relevance to people the ages of James and Joyce.

"First, I will start off with a very basic question for you. Imagine that you were just starting your work career. This shouldn't be a stretch for you two. You are 22 years old and you decide to save $2,000 per year, or $40 per week. You decide to save the $2,000 per year for ten years and then you decide to stop saving any more money. Why? Maybe you get married. Maybe you buy a house. Maybe you have kids. Maybe you get bored of saving your money. Whatever reason you choose. You then leave the amount you have to accumulate interest until you are ready to retire at age 65. Let's assume your annual rate of return is 10%, which might not be unrealistic to expect if you left your money within various solid, reputable financial instruments for that many years. How much would you expect to have when you decided to retire at age 65?"

"Ok, even I can figure out that in ten years you've saved $20,000, so I guess I'll go with $200,000?" Joyce didn't seem to have much confidence in her guess.

"I was way off on the penny example, so I'll just double my guess to $400,000 just to be safe."

"Well, the answer just might surprise you. Let's assume you started saving when you were 22 and you put away $2,000 a year for ten years and then you stop for whatever reason. By age 62 if you had just let compound interest work for you, you would have saved over $672,000!" I went to the whiteboard and started to write, "Let's build a chart showing the power of interest and compounding. I'll build it in five year segments to avoid writer's cramp, I think you'll be impressed."

Age	Opening	Additions	Interest	Closing
22	0	2,000	200	2,200
27	13,431	2,000	1,543	16,974
32	35,062	0	3,507	38,569
37	56,468	0	5,647	62,115
42	90,943	0	9,094	100,037
47	146,464	0	14,646	161,110
52	235,882	0	23,588	259,470
57	379,890	0	37,989	417,879
62	611,817	0	61,181	672,998

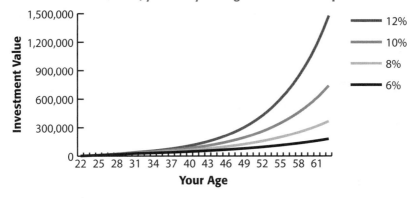

Invest $2000/yr for 10 years age 22–32 then stop

"Now, in the chart we can see that the amount we put in goes up by $2,000 for each year from age 22 until age 32. After age 32, we see that we never put any more money into our savings. Our total amount that we saved stays at $20,000 and we don't add any additional money.

"I rounded to keep the numbers whole, but I want you to focus on the big picture. As James suggested, start early. The hardest part for the vast majority is to get started on the path. So for a total investment on your part of $20,000 you created a future value of over half a million dollars by the time you turn 60."

"Does everybody know this?"

"Yes and no. Most people certainly understand the concept, it's only math. Everyone can check the numbers on their calculators and there is no shortage of financial calculators available on the Internet that will let you play with numbers. There are no tricks or magic here. But if more people truly understood it, there would be a lot more people taking advantage of it."

"But suppose I can't afford to do this right now. I know I couldn't save $2,000 a year on what I make today. What if I wait until I'm 32 instead? This compound interest magic will still work for me then, won't it? I hope there aren't any time limits."

"Certainly, but with some minor changes, as follows," I went back to the board and revised the chart to the following:

Age	Opening	Additions	Interest	Closing
22	0	0	0	0
27	0	0	0	0
32	0	2,000	200	2,200
37	13,431	2,000	1,543	16,974
42	35,062	2,000	3,707	40,769
47	69,899	2,000	7,190	79,089
52	126,005	2,000	12,800	140,805
57	216,364	2,000	21,836	140,805
62	361,887	2,000	36,389	400,276

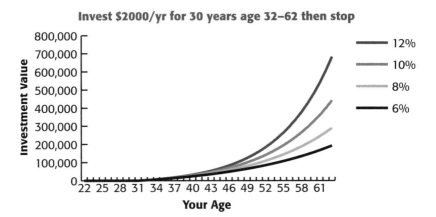

Invest $2000/yr for 30 years age 32–62 then stop

"The difference is pretty clear, about $270,000 less by age 62, about $350,000 by age 65. You've certainly managed to save a lot of money, no doubt about that, but you've managed to miss out on a bit as well."

"You're calling $270,000 a bit?"

"It's all relative James, look at the big picture, you've still got $400,000 in your favour. That is still a substantial amount of money."

"But wait a minute, something else is different in the second chart. You have James contributing $2,000 per year all the way to 62 years old."

"Very perceptive Joyce," Richard took a long sip on his coffee and continued, "by waiting those ten years, you end up having to save not just for ten years, but for 31 years, saving $62,000 in total instead of $20,000, and you still end up with $270,000 less at the end of it all. Please don't misunderstand what John and I are trying to show you here. We aren't saying don't start at all if you don't start early—far from it."

"Exactly Richard, all I am attempting to show in these charts is that procrastination is the enemy here, and that time is your best friend. I could run you through a hundred different examples. You pick the age, you pick the amount you want to save, and from there it is merely a math exercise once you understand the concept. The numbers and the amounts aren't the important parts. By the way, what are the important parts?"

"Compound interest, the eighth wonder of the world."

"Starting early, allowing time to be your friend."

With that, James and Joyce slapped a high five with each other, and Richard sat back with what appeared to be a contented smile on his face. I think we had successfully taught them an important lesson.

> **Start early. Allow time to be your friend.**

"These charts are great John, but at the end of it all, everything just blurs together and all I see are numbers that don't mean a lot to me except they keep getting bigger on the right hand side." James' excitement seemed to be fading.

"Ok, what if I can give you a quick 'rule of thumb' that will help you determine how fast things will grow without having to do a lot of math or stare at a lot of numbers. Would that help?"

"That would be great, quick and easy is always good."

Back at the board I wrote the following:

$$72/ROI = TTD$$

"Ok, thanks John, looks very simple, glad I asked," came the sarcastic response.

"Ok, it's a formula, I get that much, and know that ROI is either 'return on investment' or the French word for 'king,' I'm suspecting the former. I have no idea what TTD is though."

"It's not something that's likely to turn up in your schoolwork Joyce, but John is right, it is pretty simple," Richard grabbed a pen and added the following:

$$72/ROI = TTD$$
(Return on   (Time to
Investment)   Double)

"People call it the Rule of 72. It's a great way to quickly figure out approximately how fast your money will double in X number of years. Some quick examples are in order," and with that Richard was back writing at the board:

$$72/12 = 6$$
$$72/4 = 18$$
$$72/9 = 8$$
$$72/6 = 12$$
$$72/4.78 = 15.06$$
$$72/10 = 7.2$$

"Very cool, even I can do that sort of math," James was back, excitedly writing the formula down in his notebook.

"Rule of 72. I like it too!" Joyce seemed amused at her rhyme.

"You don't have to like it, just accept it, and it will help you determine how fast things can grow in value, not only based on your return on investment, but also to figure out what rate you must achieve in order to double your investment in a given period of time."

"So if I know I need to double my money in five years, then I would have to earn, umm, 14.4% a year to do that."

"Good James."

> **Rule of 72 shows approximately how fast your money will double in a given number of years.**

"Ok, so how do I do that? I mean, how do I earn a return of 14.4%. I'm sure you have some easy formula for that as well? Right?" Richard and I looked at each other, then back at James.

"Actually, no. No easy formula. But that will be a lesson for another day. Something called 'risk and reward' but I'm sure we'll get there soon enough."

"John's right, a lesson for another day. The sun is finally out, the fog is gone, so why don't we call it a morning. I think we've seen some valuable lessons in action today." Nods of agreement all around.

"So when do we do this again?" Joyce, the diligent one, was already tapping at her BlackBerry®.

"I don't care what the date is, but I'm lobbying for a more decent hour. No 7:30 a.m. next time. Ok?"

"Hey James, I'm all for that." Joyce seemed quite amused by my comment.

"Ok, you two slackers, no 7:30 a.m.—at least not next time. Would 9:00 a.m. be ok *sleeping beauties*? I must admit that I like these Saturday morning sessions, a good way to kick start your brain on the weekend. Should we try another Saturday morning?" Nods all around.

"How about Saturday, November 18th? That gives us three weeks to digest today's information and to generate some new questions."

"Excellent idea John, does that work for everyone?" Two quick affirmative replies and that was settled. Everyone was in the process of packing up their belongings when Richard gave a gentle "ah-hem" to get our attention.

"Before we go off on our merry way today, I thought I'd toss this out as some sort of thought generation material prior to our next gathering." With that he offered up another four 5" × 7" cards, covered with two word questions:

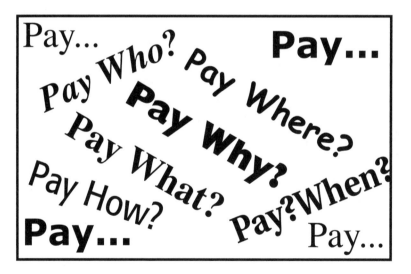

"There are a lot of questions Richard, are we covering all of these in the next session?" Joyce was spinning the card around in her hands.

"Oh, probably."

"Probably?"

"Yes James, probably. It all depends. If we have to take them one at a time, probably not, we won't be able to get to them all. That said, if you come up with the right answer to the right question, you'll have arrived at the answer to all of them. In that case, one session will suffice."

"Answer six, or answer one which will answer them all. That is an intriguing proposition Richard."

"It just sounds complicated to me."

"It's not James, really it isn't. Just don't think too seriously about it. The more you think about it, the more complicated it gets. Most of the basic truths about life are pretty simple when boiled down to their core elements. This one really isn't any different. Right John?"

> The more you think about it, the more complicated it gets.

"Umm, right. Sure. What he said." I made an awkward pointing gesture at Richard. My comment brought laughter from James and Joyce and a smile from Richard. I considered it a comment well made.

At this point, everything had been packed up and we all left together as a group. I locked the office door and we all exchanged a quick goodbye, then we were off in four different directions. Richard had a point about starting early and still having the whole day ahead of you. I hated to admit that he just might be right.

Who Else Would **You Pay?**

Richest Man: What are you paying yourself?
Young Man: Why nothing, of course! I'm busy paying everyone else.
From The Richest Man in Babylon

Brisk.

For a mid-November Saturday morning, I think brisk was the right word. There was a stiff wind blowing in from the north, not a cloud in the sky and a temperature of about 5°. Not quite the bone-chilling cold that January or February brings, but certainly enough to really open your eyes and let you know winter is on its way.

I was looking forward to this morning's meeting, not just because of the more reasonable start time, but because James and Joyce seemed to get quite a kick out of the last one, especially when they saw how compound interest can be the key to creating a successful financial future. However, I was intrigued by the question that they didn't ask. Where does the money you save come from? Perhaps that question would show up this morning?

I hadn't really looked at the 5"× 7" card from the last meeting prior to this morning, so I figured that this would be as good a time as any, in order to put myself in the right frame of mind.

They were interesting questions, the six of them—who, what, where, when, why and how—all relating to the word 'pay.' It would be interesting to see how the kids deal with this, especially since most at their age related the word 'pay' to receiving, not necessarily to be the one paying. To me it was obvious what Richard would want to talk to them about.

Canadians had always been known as a nation of savers. As a country the savings rate of Canadians in the 1970s was a healthy 7.6%. From there it seemed to be a downward slide, with the most recent figures showing that we were saving a meagre 2.8%. There were various reasons offered for the decline, among the most popular were rising tax rates, lower earnings in real dollars, increased cost of living, inflation, and the list goes on. I was clearing the whiteboard of yesterday's thoughts and drawings when a quick rap on the door signalled the arrival of someone.

"Morning John!"

"James. How are you this morning?"

"Chilled. But fine thanks. It's getting a little too cool to ride. Especially when I'm not being paid for it." James was bundled pretty much head to toe. I had just finished clearing off the last of the board when two voices drifted in from the hallway. Given Joyce's laughter, it must have been something pretty funny.

"Ok, share the joke with all of us."

"These two financial planners go into a bar …"

"Ok, that's enough, sorry I asked. I know all of your 'two financial planners' jokes and none of them are any good."

"Hey, what about me then? I don't know them."

"James. Save yourself. You'll just have to trust me."

Richard was busy loading the table with snacks from his traveling picnic basket.

"So it's been a quick three weeks, what have we been up to?"

"Well, I've won three bets using that penny doubling math trick—I mean example. Everyone seems to want the quick million rather than being patient."

"Me too, well, not three bets as James has, but a couple of teas from my friends at school. They were amazed how quickly the numbers grew."

> **The savings rate of Canadians in the 70s was a healthy 7.6%, but recent figures show that we are now saving only 2.8%.**

"That's great work. I'm glad to see you applying the principles for your own personal gain, nothing wrong with that. Something to keep in mind James is that there is no trickery involved. It's just a mathematical example that many people don't get until they see it in action for the first time, and I can guarantee you, once they see it, they won't forget it."

That opened a spirited conversation and discussion of events since we last met, social and otherwise. Richard was stacking Oreo cookies, when he produced the card from the last session and tossed it onto the table.

"So what do we think about this?" It was quickly becoming his standard opening to each session. The card was leaning up against the dozen or so Oreos piled in the middle of the table.

"Interesting questions, that's for sure."

"Agreed. But in what way?"

"Well, I answered them all for myself."

"Enlighten us James."

"Pay who? Me. Pay when? Now. Pay how? Cash. Pay what? Lots. Pay why? I earned it. Pay where? My wallet. What do you think of that?"

"Interesting," Richard gave a slight grin, but nothing more than that.

"That's all I get? Interesting?"

"Yep. How about you Joyce?"

Joyce flipped open her notebook, the card from the last session was taped to the top of the page she opened. She was consistent.

"I didn't take the same approach as James, which probably won't surprise anyone, but in thinking about the six questions, I think I have the key question identified."

"Enlighten us Joyce."

"It's *Pay Who*, right?"

"Why that one?"

"Hmm, because that just seems like the logical place to start. If you get the right *who*, then the rest of the questions can flow from that. You suggested in an earlier session that money was a very individual thing, so pay who starts with the individual. Am I right?"

"You could be."

"Could be?"

"Yes. Could be."

"As in might not be too, right?"

"Perhaps?"

"Are you always this non-committal?" Joyce seemed frustrated.

"He's only this way when he's trying to get us to think about it Joyce. He's committed. He has an opinion on everything. In this case, he doesn't want to give us his opinion; he's trying to find out what ours really are."

"Why did I ask you to be a part of this John? You're letting all of the secrets out of the bag."

I hated to take the fun away from him but the kids didn't just look puzzled, they looked frustrated too. "Instead of looking at the result of the last meeting, since we usually build on them, could you be making reference to what comes before it? Sort of like the chicken and the egg?"

"Well said John!"

"Ok, now I'm really confused," Joyce had stopped writing in her note-book. "Chickens and eggs, what are you two talking about? Please?"

"Ok, I was wondering if it would evolve into this. I guess the point I was trying to make is that one way to look at the future is to look backwards and see where you came from. We went through a number of examples in our last meeting looking at compound interest and showing how you can accumulate some substantial amounts of money. This happens *if* you start to plan, letting compound interest work for you. However, there was one question that didn't get raised and it's one of the first questions asked by 90% of the clients that I start to work with. Any ideas what that question is?"

"When will I be rich?"

"Nope, but since you asked James, let me just say that rich isn't some-thing you attain, it's something that you become, it's part of a larger process, and you can't buy it. You don't suddenly become rich overnight, it happens over time and it will happen slowly and almost predictably with the proper plan-ning in place. When it happens this way you will be better able to deal with it. This will save you from the fate of the lottery winner who has sudden wealth thrust upon them.

> **There is no time like the present to begin to take care of your financial future.**

"The question isn't 'When will I be rich?' It isn't about winning the lottery. We already said that it's not about the result of the compound interest discussion, it comes prior to that and it's a question that many of my clients ask when I first meet with them. The question we are looking for is …"

The room got very quiet. I knew the question but I didn't want to spoil Richard's attempt to get them to think. I liked the silence that these ques-tions created because I could see, as Richard could, that they were thinking about it.

The silence had almost reached the point where I was tempted to speak, when James jumped out of his seat and grabbed a pen at the whiteboard. With a few deft strokes he left the following questions:

How do I save money?
How much do I save?

"Excellent James, where did you come up with those?"

"I started thinking about what comes before producing larger amounts of money with compound interest. It had to be, 'How do I go about saving some in the first place?'"

"I think the second is logical once you see the first, how much do we have to save, and I guess we could add this," Joyce repeated the efforts of James, leaving the following beneath his writing:

When do we start?

"What do you think John?"

"This will be a great place to start. I'll tackle the easiest one first. Is that ok?" A quick nod in agreement was my confirmation to proceed. "The easy one is the 'when' question. Let me answer it for you, by asking you one. What is the date today?"

"Today? November 18th."

"Good," I decided to leave a pause hanging.

"Good? Good what?"

"Not good what, good when."

There was a pause as Joyce's face went from puzzlement to understanding. "Ok, ok, I get it. What is the date? November 18th. When do we start? November 18th. You could have just said, 'start today.' Geez."

"Yes, we could have Joyce, and you wouldn't remember the lesson quite so well. Ok, so we have that one pretty much covered I think."

"It isn't really that easy is it? You don't just say today is the day, and it starts, do you?"

"Actually James, I feel it is. At some point everyone has to make the decision to save. I always pick today because there really isn't any better day. It's not easier next week, next month, after your next raise, after you get a new job, or any other event that you are waiting for."

"John's right. The right day is today. If you are going to begin to take care of your financial future there is no time like the present. I can pretty much guarantee you that it won't be any easier tomorrow or the next day. Since it won't be any easier later you may as well start now."

"So in a nutshell it's not going to be easy is what you're saying, right Richard?" James was frowning.

"That's not exactly what I said James. I said it wouldn't get any easier, not that it wasn't easy. It seems whenever I talk to someone about money, or when John talks to a prospective client, everyone says pretty much the same thing or has the same basic goals in mind for their finances. People would like to be able to be in control of their finances. People would like to have the flexibility to do things they want to do today and they want the stability to grow toward the future and plan for the long term. The numbers are secondary at this point, but to meet their needs they have to be able to do one thing first—save money."

"I've always found it interesting that given people's desire to control their finances, you would think saving money would be at the top of their financial priorities. You'll remember from the first time we met here that both Richard and I shared with you the key strategy that our parents shared with us about personal finance: Spend less than you earn. That said, for many people the concept of saving falls someplace between buying a take-out coffee or paying their overdue cable bill. In short, the concept of saving money is foreign to many of those who claim to have saving as a key priority for their financial health."

"Ok, so I get the point that saving is important and I get that you have to start today, but I'm working part-time, almost full-time, and I really don't seem to have all that much money. So how do I do that?"

"It is a popular question that I get from people ages 20, 35, 50 and older. It's not easy, but I've told you that. Well, actually it is easy—the concept is easy, but the psychological aspect of it is not that easy. We talked early on about money being very emotional for people."

"What John is heading towards I suspect is that we have been conditioned in the past 20 years to be the perfect little consumer. Almost everything we read, listen to or watch bombards us with advertising, all day, 24/7 if you will. While we are asleep we are dreaming of things to buy, which drives the reason why many people work. We work to make money to buy stuff. James suggested back at our first meeting that being rich was the ability to buy stuff. That being said, I don't meet too many people who dream about saving money."

"Hey!"

"John does, but he's weird."

"So, how do we do this?"

"Let's say that tomorrow you walked into work James and your boss took you aside and said, 'times are tough at BMX Courier, I don't want to let anyone go, but in order to do that I need to cut everyone's pay by 15%.' What would your immediate reaction be?"

"Quit."

"Really? If times are that tough for your company, let's make the assumption that times are tough for every company."

"Ok, I might not quit immediately, that day, but I probably wouldn't like it very much."

"That's fair. But what would happen in the short term in the way you'd handle your money?"

"I'd spend less. I'd have to."

"Welcome to the world of saving!"

"What do you mean?"

"Effective tomorrow, you just got a 15% decrease in pay. You know what? It will be unpleasant, the first two months you probably won't like it, in fact, you'll hate it. But I can guarantee you that you'll be better for it in the long run, and you'll thank me when you're older."

"It's that simple?"

"I didn't say it was simple. Sit down and figure out how you'll get by on 15% less income, I can guarantee you won't like the process very much. Especially when you see your friends, who don't do this, spending their additional 15% on stuff that you'd like to have. So it's not necessarily simple, but it is that easy."

"John always says it is easy, but he's less emotional than most when it comes to money. I do like his example of a 15% drop in income being a tool for saving. We are a resilient bunch, us humans, we adapt to lots of things. Adapting to a 15% decrease in pay is just one. Now you might be thinking, 'Hey, I can't live with a 15% pay reduction, I'll just find a job that pays 15% more and I'll save all the additional income.' Nope. Won't work. It doesn't matter how much money we earn, we all think we'd be on easy street with just 15% more because we'd save it all. You won't. Trust me. Our ability to spend is infinitely more adaptable than our ability to earn more. That said, the moment you apply the 15% factor to your present situation you'll begin to stop spending money mindlessly and start setting it aside for your future and the things that really matter."

I was sitting back, taking a large sip of Diet Coke while I watched Richard in action. He was very passionate about the concept of saving money and it showed whenever he talked about it.

"The biggest and most important decision then becomes—Do I really want to make this happen?"

"Ok, I still think I get it. I get that it's not easy to start, but that it gets easier once you get started. But why 15%, why not 8%, 12%, or 22%?" Her expression showed some puzzlement at the concept, but I could tell that Joyce was certainly thinking about it, so I decided to jump back in.

"Good question. Why 15%? Mostly because it's an easy and round number, a number people can adapt to, one they can easily identify with and, given my example of the employer rolling back your earnings, a 15% rollback is certainly something people have lived through in the past. There is a tie-in to the second question James had, 'How much money do I save?'"

"15% right?"

"Let's start there. But we also have to look at those pesky goals that we talked about previously. Remember those?" Nods from all three. "A great place to start is how much those goals are going to cost you. Even if your goal doesn't appear to be financial in nature, they all have a cost associated with them. If we remember from the last session, saving $2,000 per year for ten years gave you a future value of $672,000 at age 62. You both seemed to like that amount, so let's say that is your long-term financial goal. If it is, you have to save $2,000 per year or about $40 a week to do that. If you are making $13,500, saving 15% would give you your $2,000. If you are making $35,000 a year it would only take about 6% in order to save your $2,000."

"So the more you make the less you have to save?"

"Not a chance," I couldn't help but stifle a laugh.

"Why not?"

"Because everything changes in unison James. The more you make, the more you'll need in the future to have the lifestyle you'll want later. Some of these changes will take us back to Joyce's psychological issues. A key factor for saving is simply creating the habit."

"John's right again."

"Thank you!"

> A key factor for saving is simply creating the habit.

"Especially about the habit part. There is a school of thought that would say—since you two are still relatively young—you are just starting to work, enjoy making some money, you don't need to save now, you can save later, in the future when you are more settled. Enjoy your freedom and your youth."

"Here it comes Joyce, *the speech*."

"Au contraire James, no speech. These are just ideas. I can't make you actually implement them, neither can John. All we can do is set the stage for you and offer suggestions. That said, let's assume you start saving 15% today, ten years from now how hard will it be to continue saving 15% since you've been doing it all along, then to keep doing it for 20 years, then 30 years? It's easy once it becomes a habit. I hate to keep bringing up the past, but last time we saw that when you waited just ten years you were left $270,000 behind, and you had to save for 21 additional years to even get that close. But it's always your decision to make. You could choose to enjoy your younger earnings, save nothing; after all you can always catch up later. But when is later? Don't be confused by the common perception that saving today means you'll be living a life of disappointment, or suffer from an extreme case of *want*. What we're trying to get across here is this—what do you think the likelihood is of saving 20% of your income will be ten years from now when you've never saved any money before that time?"

> **Start early—time is your friend.**

"I'll tell you what I think; it'll be pretty slim Jim. Saving money does not get any easier just because you are making more. In fact it gets harder because our expectations of what we can do with all that extra income is higher. You made a key point for us last time James, regarding compound interest, would you care to repeat it?"

James looked puzzled at first, but after a quick flip through his notebook he proudly stated, "Start early, time is your friend."

"Well said. So once you learn how, once it becomes a habit, it will serve you well into the future. I'll be the first to admit that you have to learn to save—it just doesn't seem natural for many of us. "

It was my turn again. "We aren't trying to teach you this in order to punish you, just to get you to think a little differently. Please keep in mind, that the reason we're trying to teach you this isn't that money is the most important thing in life, it's not. There are many, many things in life more important than money. Money is a great slave, but a lousy master."

"What does that mean?" In unison. Since it was drawing some confused looks, I decided that this better get added to the board:

Money is a great slave,
Money is a lousy master

"I like that John, have you used this before?"

"Sure. I can't believe that you haven't heard me use this before. I think it means that money can do a great many things for you, on your behalf, and at your command. It's as if you can say to money, 'buy me this,' 'take me there,' and 'do the following.' Keep in mind that the only command money will not obey is 'make me happy.' That function isn't up to your money, it's up to you. As for the master part, many people, in their quest to attain certain things, or a certain status, will do things for money that are counter-productive or just plain dumb. I have clients who stay in jobs they despise because they are enamoured with the lifestyle that their income gives them. At the same time I have clients who have done very well for themselves, have amassed a significant pool of assets, but are so afraid of losing it or spending it that they don't enjoy life to the degree their effort and hard work have rightfully earned them. In either of these two cases, money seems to be in control of them, not the other way around."

"John's right—it's a good thing he doesn't get tired of hearing that," Richard shot me a quick grin. "The current thinking among many people seems to be this."

Saving is punishment,
Spending is reward

"Hence the thoughts about spending what you have, enjoying life, letting tomorrow take care of itself. John and I are not frugalists or spendthrifts trying to preach some form of punishment. But if you begin to save today, and continue to do so over the long term, you'll eventually get to spend as much as you like once you get older. By building the habit today, you will give yourselves the opportunity to do the things you want even ten, 15 or 20 years from now that your peers will be unable to do because they never got the habit. Imagine being able to take a sabbatical from work, go back to school to try a different career, travel extensively, whatever you might desire."

Money can do a great many things *for* you, on your behalf, and at your command.

"I put a few bucks away, but I don't think too much about it. I know I'll be able to save more once I make more."

"You said yourself James that time is your friend, and you were right. I'm sure that John will be happy to draw up a chart to explain the concept." I had already headed to the board while James was speaking because I wanted to reinforce this concept for them.

Age	Monthly	Yearly	Total	Return	Value: Age 65
20	95.83	1,150	52,190	10%	1,001,621
30	253.33	3,040	109,440	10%	1,000,280
40	694.17	8,330	216,580	10%	1,000,433
50	2,108.00	25,300	404,800	10%	1,000,481

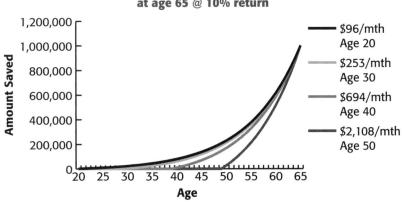

Amount of Saving Monthly to reach $1,000,000 at age 65 @ 10% return

"I'm not sure I can relate it any simpler than that. The power of starting early, the power of compound interest, all snowball up to the same amount, but I can pretty much guarantee you that saving $2,108 each month is a lot harder than saving $96 a month. To tie this back to the earlier part of the discussion, saving 15% of your income for a total savings of $1,150 per year, you'd need to earn an income of $7,800. Assuming that same 15%, to save $25,300 per year you'd have to be earning approximately $170,000. You tell me, which is easier?"

"Saving $1,150."

"Great. Then it's settled. Lesson over. Thank you for your time. Please take your personal belongings with you."

"What do you mean over?"

"Aren't you going to tell us how?"

"How what?"

"Ok, so we get why, we get the 15%, we even get the early part, but *how* do you save money?"

"Ah, the plan!" Richard was rubbing his hands together. "Show us the plan John." I hate it when Richard did things like this, building up people's expectations of what I was about to tell them such that they'd probably be under whelmed when they finally saw what I was going to show them.

1) Make the decision to save money
2) Set the objective, $ or %
3) List the 'whys'
4) Create a siphon
5) Review, Relax & Enjoy

"That's the plan?"

"What were you expecting Joyce?"

"I'm not sure, something more…"

"Complex? Convoluted?"

"Yeah … this just doesn't look …"

"Hard enough?"

"That's it. Hard enough."

"Because it really isn't that hard. The logic of it is blissfully easy. The single biggest decision is the decision to save. Telling yourself, 'I will save. Period.' That decision made and committed to, the rest of the decisions that follow get easier and easier. If you can't commit to saving, the rest of the steps really don't matter. If you've done that, we move to setting the rate.

> **The single biggest decision is the decision to save.**

We've arbitrarily set that at 15%, I think using a percentage rather than a dollar amount is psychologically easier. Let's say that you are making $20,000 per year and spending all of it.

"At this point in order to get with the plan, you need to go from saving zero to $250 per month which will seem like a huge jump. Given that, it probably won't happen. However, if I told you that you need to save 1.25% of your annual income each month, the reaction will probably be, 'Sure 1.25% is not a big deal. I can handle that.' It's the exact same amount, just easier to grasp psychologically. Are we ok so far?"

Nods from all.

"List the *whys*. This ties back directly to your goals. The car you want, saving for a house, a trip to Europe, planning a wedding, your kid's education …"

"Gifts for Uncle Richard."

"…a nice card for your uncle. Whatever you are saving for—perhaps to start your own courier company James. For Joyce it might be doing a graduate degree in Europe. In fact your whys will probably tie in very nicely to your goals. Once listed, prioritize them and assign dates to them. Once you are done, realistically figure out what they'll cost and factor that against how much you are saving. I'm sure that you'll be in a position where you could save 50% of your income and still not meet all of your whys. So we are forced to make choices. You'll have to determine some priorities. Once some whys are written down they look less appealing than they did floating around your brain. The point of all this is, if we don't know why we are saving the money, we'll lose focus on why we should keep doing it. It's part of thinking about the bigger picture. That done we need to create a siphon."

"A siphon? The only thing I think of when I hear that is removing gasoline from a tank with a hose."

"Yep. Same concept, different application. In this case the gas tank is your bank account and the siphon is a direct deposit, automatic transfer or pre-authorized chequing to take money out of these accounts. The key phrase that everyone seems to like to use is ..." I decided this was probably worthy of their notebooks, so I reinforced it by putting it on the board.

Pay Yourself First!

"Pay yourself first. I like that." James was writing it down as I predicted.

"I'm glad, but not surprised. It's the key to getting where you want to be in the future. The purpose of the direct deposit or pre-authorized chequing is to remove the funds from your account without you having access to them, before you are tempted to spend them. Many employers allow you to split your payroll deposits into multiple accounts, which is an ideal way to do this."

"So, it's pretty much out of sight, out of mind?"

"Exactly. You don't see it, you don't have it, you don't spend it."

"Where does it go when it gets removed from our account?"

"We'll get to that in a minute James. The final step is the most fun— review, relax and enjoy. Periodically check in on your goals, add some new ones, take off the ones that no longer inspire you, cross off the accomplished goals and watch your savings grow knowing that you are preparing yourself for the future."

"But you haven't said anything about budgeting John. Isn't budgeting a key issue? My Mom and Dad are always talking about their budget, and how they can't seem to stick to it."

"To be honest Joyce, I'm not a big fan of budgets. I'm not convinced they work, and they tend to reinforce the pain versus pleasure aspect of finance. I do think it is important to know where your money is going. If you have no idea, figure it out; it doesn't matter if you use personal finance software, a spreadsheet or pencil and paper to do it. I like to have clients keep track of their spending for 30 days, not just the big stuff, all of it, lattes, donuts, teas, magazines, movies, video rentals, pizza slices, gas for the car, clothes, I mean everything. The big things are easy—rent, mortgage, car loans, student loans, they are fixed and you can plan for them. If you are like most people, it will surprise you when you see where all of your discretionary money goes. In fact, here is a challenge for the both of you. Between now and our next meeting, I'd like you to track everything you spend, any expenditure over 50 cents and bring it to the next meeting. Just remember because you are paying yourself first, you are free to spend the rest, every last cent, but only *if* you are paying yourself first." Richard got up out of his seat, a sign he was going to share something.

"The biggest problem I have seen in my travels is that everyone tries to control their spending with a budget. They start with their income, and then start removing all their expenses with the committed belief that they will save whatever is left over. Surprise! There isn't any left over. There never is. In this way budgeting is a lot like dieting, if only in the sense that the success rate is about the same. You start out very committed, confident. After a whole two weeks, you're still committed, but decide a little $10 splurge won't hurt. Then within a month, once you've been denying yourself things you did all the time before, you blow the budget out. You vow to get back on it next week, next month, next year. Here's the point that people seem to miss entirely about the two concepts."

> **It surprises most people to see where all of their discretionary money goes once they track it for a month or even a week.**

Diet: Eat Less, Exercise
Budget: Spend Less, Save

"It's the concept of less that people have a problem with. It's the not-so-trendy concept called 'delayed gratification.' The ability to not do something today, or have something today, for the ability to be able to do it tomorrow and a whole bunch more because you were patient and committed enough to wait. I remember reading a quote years ago that basically summed it all up like this: I want a comfortable financial future more than I want 'stuff' today.

"That said, should you become extremely successful, have great careers, earn huge incomes, save 15%, max out your RRSPs, buy all of the things you want while preparing for your future, and still have cash left over at the end of the day, then you can disregard everything John and I are saying. I didn't mean to take John too far off topic, but I think the point has been made. You can't save, unless you first plan to save, and you can choose the easiest method of saving by choosing to pay yourself first. Stay committed to the plan and you will be on your way to building a secure financial future for yourselves."

"Excellent summation Richard, well said. You know, I think this would be a great place to cut off the session for today. We've been at this for a couple of hours now and I think that this is a proper place to end. Any thoughts?"

"But we never talked about where we put this money we are saving?"

"Right you are James, we didn't, but we will and I suspect that you won't mind being kept in suspense until next time. But I do have a second request to make, for both of you."

"Second?"

"Yes James, tracking your finances for 30 days was the first," Joyce reminded him.

"The request is for you to go and open a new bank account, a savings account, and do not have it added to your bank card. That way you cannot access it via an ATM or debit machine. Take 15% of all the money that you receive from your earnings until the next meeting, or have your employer split your payroll deposit, siphoning off that 15% into the new account. That will get you started on the saving habit and soon enough we'll start talking about what to do with it. I think we've accomplished enough for today."

"Whew! Good, I think I have a brain cramp."

"Me too, but it's a hand cramp from writing—it's like taking notes in school."

"With the possible exception that what you are learning here will be far more applicable to real life, but I'm sure that sounds harsher than I mean it to be Joyce."

"I hope so Richard. Do you think I'm wasting my time at school?"

"Not at all, learning is great, an education will open many doors for you. But until schools start to teach this type of material, I'll remain biased."

"I can live with that," Joyce was smiling again. "So when do we do this again?"

"Well, if we stick to the three week concept, that would take us to December 9th which I can't do, but I'd be game to meet on December 16th. I know that's pretty close to Christmas, but I'm in if everyone else is."

"I'm in, as long as we stick with the 9:00 a.m. start time."

"Ok James, I get the point, no 7:30 a.m. start times."

"Well done James, I can never get him to bend to my time wishes, I'm impressed." James had a big grin on his face.

"I was thinking we might meet at the cabin for a change." Richard rarely, if ever, referred to it as his house or home, almost always as 'the cabin.' I liked it, and the term certainly suited him.

"That would be great!" a unison agreement from James and Joyce. I liked the idea myself, I spend too much time in my office and I like to get out once in a while.

"Sure, I'm all for a change in venue, it might change our perspective."

"December 16th, 9:00 a.m., the cabin it is." There was a sudden silence as we all looked at Richard. We seemed to be expecting some sort of direction from him.

"What, you thought I had forgotten something?" Richard opened his folder and produced what we were expecting; four 5" × 7" cards, but they had no words this time, merely a picture.

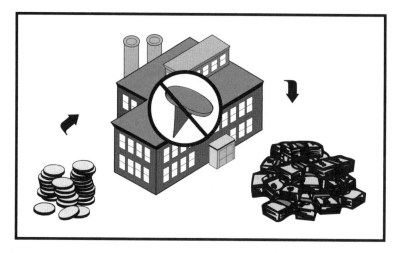

"Quite artistic don't you think?"

"No words?"

"No words. After all, a picture is worth a thousand words. Especially this one."

"Is it some sort of transformation process or something?"

"That's enough James, it's not for today's discussion, this is for next time."

I found Richard's new card quite intriguing. He had told me he had been playing around with some new computer graphics software, but he hadn't told me why. I guess I had the answer to that in my hand.

Richard, James and Joyce packed up their belongings and all the leftovers from breakfast—at my insistence—and before I knew it they were waving goodbye from the doorway. I cleaned off the wall; with the exception of 'pay yourself first.' It was a key, fundamental concept and a building block for creating a solid financial future. It was worth leaving up there as a reminder to anyone who came to visit.

8

The Money **Factory**

The entire essence of America is the hope to first make money—then make money with money—then make lots of money with lots of money.
Paul Erdman

Snow.

There are few things that bring a grin to my face more than the first snow fall of the year. I had been intrigued by Richard's suggestion to change the location for this meeting; I certainly didn't mind getting out of my office. I needed a different perspective. I think the 'kids' were looking forward to it as well. There was a thin film of white covering the road, and a set of tire tracks led the way.

My wipers were clearing the build-up off the windshield as I turned into Richard's drive. Parked next to his pickup truck was a black Audi A6. As was our custom, I simply knocked twice and opened the door; it was an informality that Richard and I enjoyed.

"John!"

I felt like Norm when he entered Cheers. I was in a place where everyone knew my name and was glad to see I arrived. The three of them were seated around the granite fireplace; the dominant feature in what Richard has always called the 'great room.'

"Greetings all!"

"Why do you have that stupid grin on your face John? No, wait a minute; it's the first snowfall of the year isn't it? John has this thing about the first snow of the year kids, he'll get over it soon and be back to his not so emotional self."

"Nice to see you too Richard."

I couldn't help but laugh, a grown man sitting in front of the fireplace wearing a red and green elf's hat with 'Santa's Helper' stitched across the front. Appropriate I guess, as we were only nine days away from Santa's arrival. A punch bowl of what I assumed was eggnog sat on a tray overflowing with baked goods. I plopped down on the couch next to Joyce and ladled myself a mug full.

"This is certainly much more festive than my office Richard, this was a great idea. I'm sure you'll miss the whiteboard, but you'll get over it."

"Oh ye of little faith," Richard jumped to his feet and disappeared into his office. The next thing we all saw was a large brightly wrapped object about six feet tall by six feet wide being wheeled into the room. "Consider it a Christmas gift to us if you will. I need a couple of Santa's helpers."

James and Joyce rose to the occasion, looking slightly puzzled, each proceeding to a side of the object and at Richard's urging grabbed a protruding piece of wrapping and pulled. To paraphrase: *'Twas the night before Christmas—and what to my wondering eyes should appear, but a shiny whiteboard on wheels, covered with eight tiny reindeer.*

"It's the latest in portable whiteboard technology. Isn't it great? Check this out." Richard pressed a button at the base of the board and an 8½" × 11" sheet of paper emerged, a printed copy of his crude drawing of eight little stick-like reindeer, which he handed to me with a large grin. "Now Joyce won't have to break her wrist writing everything down, we'll just print what she wants to capture. Or any of us for that matter."

"Very cool Richard." I admired his spirit; the kids seemed to as well. As he wiped the board clean he was humming, *it's beginning to look a lot like Christmas.* Through the windows at either side of the fireplace we could see the snow was continuing to gently fall.

> I nickel and dime myself to being broke!

"Ok, we'd better get going before John slips into snow coma. So what have we accomplished since last we met?"

"Well, as you requested, I decided to keep track of my spending, in order to find out where the money goes. It was tougher than I thought it would be."

"Keeping track was tough?"

"Well, not so much tough as just annoying," Richard grinned in my direction. "Especially since you wanted it at the 50¢ level or above. What can you buy for less than 50¢?"

"Perhaps that was too harsh, my apologies. So what did you find out?"

Joyce produced a small spiral notebook from her backpack, opened it, and tossed it onto the table in front of us:

Dec 1, 2008		Dec 5, 2008	
- Coffee	$2.25	- Loan Julie	$10.00
- Gum	$1.00		
- Photocopies	0.50	Dec 7, 2008	
		- Lunch	$7.50
Dec 2, 2008		- Christmas cards	$11.75
- Movie + drink	$12.85	Dec 10, 2008	
- Coffee + muffin	$4.75	- Coffee	$2.25
		- Magazine	$3.75
Dec 4, 2008			
- Magazine	$4.75	Dec 11, 2008	
- Coffee	$2.25	- Gifts	$25.00

"Mostly that I nickel and dime myself to being broke—lots of little amounts, buying coffees for friends, too much junk food, and too many fashion magazines."

"This led you to what conclusion?" Richard had moved up on the edge of his seat.

"That I have to focus more on where the money goes. To start, I did set up the new bank account, Bradley Jarvis does allow you to split your payroll deposit, so effective on my last payday 15% of the money went directly into the new account. As you also suggested, I didn't add it to my bank card. Good thing too. I would have used it late last week."

"Do you miss the money?"

"Duh! Sure. But I think that I'll get used to it. After all, you said the hardest part was just to get started, so it should get easier from here, no?"

"Yes, it should, but keep going on the tracking for at least another month, and keep us posted; I think it is an intriguing project. James?"

"Well, I did the easy part. I have a new bank account. I signed up with one of those new Internet banks that seem to offer higher interest, not to mention the whole concept of on-line banking, which is pretty cool. We don't get paid by direct deposit, at least not the part-timers, so I deposit my cheque, then transfer the funds over on their Web site."

"Excellent. How about the tracking?" Silence.

"Well, Joyce has me on this one, but, I might have an out. John said that he didn't like budgets, and I guess I see tracking like budgeting. So I figured that if I pay myself first, and stick with it, I can just spend the rest as long as I don't touch what I've saved. So, that's what I'm doing."

"Ok. You were listening, that is a good sign. We did say that you got to spend the rest once you have paid yourself first, so keep doing that. But if you find yourself running short, or feel a financial pinch, a good way to determine why is to track it the way Joyce has done." Richard was nodding in agreement; seemingly happy that both of them were making progress and sticking to the program we suggested last time. Then he pulled out the picture from the last session and tossed it on top of Joyce's spending notes. That could only mean one thing.

"Ok, enough about that, how about this? Any thoughts?"

I was slowly turning the card over in my hands, looking at Richard's artwork. It was a good representation of what appeared to be a money factory, small amounts of raw materials in, larger amounts or finished products coming out, in Canada that could only mean ...

"It appears to be a process of some sort, stuff going in, stuff coming out."

"Stuff James?"

"Well, money of some sort, coins in, dollars out."

"Meaning?"

"Growth? Small change to big bucks?"

"Excellent Joyce."

"So what about growth? Good or bad?"

James and Joyce looked at each other, seemingly puzzled by the question.

"Good?"

"Good. Growth is good. Keep that in mind."

"What's that symbol on the side of the building?"

"What building?"

"On the card, isn't it a building?"

"You tell me James."

"What is it supposed to mean?"

"You've grown up in the 'information age,' the picture is a sign of the 'industrial age,' and something you might have read about in school."

"So it is a factory—told ya Joyce!" It would appear that they had been discussing things outside these sessions as well. That would certainly make Richard happy.

"A money factory, turning coins into dollars, something allowing or helping your money to grow."

"Excellent James."

"So it's a money factory, we all agree about that, right?" Nods all around.

"So that only leaves the symbol on the side of the building."

"I can't really make out what it is."

"Geez you two, you're the ones with the young eyes, perhaps this will help." With that, Richard went to the board and drew the following:

"No thumbtacks?" James asked quizzically.

"Less literal James."

"No, not thumbtacks, just tacks, right?"

"You're getting warmer …"

"Your uncle likes to play with words remember?"

"I got it, not 'tacks,' but 'tax,' as in taxes."

"Bingo!"

"So put it all together."

"A money making factory, allowing you to grow small amounts of money into larger amounts. With no tax," in unison.

"Well done. So this means what?"

The joy that James and Joyce had experienced was short-lived. They seemed unsure of where to head next, so I hoped that I could prod them along the path.

"Think about your goals from a few sessions ago James, one in particular should come to mind." As usual, Joyce was right on it, flipping back through her notebook, as she scanned the list James had offered she hit on the key one.

"Open an RRSP, followed by a question mark."

"Right, I remember writing that down."

"So why did you write that?"

"Because there are ads for them everywhere."

"Why?"

"Because they seem important."

"Why?"

"Because everyone talks about them."

"Why?"

"Do you ever stop asking why?"

"No James, and you should never stop asking why either. It's the best question in order to get more information. So everyone talks about them, they seem important, there are ads everywhere. So, is a Registered Retirement Savings Plan or RRSP important?"

"I guess so."

"Yes! They are important" Joyce was jumping into the fray.

"Ok Joyce, since you seem more convinced, why are they important?"

"RRSPs allow you to build a pool of money, for retirement, and the 'no tax' concept allows for the money to grow tax free until you need to retire."

"You've been reading the ads, good."

"Did I miss something important?"

"No, but we'll get to the details in a bit, the only concept I would caution you on is the 'tax free' notion. An RRSP is not truly tax free, although many people use that language when describing them. But they are not tax free, they are, in fact, *tax sheltered* such that the growth is not taxed as it occurs, but you are taxed when you remove money from the plan at some point in the future. There is another option available now called the TFSA or Tax Free Savings Account, but that is a discussion for a later time (see Appendix B)."

> **RRSP—A money making factory, allowing you to grow small amounts of money into larger amounts, while sheltering it from taxation.**

"But why are people so interested, some might say obsessed, with these RRSPs John?"

"Well James, at your age, the future pretty much appears as a distant speck on the horizon, but we all know that it's out there and we have to prepare for it. RRSPs allow people to take responsibility for their own future. For those people who are self-employed, like your dad, Joyce, or who work for a company without a pension plan, an RRSP is a good way for people to save for their future in a tax-deferred form. The hope for people using RRSPs is that they can avoid being dependent on the government or their families as they get older. You might find this interesting." I strode over to the whiteboard, picked up a pen and wrote the following on the new board:

Men @ 65	Women @ 65
1—Rich	1—Rich
8—Lifestyle = Work	2—Lifestyle = Work
14—Working	4—Dead
24—Dead	11—Working
53—On Assistance	82—On Assistance

"So what do you think? The breakdown is of the typical survey of 100 people, male and female at the age of 65. The key is to look at the bottom numbers, with 53% of males at age 65 and 82% of females at age 65 requiring financial assistance in various forms from the government and/or family members."

"My personal belief is these numbers are pretty scary," Richard got up and circled the top two lines in each column. "Of 100 men, only nine will have a lifestyle equal to or greater than when they were working full-time, and only three women will be in that category as well."

"So what you are saying Richard is that the future doesn't look bright?"

"No, the future can be incredibly bright, for anyone who happens to plan for it properly. That's what these lessons are all about. The future will be a scary place if people don't prepare. It's often been said that people don't plan to fail—they simply fail to plan. Nowhere is this more relevant than in preparing for one's financial future. Everyone has an opportunity; it's just that many chose not to do anything about it."

"Using RRSPs is the way to avoid this failure?"

"It's part of the plan James, certainly not the only piece, but part of the plan for a significant number of people."

"We talked earlier of the tax sheltered nature of the money invested in an RRSP, which is a very good thing, but there is a second significant benefit as well."

"More benefits?"

"To encourage people to invest in their own futures, you get a tax break from the government for the money you contribute to your RRSP."

"So you get money back for investing in your future?"

"Exactly. It's a pretty good deal. One of the reasons that RRSPs have become so popular is that with the rise in personal income

> By age 65, it is estimated that 53% of men and 82% of women will require financial assistance from the government and/or family members.

tax rates over the past 30 years, the RRSP is one of the only tax breaks that Canadians have. So you'd think they would make better use of it."

"People don't use this?"

"They use it James, just not to the degree that you'd think given the amount that people talk about them and the amount of advertising that exists every year for them."

"Recent surveys," Richard stood up, "indicate approximately 70% of people believe that they will only have their RRSPs or TFSAs to fund their retirement plans. No company pension, no CPP, RRSPs or TFSAs will be it. So given that, why do only 57% of those people, and only 51% of the people who are eligible, contribute? Of that 51%, even fewer contribute the allowable maximum amount on an annual basis. Considering it is their own future they should be concerned with, I don't have an answer for that one. Do you John?"

Of the Canadians eligible to contribute to an RRSP, why do only 51% do so?

"I can't explain it either. It's unfortunate that people don't contribute when the tax breaks can be quite substantial. The math is similar to this." As I turned to the board I heard a gentle click and whir of the printer as the page emerged from the base of the board. Richard was grinning as he handed me the page.

"Here, now we can keep your notes John, I'll make copies for everyone later."

"Kids, your uncle is Exhibit A in the argument against the notion that old people are afraid of technology."

"Hey, easy on the 'old' thing, will ya?"

"Sorry," as I stifled a grin. "As I was suggesting, here are some examples."

RRSP Contribution	Assumed Tax Rate		
	19%	35%	50%
1,000	190	350	500
2,500	475	875	1,250
5,000	950	1,750	2,500
7,500	1,425	2,625	3,750
10,000	1,900	3,500	5,000
15,000	2,850	5,250	7,500
20,000	3,800	7,000	10,000

"You get money back just for saving money. I like that." James seemed to be writing that concept down in his notebook. "So why stop at $20,000, why wouldn't people put in $30,000 or $40,000 if they had the money to contribute. After all, they'd get more money back."

"Because you have to. There are rules."

"Rules?"

"Yes, to your dismay, and the dismay of many investors as well, there are rules to contributing to RRSPs. Some of the key ones to consider are the following." I turned and wrote the following on the whiteboard below the tax calculations:

Who? Less than age 71 with "earned income"
How Much? 18% of "earned income," max $23,820

"Anyone with earned income can contribute? I made about $4,500 last year, so I didn't bother filing a tax return as I was below the basic exemption, at least that's what my dad told me."

"He's right Joyce. Currently you can earn about $7,000, subject to change, without paying any tax whatsoever. But by filing a tax return you are generating RRSP contribution room, the benefit being that you don't have to use it immediately. You can carry it forward until a point in the future when you do decide to make a contribution in order to help reduce the amount of taxes you'll pay when your income is higher. But if you don't file, you aren't building that room to be used later."

"What about the time factor John?"

"Thanks Richard, there is a point to be made for that as well. For example, if you file a tax return and you are below the basic minimum tax threshold, contributing to your RRSP will not generate any tax advantage for you—you can't get back tax money that you haven't paid. The flipside is that your money can start to grow within that tax sheltered environment sooner, which means …"

"The earlier you start the better, based on our compounding discussion from before."

"Exactly. Even if your earned income is only $5,000, 18% of that is $900 and you could contribute that to your RRSP and have that start to grow for you. Or, you could choose to carry forward the $900 to a future year when that $900, might yield you a tax break. Trust me, it's not as far-fetched as it sounds. Even though tax rates have been falling, they are still too high for my liking. Don't get me started on taxes, at least not today. I suspect you still have more questions, so fire away."

"Does an RRSP replace the Canada Pension Plan?"

"Interesting James, where did you hear that?"

"Just something I overheard mom and dad talking about. I'm not really sure that I know what they were talking about."

"I can't be sure either, but RRSPs are not a replacement for the CPP, but they can certainly enhance your income in the future. In fact, if you plan well enough, you may have enough income generated by your RRSP and other investments that it could make you ineligible to collect CPP & OAS payments—well, not ineligible to collect, but they could be "clawed back," which would have the same net effect."

"We talked in school about the potential for the CPP program to be bankrupt by the time James and I, or even our parents, might be ready to retire. Is that true?"

"Well Joyce, I don't have a crystal ball for that one, but I do know this: at some point in the past the government figured they'd better give people a chance to save for their own retirement rather than the government being responsible for it. The biggest reason for that is primarily the 'baby boom generation' and its impending effect on the CPP system. It looks like this."

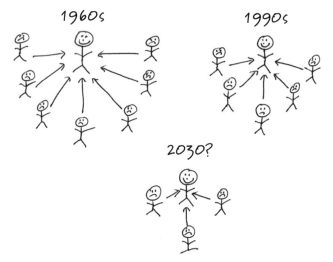

"Let me guess, the smiling stickperson is retired collecting CPP."

"Right you are Joyce."

"The frowning stick people are paying into CPP?"

"And by 2030, only three people are left working for every single person collecting?"

"Well, not exactly James. Joyce was right; they are paying into CPP because the work force will be supporting a far higher number of people who are dependent on the government for assistance. Remember the numbers from earlier about which people need assistance at age 65. There will be 53 men and 82 women who will be requiring some form of assistance. CPP is a part of that, along with Old Age Security (OAS) and the Guaranteed Income Supplement (GIS)."

"But they paid their share right?"

"Yes, to some degree James. People collecting CPP today have paid ever since they started working and deserve to draw out of the system, no argument there. The issue is that when it all started, there were over a dozen Canadians working to support a retiree and when CPP was created life expectancy was approximately 60 to 63 years. So giving people who turned 70 a pension seemed like a grand gesture on behalf of the government. Today, the age has changed to 67 while life expectancy is approaching 77 to 80 years. It's a huge obligation the government has. It's called 'demographics' and I'll point you in the direction of two books: *Boom, Bust & Echo* by David Foot and *The Pig and The Python* by David Cork for a discussion of the boomer generation and their effect on pretty much everything and everyone in the coming years. It's interesting reading and you'll be feeling the effects even though you did nothing to contribute to it. The long and the short of it is, it will become more important than ever for people to take care of themselves and RRSPs are an important part of that."

"So when do we open one?"

"Good question James, especially since you listed that as your goal. You can open one anytime you like since you are working and have earned income. That applies to Joyce as well."

"How do I open one?"

"Many options. Banks, trust companies, insurance companies, mutual fund companies or, might I be so bold to suggest, I could open one for you."

"There are advantages to doing that kids. John, as an *independent* financial planner, has access to a vast array of investment options and can select the appropriate vehicles for you, regardless of whose products they are— mutual funds, stocks, government bonds, if they are licensed for them. If you are dealing with a specific financial institution you may be limited to their private brand of product. The advantage of dealing with a planner is you get specific advice tailored for you, with the widest array of options to invest in."

"Thanks for the plug Richard. Using a financial planner is always a good idea."

"When do we have to put our money in?"

"Anytime during the tax year James, or in the first 60 days of the following calendar year."

"We can invest in anything?"

"No. More rules. But the limitations are pretty broad—cash, GICs, stocks of Canadian companies, mutual funds registered with the government, exchange traded funds which are commonly called ETFs, bonds of Canadian companies, government treasury bills, and government bonds, to name just a few. You can also invest in stocks and mutual funds outside of Canada traded on registered exchanges, which is something we'll call foreign content. There are other things that you can invest in, but this covers the basics and, for the vast majority of people, this will cover everything they will want to invest in. If you start here, you'll be doing well."

"What's foreign content?"

"Because we are Canadian, RRSPs are Canadian and we are Canadian taxpayers, the government has determined that it is a good idea for us to invest our money in Canadian assets to help Canadian companies. This isn't a bad thing, but, and it's a big but, Canada accounts for barely 4% of the available world stock market for investing, so there are plenty of options to be had outside the country. The rules, as they exist today, allow you to invest 100% of your money outside the country. In the past it was only 30%—it could be different again in the future. Determining what your split is depends on your goals and time horizon. Decisions like these are best discussed with a financial professional, as with all things there are pros & cons to everything. The key takeaway from all of this discussion would be?"

"Start early!"

"Excellent James. Start early is the key, there is absolutely no substitute for starting early."

"So what about the compound interest we talked about, does that apply to RRSPs as well?"

"Certainly, your investments can grow in exactly the same way in your RRSP, compound interest included, and all the growth is subject to no taxation until you remove money from the plan."

"Cool." James seemed pretty pleased by this discussion, and that was reflected in his attitude.

"When can you take your money out?"

"Anytime you like Joyce, but I would counsel against that most of the time, although there can be situations when it makes sense."

"If you are saving for the future, why not take the money out in the future?"

"Yes, you will take it out in the future, agreed. But the future isn't three years from now when you need a new digital flat screen television set, or a couch and microwave for your first apartment. Remember that when you remove money from your RRSP you'll be taxed in two forms. First, there is a withholding tax when you remove the funds, to cover some of the non-taxable growth that you have benefited from. Withholding rates are constant for all provinces except Quebec and the rate varies by the amount you choose to withdraw from the plan. The current amounts, subject to change, are these."

Amount Withdrawn	Tax Rate All Other Provinces	Quebec
< 5,000	10%	5%
5,001 – 15,000	20%	10%
> 15,000	30%	15%

"What that means is if you want $4,000 cash from your plan, you need to withdraw $4,450, then pay a withholding tax of $445 in order to get the $4,005 you wanted."

"Yeah, but that is not so bad if you need the money."

"Wait, there's more. You also have to declare the entire $4,450 as part of your taxable income for the year in which you take the funds out, this means that you'll pay income tax on that amount at tax time."

"Does everything get taxed?"

"Ultimately yes, but don't get me started!" Richard's voice boomed out, catching us all by surprise. We had been having a rather soft-spoken discussion until his interjection. He seemed quite surprised at the volume he generated. "Sorry, I didn't mean to yell, John knows how I feel about taxation in Canada."

"Ultimately James, everything you earn does get taxed, the key is to reduce the amount and the impact whenever you can. But it's not just the taxation issue; it's also the effect on future growth that has to be considered as well. Removing $5,000 or $10,000 today can have a large impact on your potential to grow your RRSP funds in the future. If you remember our discussion about starting early versus starting later from our talk on compounding, you'll be able to understand the long-term effect of pulling money out. So it should be considered with the utmost thought before you decide to pull funds out."

"There are a couple of exceptions you might want to mention John, regarding tax free removal of funds."

"Tax free? I thought you said …"

"Hold on a second, I know I said it was all taxed, but there are two instances when you can remove money from an RRSP without a tax implication, but they are very specific and probably will not apply to you for a few years yet, but they are worth mentioning. The first is called the Homebuyers Plan and lets you remove money without tax to finance the purchase of your first home. Not a bad thing necessarily, but it is subject to some restrictions. First the amount you can withdraw is $25,000 per person or $50,000 for a couple and those funds must be repaid back into the RRSP 1/15th a year on a 15 year schedule. If that schedule is not adhered to, it makes the funds withdrawn subject to tax in a lump sum—very painful from a tax perspective. Second, when you repay the money to the RRSP there is no additional tax benefit because you already received that when you contributed the funds the first time. There are some instances when I think this might be a beneficial strategy, but it varies from person to person, and couple to couple."

I paused to take a sip from my cup of eggnog. The snow was still falling gently outside and everything within sight had a pristine blanket of white. I was marvelling at the progress that James and Joyce were making. I had been firing a lot of information at them today.

"The second one is?" Joyce was poised, pen in hand, ready for me to continue. The addition of a new whiteboard with a printer didn't stifle her desire to take notes on everything we were talking about.

"The second is called the Lifelong Learning Plan and is used to allow people to fund a return to school to continue their education, to learn a new skill or trade, which could be very useful to those in the midst of a career change or to help those who may have been downsized out of a corporation for economic reasons and want to pursue something new. You are allowed to remove $20,000 over a four-year period, with a maximum of $10,000 in a given year. Repayment occurs over a ten-year period; the start period depends on the program you are registered in. Like the home ownership plan, each situation will be different and it will make sense for some people and not for others."

Do not discount the power and value of lifelong learning!

"Do not under any circumstances discount the power and value of lifelong learning you two," Richard was wagging a finger at James and Joyce.

"Richard, we're here aren't we?"

"Yes you are, James. Yes you are." Richard and the kids were smiling; everyone was in a good mood this morning. Aside from the first snowfall, I think the proximity to Christmas might have had something to do with it.

"So what happens at age 71?"

"What do you mean?"

"In terms of RRSPs. You said everyone less than 71 can contribute, so now I'm 72 years old, what happens?"

"Well, Joyce, for starters, you can no longer contribute any more money to your RRSP, even if you are earning income. I suppose the government has just assumed by the time you have made it to age 71 that you won't want to be working anymore, and I guess they had to draw the line somewhere."

"So your money just sits there?"

"In a manner of speaking, but not exactly." I was getting curious glances from James and Joyce sitting on the couch, wondering where I was going with this discussion.

"It's at this point that you start to take money out of the RRSP and hopefully do something creative with it, like spend it on your uncle Richard."

"That would be a splendid idea if you ask me." Richard was laughing as he rubbed his hands together.

"And you'd be just about …"

"Don't even go there James!"

"Let's try to stay on topic here, I think this is the last point we'll cover today. In the year that you turn 71 you can make your final RRSP contribution, assuming you have earned income. By December 31st of that year you must make a decision about what happens with your RRSP. Should you fall into a financial slumber, ignore the fact that you are 71 years old, or simply forget—well, you are in for one of life's most expensive lessons. On January 2nd of the following year, only three days later, all of your RRSP assets cease to be tax sheltered and all the money you have contributed, and all of your tax sheltered compound growth becomes taxable in that tax year in one large lump sum. So imagine if you will, being asleep at the switch and doing nothing. If you had an RRSP worth $1.2 million on December 31st, on January 2nd you are now in a position of paying tax on the entire amount in that tax year. Tax on an amount that large would be sure to put you in the highest tax bracket in the country, and I'll just make a wild assumption that it would be close to 50% regardless of the province you lived in. So, that indecision just cost you $600,000. What do you think about that?"

"Yikes, that bites."

"So assuming we aren't going to be asleep at the switch as you said, what options do we have?" Joyce was once again at the ready to take some more notes. I must admit, I admired her enthusiasm for a topic that conceivably wouldn't affect her for close to 50 years.

"You have two basic choices if you don't want to cash your RRSP at that point Joyce. You can use a RRIF or an annuity."

"RRIF or annuity? Sounds complicated."

"Not really, but for most people it will be one of the largest financial decisions they make assuming that they have done all of the proper work in the years prior to accumulate a store of wealth. There is actually much to consider—How long will you live? What level of income would you like to have? Will you need money to take care of other family members? What is your health like? What about emergency funds? Are you going to be traveling? The list of questions can go on and on. Key questions when it comes to trying to determine what you should be doing with your RRSP would be the following:

1) How do I minimize tax for the longest period possible?
2) How do I maximize the value of my estate?
3) How do I maintain a steady income stream?
4) How do I continue to grow my assets?
5) How do I keep the most control?

"Given these questions, how do we choose what to do with the funds? Well, let's start by looking at the RRIF. A RRIF, also known as a Registered Retirement Income Fund, is the natural extension of an RRSP and it is a popular option as your funds remain tax deferred until withdrawn, and as such they let your funds continue to earn income on a tax deferred basis. In fact, all of your money can remain in the same assets and investments you owned while they were in the RRSP. The major difference is the objective. The objective of an RRSP is to accumulate as much money as you can, while for the RRIF it is to pay money out of the plan for income. How much money gets paid out? Well, it won't surprise you to find out there is a formula and the formula determines your MAP.

"What's MAP?"

"Minimum Annual Payment. It is the minimum amount that you must take out of the plan in any given year. Let's assume you were 71 years old, your MAP is 7.38%. Therefore if you had a RRIF valued at $800,000 you have to remove $59,040."

"Cool. I get to take $59,040 out of the plan tax free."

"Not so fast James. No tax-free holiday here. Now that you are pulling funds out, you start paying tax on the money that you have been sheltering for an extended period of time. That $59,040 becomes taxable income in the year that you pull it out and, what's more, you don't have a choice but to pull out $59,040. Even if you only wanted or needed to take $20,000 of income, you have to take a minimum of $59,040 out."

"That's not fair! It's your money, isn't it?"

"Joyce, Joyce, Joyce. Who planted the mistaken notion in your head that life was going to be fair?" Richard was laughing as he wagged a finger in Joyce's direction. "Sorry pal, the rules are the rules and sometimes the rules ain't fair."

> **No tax-free holiday here. Once you begin to pull funds out of your RRSP, you start paying tax on the money.**

I continued. "Fair, not fair, that's not for me to decide Joyce. It's just the way it is. Keep in mind that the rules can and probably will change before this affects you in the future, as just about everything else will. Before 1993 the MAP was calculated based on a different formula which has been replaced by a defined schedule of minimum payouts, based on percentages allowing your money to last your lifetime. Here is a table of the calculated MAP values as they currently exist today. The 'Old Map' is used by anyone with a RRIF in place before 1992. Everyone since 1993 uses the 'New Map' value." I removed copies of the MAP payment tables from my briefcase; there were just too many numbers to be writing this out on the board.

Age	Old Map%	New Map%	Age	Old Map%	New Map%	Age	Old Map%	New Map%
71	5.26	7.38	72	5.56	7.48	73	5.88	7.59
74	6.25	7.71	75	6.67	7.85	76	7.14	7.99
77	7.69	8.15	78	8.33	8.33	79	8.53	8.53
80	8.75	8.75	81	8.99	8.99	82	9.27	9.27
83	9.58	9.58	84	9.93	9.93	85	10.33	10.33
86	10.79	10.79	87	11.33	11.33	88	11.96	11.96
89	12.71	12.71	90	13.62	13.62	91	14.73	14.73
92	16.12	16.12	93	17.92	17.92	94+	20.00	20.00

Current tax data available at: www.cra-arc.gc.ca

"Again, keep in mind that the MAP only defines the minimum amount you have to withdraw each year. If you decide to withdraw more and you certainly can, there will be a withholding tax on the amount in excess of the MAP and all the amount withdrawn will become taxable income in that tax year." I paused to do two things, catch my breath and take a sip of my beverage. It had been a fairly long and rambling bit of lecture. I was hoping I hadn't lost my audience.

"Or could you take out an annuity as an alternative?"

"Yes Richard that is an option that people can choose as well. You've taken some finance courses and accounting at university Joyce. Have you come across the term 'actuary'?"

"Sure, it has to do with a lot of number crunching in an attempt to predict the future, risk analysis and stuff like that. That's my impression at least."

"Something like that, and that is what annuities are like to some degree. An annuity is an agreement between you and a financial institution, bank, trust, insurance company, etc. You give them a lump sum of money in return for their promise to provide you with a set amount of income per year for a predefined period of time. The payments are fixed and can be paid to you monthly or annually depending on the agreement. Plenty of factors come into play here—your age, prevailing interest rates, life expectancies, long term economic predictions, etc., etc."

James and Joyce were both looking a little dazed by all of this information and Richard was giving me the wrap up signal. It was probably a good thing. After all, while this information is very important, it wouldn't directly impact them for years to come.

"There are two terms to remember: 'life annuity' and 'fixed term annuity.' Life annuities are available only through insurance companies and they offer the security of regular payments for the rest of your life. When you die the plan dies. That might mean if you purchased one and died only four months later, you didn't get your money's worth. Should you live until age 107, you'd have done very well. There are a variety of different survivor options to select as well, but a discussion of those should be left to a qualified financial advisor."

"So do you know any?" James was smiling.

"Yes I do, thank you, but that discussion can wait until you are closer to the point where you'll be needing one. The fixed term annuity provides a regular payment stream for a fixed period of five, ten, 15 or 20 years. Should you die unexpectedly four months into it, payments would continue until the end of the term. If there is no spouse, the payments are turned into a commuted value and are paid to your estate. For now, that is pretty much all I want to say about this topic, if that is ok with you guys. Your thoughts?"

I could tell they weren't lost, just in information overload at this point; we'd covered a lot of ground today. Richard was standing behind the couch, his hands spread out on the back, between James and Joyce who were sitting on the couch. It made a great family picture. I decided to add the following to the board as a final thought:

Money from your RRSP
Cash   Advantage: You get cash to use
          Disadvantage: Huge tax liability
RRIF   Advantage: Money grows sheltered
          Disadvantage: Have to take minimum amount out each year
Annuity   Advantage: Guaranteed monthly/annual payment
          Disadvantage: Lose ownership of the assets

"You know John, I think we've all had enough for today. How do we feel about that?" Richard leaned over and pressed the button to print the last page of material from the board. James and Joyce hadn't said anything, but both had closed their books, so I guess the point had been taken. We were all relaxing, enjoying the company and the view.

"Right now, it's time to celebrate." With that Richard went over to the large well-decorated Christmas tree to the left of the fireplace and returned carrying two presents.

"Merry Christmas Joyce. Merry Christmas James."

"What is this?"

"They're called presents Joyce. People sometimes give them to each other as signs of affection on special occasions."

"I know that, but I wasn't expecting … I didn't bring …"

"Which is fine, I didn't give these to you in order to get one, go ahead, open them."

James tore into the bright wrapping paper as I noticed that both gifts were approximately the same shape and size. Joyce was more meticulous, carefully taking the wrapping paper off with slow and deliberate action.

"Cool. *Boom, Bust & Echo*. Thanks Richard. I guess I have some reading to do over the holidays. What did you get Joyce?"

"*The Pig and the Python*. Thanks Richard. You didn't have to do this you know?"

"That's the fun thing about gifts, you never have to. It's best done when you simply want to. I think you'll find they are a nice tie-in to today's conversation. Feel free to share them with each other."

"Share? But I don't wanna share." For his comment, Joyce punched James in the shoulder playfully.

"Yes, you have to share with me. You hated it when we were kids, you should be over it by now."

"So what do we think the New Year will bring us with this project Richard?" I asked grinning, amused by watching James and Joyce interact.

"Good question, perhaps better asked as when do we think the New Year should bring us something for the project. Do we like meeting here? Does this work for everyone?"

"This is great, I vote for here!" James didn't even hesitate.

"Me too!" Joyce certainly wasn't far behind.

I liked it as well and offered, "Sure, I'm in."

"Well, a month from today is January 16th, but that's a Tuesday, so how about Saturday the 20th?" Everyone was checking their calendars, I knew it would be fine for me; I figured that we might pick that date so I had cleared it in advance.

"Good for me."

"Me too."

There was a pause in the conversation; we all seemed to be looking at Richard. He seemed to sense that as well.

"What? What do you need now?" Richard was laughing.

"Some direction. A topic maybe?"

"Page 25 James," James picked up his gift and when he opened it to page 25, four 5" × 7" cards spilled out onto the floor. James picked them up and passed them out to us. Like the last set, these new cards contained no words, just a picture, and this one seemed far more cryptic than the last one.

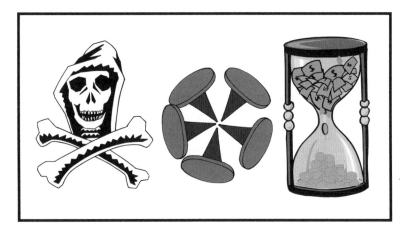

"What sort of message is this?"

"No hints before we go?"

"There are three guarantees."

"Guarantees of what?

"That's the hint."

"What? You lost me Richard."

"There are three guarantees. That's the hint."

We spent the next several minutes tidying up the great room, and before we knew it we were all standing at the front door, making our exit. We must have been in the Christmas spirit. There were Jarvis Hugs and handshakes for everyone. Then we were off to clean the fresh blanket of snow off our vehicles.

9

The Three
Guarantees

The Promised Land guarantees nothing. It is only an opportunity, not a deliverance.
Shelby Steele

Sleet.

Call it what you like, some use 'sleet,' others use 'freezing rain,' some people use much more colourful language than that. In any case, it makes for particularly nasty driving. The drive was taking an exceptionally long time today, but I was in no hurry. Richard's retentiveness about time wasn't about to make me move any faster under these conditions.

The days since our last meeting had been full of activity. First were the Christmas preparations, followed by New Year's celebrations. Richard had rung in the New Year in Bermuda, resting his toes in the pink sand and enjoying the sunshine. I opted for the thrill of a double black diamond run at Mt. Tremblant and living to tell about it.

Brad's car was parked in the driveway. I instinctively put a hand on the hood where the melting snow was sliding off into a pile on the front bumper. Still warm. They hadn't been here long and I was only a little late. I bounded up the porch carefully, no sense falling on my head to announce my arrival. I knocked twice and opened the door.

"John!"

The three of them were seated around the granite fireplace, almost an exact duplicate of our last meeting. Three pitchers of juice and a huge plate of sliced fruit covered the table. Piled in the middle of the plate, pretty much the entire contents of a large bag of Oreo cookies. At least he was consistent. Richard was wearing a yellow sweatshirt with 'Bermuda' stitched across the front, along with a wide-brimmed straw hat. I guess he was still in vacation mode. "So I was sitting there with my toes dangling in the surf, two dolphins were lazily swimming just out beyond the wave break. Ah, but enough about me, John is here. He'll make us work now."

"Boo. Hiss." Catcalls from Richard's audience.

"Sure, ruin a good story, that's what I pride myself on. Sorry I'm late; I didn't want you to think that I had forgotten about our punctuality pledge."

"Not a problem John. You know I like punctuality, but I'm not stupid about it, especially in this weather." While Richard ribbed me for taking the fun away it was obvious that everyone was ready to go. The whiteboard, fresh off its debut last month, was situated to the left of the fireplace and both James and Joyce had their notebooks out. It seemed as good a time as any to start. As I opened my briefcase, Richard was spinning the 5" × 7" card from the last session in his hands.

"Do we have any volunteers?"

"Pick me! Pick me!" James had his hand in the air.

"Ok James, go ahead," Joyce was shaking her head back and forth.

"You seem skeptical of his enthusiasm Joyce."

"No, just trying to temper his expectations. He thinks he has it all figured out."

"That's not what I said, I don't have it *all* figured out, but I think that I have the card figured out."

"Ok James, the stage is yours, tell us what you think."

"Well, when you gave us the card and we badgered you for a little guidance, you offered up three guarantees as your hint. So, given that and a little research, this is my best guess." James popped up out of his chair and wrote the following on the board:

1) Death
2) Taxes
3) Inflation

"I like it. Any comments Joyce?"

"No. I'm not suggesting he's wrong; I just don't get the death part. We're supposed to be talking about financial planning, so taxes and inflation make sense to me. Then again I'm not sure how he got inflation from the card either."

"James?"

"Well, I'll admit, mom helped a little. I asked her what she thought life's three guarantees were. She said 'death and taxes, but that she didn't have any clues as to the third.' Since the first two seemed to make sense, I started looking at the card a little closer. You have money in the form of bills in the top of the hourglass and coins in the bottom. Looking at this card," James pulled out the card from the December session, "it showed coins to dollars or growing the money with an RRSP."

"Nice going, Mr. Smarty-pants." Joyce smiled.

"So now it's reversed. What would take money and do the reverse, shrink it, assuming we weren't spending it. Inflation will do that, right?"

"Right you are James. Well done. If I had a gold star I'd give you one. So we have death, taxes and inflation. The three guarantees. To Joyce's point, death does seem like an odd one and, while most people don't want to admit it, it's guaranteed that we'll all die, the big unknown is when."

> **There are three guarantees in life—death, taxes and inflation!**

"Believe it or not, that fact will have an impact on your plans and everyone else's plans at some point, but I suspect that isn't what we are talking about today."

"Right you are, John. We'll save death for another day—perhaps a grey and rainy one at that, no sense spoiling today with that topic. So let's gloom it up talking about taxes and inflation instead, ok?" Richard made a face, which I can't really describe, but the three of us cracked-up laughing.

"Ok. Ok. Focus people. Which do we tackle first?"

"I vote for inflation."

"Why?"

"Because I know less about it. Taxes I think I have a handle on. Inflation is something we hear about in the news all the time, but is still a mystery to me." Since nobody seemed to offer any other opinion, Richard took that as the place to begin.

"Inflation is an interesting, yet easy concept to comprehend." He withdrew a yellow balloon from his pocket and proceeded to blow it up. "Inflation is taking something smaller and making it larger," then he blew more air into it, "and larger again," he repeated the process a third time, "until ..." he blew one final blast of air into the balloon. Bang!

"It explodes? Inflation is an explosion?" questioned James.

"I think it's a metaphor or something," offered Joyce.

"Right, the balloon is an example of the price of things—what it costs to live. Richard was showing us that over time, it costs more to live, and that increased cost is due to inflation. If inflation remains unchecked, the economy, or your spending, blows up."

"Inflation would seem to be a very bad thing, especially if it blows up."

"If left unchecked, inflation can be very bad James. That said, the economy does need some inflation in order to maintain growth. The concept of trying to hold things the same for an extended period has never worked. Various governments have tried wage and price controls, much to the dismay of those who elected them. Workers want higher wages, the stuff they produce then costs more, we see prices go up, we ask for more money so we can purchase the things we want to buy."

"Just as an interesting aside, and because it is something we can all relate to, let's take a look at these." Richard opened a folder and tossed an assortment of postage stamps on the table.

"I sent out some letters the other day. Yes, some people still don't do everything by e-mail," he cast a glance in my direction. "It got me thinking about what stamps used to cost. You know, those things we used before e-mail," Richard grinned slightly as he continued. "Just under 40 years ago, in 1974, it cost only eight cents to send a first class letter in Canada. Today costs 63 cents, 66 to 71 cents when you add on the HST, depending on province. An increase of almost eight times the cost to mail the exact same letter, to the exact same place. That works out to an inflation rate of approximately 5.29% per year, compounded."

"*Approximately* 5.29%?"

"Ok, I figured it out; I was trying to make a point John."

"So it's a vicious cycle then, more, more, more?" Joyce looked dismayed at the thought.

"It can be, but not always. Some things naturally go down. When I bought my first computer in 1985, it cost me over $5,000. I can purchase a machine today with 200 times the functionality of that one for under $1,000. New technologies and efficiencies will drive the prices of many things down over time. Other things, those with a high labour content get pushed up, or items that become scarce get driven up as well."

"The point of all this is what?" James seemed puzzled.

"Good question. What is the point? John?"

"Oh sure, drag me into this. I suspect the point that Richard would like to make is that you can't just sit under a rock and do nothing. We spent the last three meetings looking at how to generate assets and future wealth and a big question, especially for someone in your age group, might be 'why?'"

"I get why, because I want to buy stuff in the future, have a house, travel, etc."

"Exactly. So we invest our money, we hope we watch it grow and to be successful we have to be able to deal with inflation because it eats away at the gains that we are making."

"Eats away? How?"

"Think of the last bike you purchased James. How much did you pay for it?"

"About $400 or so."

"When?"

"Two years ago."

"If you had to replace that same bike today, what would it cost you?"

"About $500. It's electric blue, titanium rims, double shift ..."

"Ok. About $500. In just under two years the inflation rate is about 12% a year."

"So?"

"That means if you had taken $400 two years ago and invested it, you would have had to earn 12% or better on the money in order to buy your new bike." Before I could continue, Richard jumped back in.

"If you had just put the money in your sock drawer or under your bed, or wherever you hide stuff, and did nothing with it for two years, you'd still have $400 and you'd need to come up with another $100 to buy your bike. In short, inflation erodes your purchasing power as you move to the future."

"You two are depressing me for what reason?" James didn't seem to be enjoying this at all.

"Not trying to be depressing, just being realistic about life that's all. Remember the numbers we were looking at from RRSPs and compound interest, the impressive bottom of the chart numbers?"

"Well, what Richard is setting you up for is the potential that having $1.5 million today would be a tremendous thing, or perhaps just a good thing depending on your perspective. Now, if we look 30 years down the road, I suspect that it will still be a significant amount of money. However, your expenses will be rising accordingly, but hopefully less than your investments rise." I liked the interplay that Richard and I were having in discussing this topic. It was a little like tennis, and we were volleying back and forth. James and Joyce kept alternating their glances back and forth watching us.

"For example, let's look at your mom's house James. I grew up there; I know what your grandparents paid for it. Would you believe the very large sum of $8,800? That was in 1952. Should your parents choose to sell it today, they would probably get close to $275,000 or so." Joyce had pulled out her BlackBerry® from her backpack and was tapping furiously.

"That would be an average annual return of about 7.1%. That's quite impressive, isn't it?" Joyce showed us the display to make her point.

"It depends."

"Depends on what?"

"Well, if you were going to sell the house and put the money in your pocket, that would be great. But if you sold it, you'd still need a place to live and to buy another place of equivalent size, in a similar location would cost you roughly the same, so you wouldn't be any further ahead. So while your parent's house appreciated or grew in value so did everyone else's house. That's how inflation affects things."

"So how do we combat this?" Joyce seemed annoyed at the concept of inflation and its effect on our lives.

"You don't." Richard had jumped in before I could speak.

"What?" in unison.

Inflation erodes your purchasing power as you move to the future.

"You can't control it or affect it. It's the product of the economy, our country's fiscal and monetary policies, external political influences and blind dumb luck for the most part."

"What we are suggesting is that you need to know that it exists, that it will affect your future buying power and in order to have any real gains within your investing program you need to earn more than the rate of inflation or you'll fall behind. Let's look at a quick example—this chart shows the earning power of today's dollars in the future at a couple of different rates of inflation."

Impact of Inflation

Income	Inflation @	5 Years	15 Years	25 Years
20,000	3%	23,185	31,159	41,876
	4%	24,333	36,019	53,317
	5%	25,526	41,579	67,727
40,000	3%	46,371	62,319	83,751
	4%	48,666	72,038	106,633
	5%	51,051	83,157	135,454
60,000	3%	69,556	93,478	125,627
	4%	72,999	108,057	159,950
	5%	76,577	124,736	203,181

"So you can see that in order to maintain the purchasing power that you had earning $40,000 a year, in five years with an inflation rate of 4%, you need to be earning $48,666 just to stay even. If you don't stay even, you fall behind, and that is how inflation eats away at your standard of living. If you were making $60,000 a year, in 25 years you'd need $125,627 if inflation stayed at 3% a year."

"So we can't affect it or do anything about it, we just accept that it is and live with it?" James was shaking his head and looking at Joyce with a disgusted look.

"Hey, don't look at me like that! I didn't invent this."

"Is there any good news for us today guys?"

"Sure, John's going to talk about taxes now." An audible groan came from both James and Joyce and I added my voice to theirs. Taxes were never a fun thing to talk about, but Richard was insisting.

"All my dad ever complains about are taxes. Income taxes, sales taxes, house taxes, school taxes, etc."

"As do most people Joyce, but for the purposes of today's discussion we'll only be focusing on income taxes because that is an area where proper planning can have a substantial impact. First, we had better get used to income taxes because they aren't going away. It might interest you to know that income tax was implemented in 1919 by Prime Minister Sir Robert Borden to help pay for the debt incurred during World War I. A temporary measure—that has been here ever since. Second, while you are obligated to pay your income tax, you are under no obligation to pay one more penny than you have to."

"John is making a key point here. Tax evasion is illegal and if you cheat the system and get caught, you will pay. However, it is not illegal and is, in fact, smart planning to pay only the minimum amount that you have to and not a penny more. Sorry to have interrupted John."

Income taxes were first introduced as a temporary measure in 1919.

"Thank you and it's a good point. What I'm going to share with you isn't intended to be a tax seminar. For detailed tax planning and how to ensure the maximum deductions are taken, please use a professional tax accountant or take up the in-depth study of the Canadian Income Tax Act."

"No, thank you. One semester of corporate tax was enough to drive me away from accounting as a profession."

"I'm already math phobic, so don't be looking at me."

"Good, so I'll be able to keep this simple. There are four major ways to reduce the amount of tax you pay."

How to reduce taxes you pay
1) Earn less money
2) Use RRSPs to save tax
3) Use borrowed money to invest
4) Review the type of investment income

"We have what is called a sliding marginal tax system in our country. As you are probably aware, the more you earn, the more tax you pay. If you want to pay less tax, the first and most obvious way is to earn less money. I'll assume that this isn't a very popular option. Trust me, it isn't for most people."

"Gee, why am I not surprised at that?"

"Agreed, so the vast majority opt for the second most obvious one—contributing to an RRSP and getting a tax refund based on their contribution every year. You might remember this clearly; this was the focus of our last session. Your money grows in a tax sheltered fashion to be taxed later when it is removed from the plan. The third option, leverage investing, is a program where you borrow money to invest. It also has a tax benefit as the interest you pay on the money you borrowed can be claimed as a tax deduction."

"Is one better than the other John?" Joyce looked up from her notes.

"They are treated as the same deduction. A $1,000 RRSP contribution and a $1,000 claim for interest paid will yield the same benefit at tax time."

"Perhaps this might be a good time to talk about the fourth option or how investment income gets taxed John—that might answer a few questions," Richard prompted.

"Well, I've never thought of talking about taxes as a *good time*, but you're right, this might not be a bad time at that." I wandered over to the whiteboard and wrote the following:

Good	Better	Best
Interest	Canadian Dividends	Capital Gains

"While it won't come as a surprise to you since you are both working, your income is taxed by your employer and remitted to the government on your behalf. This is why you fill out an income tax return every year to make an account of what you made to the government. If too much tax was taken from you, you get a refund."

"Yay!" Richard was clapping.

"And, if you paid too little, then you get to write the government a cheque to make up the difference."

"Boo!" Richard was giving the thumbs down sign.

"Ok Richard, let's try to show some decorum in this discussion, we all know how you feel about the subject."

"Very well, carry on John."

"What you may not know is that any other income you earn, either from interest on bank accounts or income from other investments, gets taxed as well and how it is taxed depends on how the income comes to you. Income typically comes in three forms—interest, dividends and capital gains, as I have outlined on the board."

Income from interest sources is the highest taxed income you can have.

"Why good, better, best?" James was writing.

"It has to do with how the government treats the different types of income. Let's start with interest income. In short, interest income is what you earn by lending people money. Bank accounts, investment certificates, bonds, and treasury bills all generate interest income. Your income from interest sources is the highest taxed income you can have, taxed at the same rate as your employment income. Since you must include all interest you earn for income tax purposes, it gets added to your regular income from employment and is taxed at the highest marginal rate."

"It's like a double-whammy. Since the risk factors are lower for investing in GICs, bonds, etc., the government taxes it the heaviest because most people have interest generating investments—of course that is just my opinion. It is like a cash-cow for the government if you will. With that said, I'll end my sermon."

"Your uncle has a point. Interest is the most heavily taxed, which begs the question ..."

"Why would you want interest income?"

"That's a nice segue. Yes, why would we want interest income? Well, inside a tax-deferred investment such as an RRSP, where you are sheltering the interest income or any income for that matter, would be a good place to hold interest generating investments, should you decide to hold them at all. At the same time, if you are creating a pool of money for a short-term savings plan, to buy a new bike perhaps James, you'll do it in a bank account, and earn interest in the process. Any questions?"

Joyce as usual was writing furiously and James was content to make point form notes. It seemed that even with the addition of the electronic whiteboard and it's ability to print copies of the material, some people were just more comfortable doing things their own way. There didn't appear to be any questions on the topic and once Joyce looked back up at me, I took that as the sign to continue.

"Ok, the second type of income would be dividends. When you own shares or stock in a company, those companies often distribute profits back to their shareholders in the form of dividends. Depending on the type of stock you own, your dividends may be fixed or variable, they may be paid out to you quarterly, semi-annually or annually. If you own a mutual fund and the stocks that the fund owns issues dividend payments, then you will be passed those dividends via a distribution from the fund at the end of the year."

Dividends from Canadian companies entitle you to a break in taxation.

"Ok, so you are getting a payment from the investment. Why is this better than interest?"

"Thank you again, Joyce. Dividends from Canadian companies entitle you to a break in taxation; it's called the dividend tax credit. Perhaps the easiest way to explain it is by example."

Company XYZ issues dividend of 25 cents per share
If you own 1,000 shares:
Dividend Amount = 1000 * .25 = $250.00
Dividend Gross Up = $250.00 * 1.25 = $312.50

Dividend Tax Credit = \$250.00 * 20% = \$50.00
Formula: Dividend Amount − (Dividend Gross Up − 50% income tax
    − Div. Tax Credit) = What you keep
Therefore: \$250.00 − (\$312.50 − \$156.25 − \$50.00)
    = \$143.75

"Seems like a lot of math to me. Perhaps the word 'gross' is appropriate?"

"Don't let it get to you James. Whether you use a pencil, calculator, tax software or accountant, it's easier than it first appears. Your number of shares multiplied by the dividend will give you your total dividend amount—\$250 in this example. The 'Dividend Gross Up' is a multiplier set by the federal government, which requires you to increase your dividend amount by 125%—bringing you to \$312.50; this would be the actual amount of dividend income that you claim on your income tax form. Then you receive a 20% Dividend Tax Credit based on the original dividend amount of \$250—in this example it would be \$50.00. The taxpayer is provided with this dividend tax credit to account for the fact we are paying tax on an amount of money we didn't actually receive. The 20% is a combined federal/provincial average for example only. Tax laws change frequently, the latest information is always available at: www.cra-arc.gc.ca. For our example, based on \$250 in dividends you would keep \$143.75 after tax. Compare that to interest income of \$250, where you would only keep \$125. This is why having dividend income can be an important tax issue. I realize it probably sounds fairly complicated, but at tax time each year your income tax forms do a good job of walking you through the process. A financial planner or tax accountant can help as well. Any questions?"

Dividends from stocks of non-Canadian companies are treated like interest income –taxed at your highest marginal tax rate.

"What about dividends from non-Canadian companies, you seemed to make a point of saying *Canadian* companies when you started this."

"I did indeed Richard, thanks for catching that. If you are investing in stocks of non-Canadian companies and they pay dividends, the amount is treated the same as interest income, taxed at your highest marginal tax rate, no special treatment. Sorry."

"So I guess that leaves us with capital gains then."

"Yes James, so what about capital gains? Hopefully, the reason you purchased an investment, be it a stock, a mutual fund, or an investment property, is to have it appreciate or go up in value. Eventually, you will sell this investment and when you do you will realize a capital gain on the sale. The tax break on capital gains is significant compared to the other types of income. Currently, you are only required to pay tax on 50% of the capital gain and that amount then gets added to your taxable income for the year. Perhaps the easiest way to see the good, better, best would be by tracing the amount of money you'd keep by earning $1,000 of each type of income. For this example, let's assume a tax rate of 50% to make the math easier." As I turned to the board, James and Joyce were laughing at something Richard was saying, but I was focused on the task at hand, so I couldn't quite make out his comment.

	Good Interest	Better Cdn. Dividends	Best Capital Gains
Amount:	$1,000	$1,000 Gross Up: $1,250 Credit: $200	$1,000
Taxable:	$1,000	$1,250	$500
Tax:	$500	$(625 – 200)	$250
You Keep:	$500	$575	$750

"So there you have it. If you are going to earn $1,000 of income, which is your best alternative?"

"Capital gains," in unison.

"Very good class, you guys are quick," I actually laughed out loud, but softly.

"What happens if you pick a bad investment?"

"Meaning?"

"Well, I get the capital gain concept. In a perfect world things go up in value, but sometimes they don't. Right?"

"Definitely. Sometimes they don't. When they don't that is called a capital loss, the opposite of a capital gain, but there is a tax provision for that as well. You can use your loss to offset other capital gains that you have in the current tax year, or you can save the capital loss to offset gains that will come in the future. Additionally, if you have had capital gains in any of the preceding three tax years, you can use the loss to offset those gains. Given all of this, as I mentioned earlier, please do not take this as *the* taxation seminar. I'm only outlining some of the key points so you'll understand more about the topic. Are we ok with that?"

"So this is why tax deductions are important?"

"Very much so. The more you can reduce the amount of tax you pay, the more money you get to keep. The more money you get to keep, the happier and wealthier you'll be. It's never about how much you make, it's always about how much you keep. Just to show you the impact of taxation on the type of income, here are the differences in rate of return required to balance them out to the same after tax amount."

I started to write once again, hearing more laughter, louder this time than the last. I turned around to find the three of them stifling laughter when I realized that Richard must be up to something. Then it hit me. During the last part of the discussion he had walked by and patted me on the back. I reached behind me to find a small piece of paper taped to my back reading: Tax Nerd At Work.

"Very nice! You try to teach some people a key learning on the road to their financial future and this is how they repay you?" I quickly gathered my thoughts to continue the lesson knowing full well that Richard was the culprit and I would be forced to repay in kind at some point in the future.

	Good Interest	Better Cdn. Dividends	Best Capital Gains
Invest:	$10,000	$10,000	$10,000
Return:	10%	8.70%	6.67%
Income:	$1,000	$870	$667
Taxable:	$1,000	$1,087.50	$333.50
Tax:	$500	$(543.75 – 174)	$166.75
You Keep:	$500	$500.25	$500.25

"This is key learning, John, well done."

"Not bad for a tax nerd, eh?"

"It's key because many people don't realize that your tax issues will have as large a factor on your ability to create wealth as your investment returns. The average person would tell you that they'd be better off earning 10% than 6.67%, but here you've shown that a lower rate of return can yield you the same after tax earning. This is key."

Key or not key, I was getting a glassy-eyed stare not just from James but from Joyce as well. This was the first time that I had seen both of them in this state, so I figured that this would be a good time to call it a day.

"Well, I've certainly had enough for this morning. I don't know about you guys, but I'm taxed out."

"Me too! And I'm the one who likes numbers." Joyce grinned.

"Ok then, let's get out there and enjoy the rest of the day shall we?" But nobody moved from his or her seat. All eyes were on Richard.

"What did I do now?"

"You know …"

"Oh, you mean these?" With a flourish he removed four 5"× 7" cards from his folder and waved them around like a magician's wand. Finally finished, and seemingly amused with himself, he passed them out. Again, no words, just a picture.

"I'm getting better at this art stuff, don't you think?"

"What is this?" Joyce appeared puzzled.

"The next lesson gang. You'll get it. Stop thinking so literally and it will come to you. If it doesn't that is ok too. We'll figure it out together."

Richard had a big grin on his face. He was enjoying the puzzlement of his young pupils. He knew as I did, the biggest learning occurs when you figure something out for yourself, not when someone spells everything out for you. I had confidence that James and Joyce were up to the task. While we were sitting in puzzlement, Richard went back, erased the whiteboard and wrote the following:

> **The biggest learning occurs when you figure something out for yourself.**

Archimedes

"There, I can't be of more help than this—I've practically given it away, it would appear that I am still in the Christmas spirit today."

"What is an Archimedes?"

"That's it. No more. Finis. C'est tout."

"Well done Richard."

"Yes, that was just for your enjoyment Joyce."

"Richard likes to throw out a little French now and then to impress people. Don't build his ego up too much kids, we'll never be able to deal with him."

"Moi? Before we go much further, how about picking the next date? How about Saturday the 25th? Everyone free?" There was a momentary silence before the chorus replied affirmatively.

"So tell me about your Christmas kids, I already know what John did over the holidays—Mr. Double Black Diamond—ha!"

We spent the next 30 minutes discussing the past month, Christmas, New Year's celebrations, and all of the events and parties that filled the holidays. The New Year was off to a good start for everyone. James was getting more and more work at the courier company; Joyce was back in student mode after completing her fall work term. Me? I had been getting ready for RRSP season; there was no other time like the January and February financial planning and tax season rolled into one. For many, it is the only time of year they give any thought to their personal finances. I was hoping that by the time we finished with James and Joyce that we would be able to count them among the small percentage of those who were diligent year round.

> For many people, tax season is the only time of year they give any thought to their personal finances.

10

Getting a
Bigger Stick

Business? It's quite simple: it's other people's money.
Alexandre Dumas

Grey.

Anyone who has spent enough winters watching the weather knows exactly what someone means when they say it is a 'grey day.' Minimal light, extensive cloud cover, a general blanket of 'blah' over the entire landscape.

I decided that since I had been the last to arrive for the last two meetings I would rectify that today. I allowed myself plenty of time to arrive, including a stop at Timmy's for a jumbo box of donut holes. I like fruit as much as the next guy, but Richard's selection at our last gathering left me craving fat and carbohydrates.

"Morning Richard!"

"John. Nice to see you again. I see you brought some snacks, nothing healthy I presume?"

"I get this abuse from a guy who eats Oreo cookies for breakfast on a regular basis? Give me a break. If that is your attitude, then these will just be for me and the kids."

"Hey! Who are you calling kids?"

With the crackling of the fire and the noise from Richard rolling the whiteboard out of his office I hadn't heard the door open behind me. James and Joyce bounded into the living room and after surveying the offering of Richard's overflowing fruit plate and my box of deep fried non-nutritional dough, opted for the latter with enthusiasm.

"I'm disappointed James, I thought you had better dietary habits than that."

"Sorry. Can't resist."

We all grabbed a plate and spent some time discussing the events of the past month. James recounted some harrowing exploits of winter biking; Joyce was fully immersed back into her studies; I was lamenting for more time to get everything done; while Richard had spoken at a conference in Toronto two weeks ago, unveiling a new presentation he called 'Your Richly Imagined Future.' I was reloading my second plate when Richard produced the 5"× 7" card from the last session, which was the indicator that it was time to start this one.

> I didn't say it was easy, but that it got done.

"So, what do we think about this?"

"Well, it seems that Archimedes wasn't a *what* but a *who*," James had flipped open his notebook where the card was taped at the top of the page, "and an old guy at that."

"Easy on the age thing James," Richard was wagging a finger at him.

"Ok, I meant that he lived a long time ago. He said something like, 'give me a lever long enough and a place to stand and single-handed I can move the world,' or something to that effect."

"Yes he did, something to that effect. The importance of that would be?"

"Probably the lever I'd say," I didn't want to interrupt the lesson but I suspected that I knew where this was headed.

"Like this one?" Richard walked behind the couch and he reached down to retrieve something. He displayed a rusted piece of metal, almost ten feet long and at least two inches square. From how he was holding it, it seemed to have a considerable weight.

"A lever, exactly. A bar used for prying or dislodging something. An inducing or compelling force."

"Well done Joyce. So why is it important?"

"More importantly, why do you have one?"

"Well, where do you think all of the stones for that fireplace came from? Here's a hint, they were underneath the building we're sitting in."

"Really?"

"Really. This iron pry bar, or lever, was the tool that I used in order to move these stones and a couple of tree stumps from where they were, which were in the way of where I wanted to put the cabin."

"You and an iron bar. That's all?" Joyce seemed dubious.

"Well, me, this iron bar, time, patience and a desire to move them. I didn't say it was easy, but that it got done. Why did it get done?"

"Because you made it a goal to get it done."

"I told you they were quick John. You're right James."

"I understand the lever and the rocks. That's more of a physics thing, strength and moving inanimate objects. But this lever somehow applies to finance as well?"

"Very much so Joyce, and in a very powerful way." I hope that Richard didn't mind my jumping into the conversation. "What have been some of the recurring key points from our previous sessions?"

"Time is our friend."

"Start as early as you can to save money and invest to take advantage of compound interest."

"Right. Now think about Richard's card from the last session." Richard was drawing a crude representation of the 5"× 7" card on the whiteboard.

"Ok, I still see the lever, and what I'm assuming is a rock, or something to brace the lever against, but it's lifting a clock. Is the clock heavy?" James glanced toward Joyce and shrugged.

"Or the clock is big, the clock is … time? You're moving time using a lever?"

"Well, the lever is the object in use, the act of using it, or the execution is called leverage. But you are right in deducing that we are attempting to move time."

"Move time? I don't get it."

"Remember when we discussed compound interest and we saw how $2,000 a year invested over time could yield a tremendous amount of money 30 to 40 years down the road?"

"Big numbers, if you started early as Joyce said."

"Right, but you asked the question about starting later, either due to procrastination, lifestyle choices, whatever reason you choose. So you lost ten years of time in the example that we looked at."

"Those ten years of compounding makes a large difference in the totals. I created a spreadsheet at work with formulas that allowed you to manipulate the variables, how much you were saving, rate of return so you could see the changes."

"Lost time is important, Joyce." Richard continued; he read from a dictionary, "The concept of leverage from a financial perspective is to use credit to enhance one's speculative capacity. The key words there are 'credit,' 'enhance' and 'capacity.'"

"Not speculative? Isn't speculation just another word for risky?"

"It can be James, but for now we'll put the 'speculative' factor aside for purposes of our example. But we'll certainly be discussing it as we move ahead. I took the liberty of creating printed versions of the growth charts from that session. Here they are as a point of reference." I handed them to Joyce who passed them around the table. Since I was already standing, I moved over to the whiteboard.

"Let's see if we can start today with a good example shall we? On the first page I handed out is the chart where you invested $2,000 a year from age 22 for ten years. Here's the summary."

Start at age: 22
$2000/yr for 10 years
$20,000 total saved
@ 10% return compounded = $672,000 @ 62

"On the second page is the example of delaying by ten years. Summarized it is:

Start at age: 32
$2000/yr for 31 years
$62,000 total saved
@ 10% return compounded = $400,000 @ 62

"So starting on that basis we are all happy with the numbers right?"

Nods from around the table.

"Ok, leverage from the definition that Richard gave us used the word credit, which means what?"

"Credit cards?"

"A bank loan?"

"Credit cards are certainly credit, James, but for the purposes of leverage we are talking about a loan from a bank or other financial institution. When we started our last example we were saving $2,000 a year. So for this example we are going to use that same $2,000 to make loan payments in place of investing the money. If we were to borrow $20,000 we would have that amount to use as our investment base. We'll assume a 10% interest rate and a 10% return for example purposes. Using 10% on $20,000 means we pay $2,000 in interest each year. Let's see what that does to our chart and see if it helps James catch up to Joyce." The advantage of teaching these examples time after time is that you eventually memorize the numbers. When I had finished writing on the board, the result was the following:

Age	Opening	Additions	Interest	Closing
32	20,000	—	2,000	22,000
37	32,210	—	3,221	35,431
42	51,875	—	5,187	57,062
47	83,545	—	8,354	91,899
52	134,550	—	13,455	148,005
57	216,694	—	21,669	238,364
62	348,988	—	34,898	383,887

Invest $20,000 at age 32 – no additional funding

"So, what do we think of that?" as I turned to let them review the numbers.

"Not much. I have less money now than I had before. Investing $2,000 a year for 30 years I had accumulated $400,000. Now I spend $2,000 a year for 30 years paying off interest on a $20,000 investment loan and I have accumulated $16,000 less. Looks like this tool isn't that great to me."

"So what's missing James?" Silence. Richard grinned but remained silent.

"I can tell by the grin on Richard's face that there is more to those numbers than meets the eye, I just don't know what it is."

"You're getting good at this Joyce," Richard was still grinning. "So tell me, based on all the business finance classes you've taken so far, which was by far the most complex?"

"Hands down, Business 318—Corporate Taxation."

"Bingo!"

"Bingo?" in unison.

"When we discussed the concept of compound interest, the numbers look excessively large which is good, but we didn't add in the concept of taxation on the money that you were making. We covered taxes last session, so let's put both together now and see if we can ease some of James' puzzlement."

"Yeah, but taxes are negatives, that's what my parents say, which means less. And if I'm taking money away, how will that help me? I'm already behind where I was before."

> **If we borrow to invest money in qualified investments, the government allows us to deduct the interest we pay for that loan.**

"You have less James, according to the chart," Richard made a sweeping gesture to the board. "But you have also invested less and the chart doesn't show that. Care to explain John?"

"Certainly. What Richard is trying to get at is that from an investment perspective, in our summary from before, you invested $2,000 a year for 31 years to accumulate $400,000 dollars."

"And we did the same thing here. I made loan payments of $2,000 a year for 31 years—same thing, no?"

"Sort of James, but if we borrow to invest money in qualified investments, the government allows us to deduct the interest we pay for that loan when we do our income taxes at the end of the year. That interest amount combined with your personal tax rate will determine how much money you get back. Assuming you are in the 50% tax bracket, using a $2,000 interest expense would get you back $1,000. So in this example your real cost is only $1,000 a year for 31 years, or in total $31,000 instead of $62,000."

"In the original example, James invested $2,000 a year for 31 years, or $62,000. By doing it this way, he invests only half as much, but still ends up at roughly the same place." Joyce was sitting on the edge of the couch, obviously excited by the prospect of getting to the same place by investing less.

"Right again Joyce, but it can get better. Since we obviously had the diligence to make our $2,000 worth of interest payments every year, and the government is going to refund $1,000 to us, what will we do with that $1,000 dollars when we get it back?"

"Spend it!"

"I don't think that is where he's headed Joyce, even I figured that out." James rolled his eyes at his cousin.

"I know James, I was just trying to be cute," with that she flashed a toothy grin at James, then at Richard and me.

"See James, didn't we say back in the park months ago that learning could be fun? Now let's let John get back to his point—I'm assuming he had one."

"Umm, thanks I guess. My point? That we take our $1,000 rebate and invest it back into the program. After all, we were willing to invest $2,000 of our own money. Since the government has seen fit to give us another $1,000 to add back to it, why don't we? Now we'll see if things change—if at all." I returned to the board, adding in a new column to account for the additional $1,000 and after doing so was left with the following:

Age	Opening	Additions	Interest	Closing
32	20,000	—	2,000	22,000
37	37,315	1,000	3,832	42,147
42	66,812	1,000	6,782	74,594
47	114,317	1,000	11,532	126,849
52	190,825	1,000	19,182	211,007
57	314,041	1,000	31,504	346,545
62	512,482	1,000	51,348	564,830

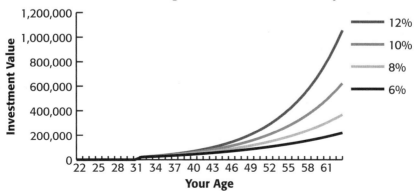

Invest $20,000 at age 32 – add tax refund each year

"So what do you think now James?"

"Let's see if I get this. I'm still investing $62,000 in total, $2,000 a year to make loan payments on the $20,000. The government gives me back $1,000 and I reinvest it since it didn't cost me anything to get it. Now I have $564,000 versus $400,000 or basically $160,000 more for doing exactly the same thing—investing the same $2,000 a year, only differently."

"Almost."

"Almost?"

"Remember, we did take out a loan after all, the bank will want their money back—so we should take that $20,000 off the bottom line figure assuming we pay them back at age 62. Am I right John? But why no $1,000 in the first year?"

"Right you are. You still owe the bank $20,000, if you pay them back the principal of $20,000 at age 62, then you drop $20,000 from the $564,830 leaving you with $544,830—still $140,000 above where you were before. As for the $1,000, you are always one year behind in terms of the tax year so I skipped the first year to account for that."

"So leverage is about buying back time. In a way it allows you to invest a larger amount of money due to the loan, that larger amount of money grows faster, helping you make up for the fact that you didn't start sooner. I like it." James smiled for the first time today.

"There is much to like. But, one key point to keep in mind is that leverage does not, cannot and will not make your investments grow faster; it does not affect your returns at all. I can't make this point strongly enough—*leverage has no effect on your returns*. What leverage will do is magnify your returns—both positively and negatively. Much like the old saying, 'when it's good it's great, when it's bad it's terrible.' But as you said, leverage in the right situation can help make up for the fact that you didn't start sooner."

> **Leverage in the right situation can help make up for the fact that you didn't start investing sooner.**

"Oh no, here we go again."

"Hang on a second before you get to the 'buts.' What if rather than buying back time to make up for time lost, you try to pre-purchase time? I don't even know what word I'm looking for—sorry John." Joyce looked up from her notebook for some inspiration.

"I'm not sure either, but I think the word you might be looking for is 'accelerate' or speeding time up. While impossible in the physical sense, in the financial sense you are onto something. Using James' original example of waiting until age 32 in order to start, we saw that we moved from $400,000 to $540,000 AL in the same amount of time."

"AL?"

"After Loan. Remember we eventually have to pay it back. So let's see what would happen if we started earlier. This button Richard?" I was pointing to the printer option on the whiteboard.

"Yep, that button. We'll bring you into the technological millennium." Richard laughed as the page emerged from the printer. That finished, I erased the board and proceeded to redraw the example.

Age	Opening	Additions	Interest	Closing
22	20,000	—	2,000	22,000
27	32,210	—	3,221	35,431
32	51,875	—	5,187	57,062
37	83,545	—	8,354	91,899
42	134,550	—	13,455	148,005
47	216,694	—	21,669	238,364
52	348,988	—	34,898	383,887
57	562,049	—	56,205	618,254
62	905,185	—	90,519	995,704

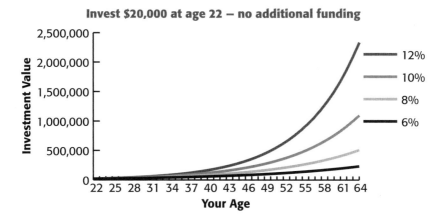

Invest $20,000 at age 22 – no additional funding

"Wow!" in unison.

I hadn't even had a chance to turn around from the board in order to gauge their reaction to the chart; I guess I didn't have to ask if they were impressed. "Any questions?"

"No, but I know there are some things here that we don't see and probably should, if the past is any indication." James was tempering his enthusiasm, but he was onto something.

"Ok, you got me."

"Ha! Told you."

"Here are the differences: First, in the original example, Joyce invested $2,000 a year for ten years, or $20,000 in total, ending up with $672,000. In this example she makes loan payments of $2,000 a year for 41 years, or $82,000 in total rather than $20,000, but ends up with $323,000 more for the effort. A significant amount, no?"

"Hey, wait a minute, what about the tax thing?"

"The *tax thing* James?"

"The interest rebate from income tax; you know, spend $2,000, and get $1,000 back."

"Very perceptive. Assuming a tax rate of 50% to keep the examples comparable, Joyce's actual cost is only $41,000. So over the time frame of 41 years she invests only $21,000 more and ends up $323,000 ahead."

"Actually $303,000, considering the $20,000 loan."

"Good Joyce. So is the $303,000 worth an extra $21,000 spread over 41 years? That would be the question. Only you or a client can provide the answer, but I suspect I know what the answer might be. I can do the chart using only $20,000 of payments just to see if you'd like that."

"I'd like that, but I'd also like to see what happens if I reinvest that $1,000 government rebate. After all, as you said I was willing to invest $2,000 in the loan payment. I may as well take the money they give me and put it back into the program."

"Good. I can do that too." Before I could get to the board Richard had already printed off the chart to keep a copy of it. Richard was talking about leverage and moving rocks and tree stumps with James and Joyce while I was busy drawing the two new charts. Joyce wasn't suffering from writer's cramp, but I was. I figured that the new charts would show them some impressive numbers and as I finished I was interested in what their reaction would be.

I turned to find them staring at the board, then at each other, then back to the board. I was pretty sure the number in the bottom right corner of the first chart had caught their eyes. It certainly would have caught my eye at their age. Heck, it still catches my eye at my age and I do this for a living.

Age	Opening	Additions	Growth	Closing
22	20,000	—	2,000	22,000
27	37,315	1,000	3,832	42,147
32	66,812	1,000	6,782	74,594
37	114,317	1,000	11,532	126,849
42	190,825	1,000	19,182	211,007
47	314,041	1,000	31,504	346,545
52	512,482	1,000	51,348	564,830
57	832,073	1,000	83,307	916,380
62	1,346,778	1,000	134,777	1,482,555

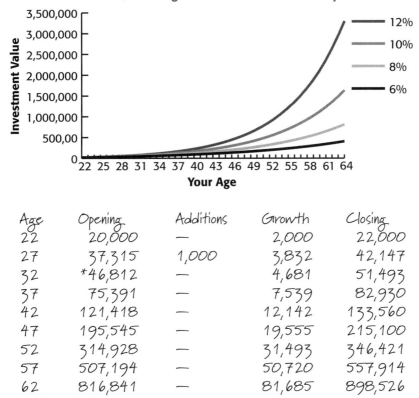

Invest $20,000 at age 22 – add tax refund each year

Age	Opening	Additions	Growth	Closing
22	20,000	—	2,000	22,000
27	37,315	1,000	3,832	42,147
32	*46,812	—	4,681	51,493
37	75,391	—	7,539	82,930
42	121,418	—	12,142	133,560
47	195,545	—	19,555	215,100
52	314,928	—	31,493	346,421
57	507,194	—	50,720	557,914
62	816,841	—	81,685	898,526

* Paid off $20,000 loan @ age 31

Invest $20,000 at age 22 – add tax refund, pay off loan at age 31

"That is huge!" James let out a sharp whistle to reinforce his point.

"All that for $82,000 plus adding back the tax refund based on borrowing $20,000 at age 22? Close to 1.5 million dollars? I don't believe it. I just don't believe it."

"Believe it Joyce. There are no math tricks here, it's merely the power of compound interest, using leverage to increase the amount you start with and then being diligent and patient enough to wait for the future to come to you."

"So everyone does this, right?"

"No." in unison from Richard and me. Now that was certainly a first.

"Why not?" in unison back at us. Somehow, I felt we were being mocked. Richard reached into his folder on the table and withdrew a sheet of paper.

"Exhibit A," as he waved the sheet around. "Remember the rules that John and I shared about what we had learned from our parents about money. One of the key rules was 'Do not borrow money—Debt is bad.' Using leverage is borrowing money after all, and borrowing is bad, so many people do not see leverage as a beneficial tool because debt is bad, leverage is debt, and therefore leverage is bad."

"There is that Richard, then there is always the real world to consider as well," I punctuated the point.

"Oh here it comes Joyce, the truth they've been hiding from us all along while painting pictures of a bright, financially secure future."

"What did you mean by real world John?"

"Each of the examples we have been using has been based on relatively easy math to illustrate our points. Interest rates at 10%, growth at 10%, all numbers moving in one direction only, and always positive. The real world unfortunately doesn't always work that way. While Richard and I could cite you chapter and verse as to why that is the case, you'll just have to believe us, or simply ask your parents. They'd be more than happy to explain to you that things do not always go as planned."

"While John and I are firm believers that you can consistently earn 10% on your money, when invested properly over an extended period of time, there is, first, no guarantee that will happen and, second, a guarantee that it won't be a straight line progression."

"Straight line progression, more math stuff right?"

"Relax James, not math, just logic. The key is that you average 10%, that doesn't mean 10% year after year after year. What it means is that you get 12%, then 8%, -7%, -6%, +19%, -3%, +9%, +12% and so on, and so on. We are talking about long-term investing here, not speculation, not gambling. If you are interested in gambling, try Las Vegas. Catch a show and roll the dice. When you only look at the short-term, leverage can be a very risky endeavour. I'll offer this up as an example. Let's assume the markets were to drop worldwide for a couple of years, say ten years running, which has rarely happened but certainly could. Let's assume a 10% drop per year. This would certainly be a long-term bear market." The following example was drawn for them:

Year	Opening	Additions	Growth	Closing
1	20,000	—	-2,000	18,000
3	17,100	1,000	-1,810	16,290
5	15,561	1,000	-1,656	14,905
7	14,314	1,000	-1,531	13,783
9	13,305	1,000	-1,431	12,874
10	12,874	1,000	-1,387	12,487

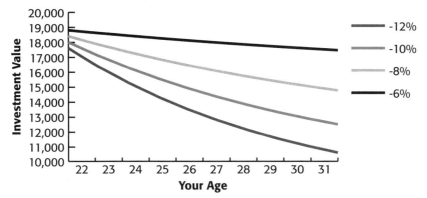

Invest $20,000 at age 22 – add tax refund, effect of declining market for 10 consecutive years

"Ugh!"

"Ugh is right Joyce, this is not a pretty picture. You are now ten years into your investing program, you owe the bank $20,000 for the loan, and your investments are now worth $12,500. Several things can happen here. The bank can ask for more collateral on the loan and they may have asked at a couple of points during those ten years. After all, your investments are worth less than the loan value. Alternatively, you could choose to panic and get out, selling your investments and you'd still have to make up the difference between what you received from the investment and what you still owe the bank."

"Or you could always do what I did kids."

"What was that Richard?"

"Decided that leverage was the way to go as part of my overall investment strategy; John and I had talked about it for several years. Finally, as always with discussions between John and me, the final decision was mine, so I decided to borrow $100,000 and invest it in the market on September 25th, 1987. The interest rate at the time was 12%, meaning that I had to make loan payments of approximately $1,000 a month. Exactly 23 days later, the largest single one-day percentage drop in the markets occurred sending investors panicking—and trust me I wanted to as well. In fact, in only five days, from October 14th to the 19th, the market lost 33.4% of its value. My brilliant leverage idea using $100,000 was now worth approximately $67,000 after only 23 days. 'Don't panic,' John told me. We were looking long term, not less than a month. Think bigger picture he told me. Yeah, right John, I'm living in a trailer surrounded by tree stumps, spending my days moving rocks with a metal bar, my investments are in free-fall and the business press is screaming the end of the world is near. Just how was I supposed to think big picture?" Richard produced some yellowed clippings from his folder and tossed them onto the table.

Richard paused in his story, calmly poured himself a glass of orange juice, took a huge slice of pineapple and settled back into the couch, obviously quite relaxed and pleased with himself.

"And then what happened?"

"Life happened James."

"What?" in unison.

"Life. Time passed, the markets went back up, then down, then up, then down again, interest rates went up, interest rates went down, a couple of wars and skirmishes around the world, I finished building the cabin, I started consulting, we had a couple of recessions, I taught a bunch of photography classes, your grandparents both passed away, I did some traveling in Europe, Quebec tried to leave Canada, the Internet revolution exploded, you discovered you had an uncle you didn't know about and here we are today."

"But your investments, what happened to your investments?"

"There are more important things than money James." It seemed strange to hear it come from Joyce rather than Richard.

"Joyce is right, but to your point. I did start by talking about the leverage program so I should at least stay on topic."

I was enjoying the interplay between Richard, James and Joyce. I could somehow envision that this was exactly what he had in mind when he first discussed the project with me.

"I don't know exactly how much they're worth today James. I'm sure John could tell you about the money. That's why I hang around with him, he's good that way. Any idea John?"

He had set me up. Earlier this week he had asked me to create a report for him based on the $100,000 he invested on September 25th, 1987, tracking only that and nothing else. I hadn't had a chance to show it to Richard so I was reluctant to share it here without him having seen it first.

"I do have it, but you haven't seen it, and you know how I feel about maintaining client confidentiality."

"You have my approval, enlighten us."

"I had created a chart, but rather than show you that, I'll just say that as of last Friday, the value was $501,754 give or take a few cents."

James and Joyce were stunned. Richard just took it in stride, as he always did. He grinned; after all, it was excellent growth and nothing to sneeze at. Still, money really didn't excite Richard as it did most people. Don't get me wrong, he liked it well enough that it was important to take care of and pay attention to, but not so much that it dominated his thoughts.

"All that in just 23 years?"

"It's been an interesting 23 years." With that, Richard and I each picked up our glasses and clinked them together.

"To the experiences," in unison. It was a phrase we used when we were toasting happy events or just when we felt like breaking the monotony of a silent point in time. James and Joyce were looking at each other as if they'd just been given an insight into Richard's private life, which they had.

> **Everything isn't for everyone. Every situation is different. Everyone's goals and dreams are unique.**

"I think class is over for today kids. To answer your question from earlier James, there are some logical and illogical reasons why leverage isn't for everyone and we can, and will, discuss those in the future. In fact, we can discuss these at the next session if that's ok with everyone. How about that?"

"Sure, this is fascinating stuff, unless there is something that I'm failing to see, which is likely. I'm not sure why people wouldn't want to do this."

"I like your enthusiasm Joyce, but keep in mind that everything isn't for everyone; every situation is different, as are everyone's goals and dreams. But just for interest's sake, this might be a good topic for next time." Before I realized it, Richard was passing out four new 5"× 7" cards to us to examine.

"Does this mean we have to choose between the two? Why can't we do both?"

"No, James it's not an either/or, but more the case why someone might choose one over the other. When we look at why people might choose not to use leverage we'll see why it might be an either/or decision, but it could certainly be *and*. How's that for being elusive? Before we go much further, how about picking the next date?

A month from today is March 25th, exactly four weeks. So how about Saturday the 25th? Everyone free?" There was a momentary silence before the chorus replied affirmatively.

"I might suggest, if we are open to it, a change in venue."

"To where?"

"Your office John, if that's ok."

"Fine with me. Any particular reason?"

"Nope. Just a change of pace."

"For the experience?" James shrugged his shoulders.

"Certainly!" Richard's enthusiastic comment was accompanied by an equally enthusiastic slap on the back.

"Ok I give, stop beating me."

"Sorry James, did I hurt you?"

"No, you just surprised me."

"Get used to it. Life is full of surprises."

"It certainly is. Look at that!"

We all turned toward the windows in the living room. A female deer was standing about 20 feet from the cabin, directly in a sliver of sunlight. I think we were surprised on two accounts. First, to see such a beautiful animal just steps away. Second, to actually see some sunshine. Richard slowly and deliberately picked up a camera from the compartment below the side table, and the continuous 'click, whir' of the automatic film advance filled the room for several seconds. Before the noise ended the young doe had bounded off into the trees behind the garage.

"And you want a change of venue for the next meeting?"

"Sure. I see this all the time. We'll be back, I promise."

"That was great!" Joyce was smiling ear-to-ear.

It was nice to see James and Joyce excited, not as kids, but as adults who had just seen something interesting and were not afraid to show their reaction to it. Richard and I had talked recently about the fact that too many people seem to have lost the ability to enjoy simple things in life.

"If any of the pictures turn out, I'll bring them to the next session." Before I knew what was happening, Richard was clicking away again—except we were the targets this time.

"Argh! No pictures!" Joyce was covering her face with her hands; as for me, I simply turned around and looked the other way. It seemed James was the ham of the group, the only one who liked having his picture taken. Finally, the flashing subsided, and Richard put the camera down, as we were making our way to the door.

The sliver of sunshine where the deer had stood was now across the middle of the driveway, and the sky appeared to be brightening a touch. Perhaps we'd be seeing more sun before the end of the day? They hadn't called for sun today, but all four of us where happy to see it.

To RRSP or Not
to RRSP?

It doesn't matter which side of the fence you get off on sometimes. What matters most is getting off. You cannot make progress without making decisions.
Jim Rohn

Sunshine.

Finally. Just when you begin to lull yourself into depression that winter is never going to end, Mother Nature delivers the antidote. Sunlight was streaming in through my office windows.

I was cleaning off the white board in preparation for the meeting when I realized it had been four months since we were last here. A change of venue might give us a fresh perspective on things, and given the topics I suspected were going to be covered today, having reference material handy would be a good thing. I took a seat at the table near the windows and decided to close my eyes and bask in the warmth.

"John? You ok?"

"Hmmm, I think so. Come on in." How long had I dozed off for? It was only minutes according to my watch, but it seemed like an hour.

"I'm already in," the table in front of me was covered by Richard's large fruit tray, the bag of Oreos and an assortment of beverages, including a can of Diet Coke that I knew was just for me.

"Ok then, sorry I didn't get up. How long have you been here?"

"Two minutes tops John, don't sweat it."

He smiled as he tossed his folder on the table and proceeded to fill a plastic plate with food. "You'll notice I'm even partaking of your offering

John. It must be the kids' influence, they seem to like these donut bites or whatever they call them."

We were talking about the impending income tax deadline, both complaining about the government's inability to spend our donations properly when I heard two voices coming up the hallway.

"Did so."

"Did not."

"Did so!"

Richard looked over and smiled. He found the actions of James and Joyce quite amusing at times and had told me so on several occasions. They had always been close, but I suspected the time they spent together as part of this project had tightened their relationship. As for Richard, I think he was getting a family connection that he failed to get from Brad or Mary. If a project such as this could accomplish nothing else, it made me feel happy to have contributed to the cause.

"Did what?" Richard yelled in the direction of the door.

"Sorry guys, we didn't mean to yell," James walked in ahead of Joyce who was struggling to remove her backpack. "I was just telling Joyce that I missed having a puzzle to solve from the last meeting, and how I didn't think you'd be able to stump me again. Joyce doesn't think that I'm that bright."

"That's not what I said James! I said that I'd be surprised because there is always a curve we don't expect, that's all. So don't get your hopes up."

"All in due time, grab some breakfast," Richard offered a sweeping gesture to the food on the table.

"Hey, more donut holes. Argh! Richard is eating them? What's wrong with this picture?"

"Relax. Everything in moderation. They're actually quite tasty even if they contain zero nutritional value. So, what have we all been up to since we last met?"

Our usual opening discussion centered on the activity of the previous four weeks. Joyce was getting some exceptional marks back from school. James was examining the possibility of starting his own courier company to get away from some of the dissatisfaction that he was experiencing. Richard had been to Ottawa, Montreal and Calgary. His professional speaking was becoming quite a lucrative endeavour. Me? Finally, although it seemed it would never end, the RRSP season had come and gone; now I was just finishing up with clients who were wrapping up their preparations for tax season. We all took a refill on the beverages, James took a heaping second helping of everything and Richard pulled out the 5"× 7" card from his folder. Time to start today's lesson. "To be or not to be, that is the question."

"To RRSP or not to RRSP isn't that the question?"

"Well, yes Joyce, but thanks for stealing my thunder."

"My pleasure," she offered with a large grin.

"Whether it is nobler to suffer the slings and arrows of financial mismanagement."

"James quoting Shakespeare, I feel faint."

"Well done James!" Richard was applauding.

"Yes, very impressive, and appropriate given this project."

"So where do we go from here?" Richard was holding the 5"× 7" card that we left the last session with.

"So why doesn't everyone do this *leverage* thing. I mean the logic looks sound, the numbers seem to work. Might there be something that you are choosing not to tell us. You wouldn't do that to us would you?"

I looked at Richard to see if he wanted to kick it off. He simply nodded back at me, so I guessed that he wanted me to begin.

"Well, James, first of all, as we said last time, not everything is for everyone, even if it is a good thing, and that is ok. I talk to many of my clients and prospective clients about leverage and not all of them do it and that is ok. An ethical financial planner does not push a client into a strategy or investment that the client is not 100% committed to or feels comfortable with. So ends my sermon on why this isn't for everyone."

"That said John, there are some common misconceptions about leverage that cause people to shy away from it, even if they do see the advantages—right?"

"Yes there are, the primary being the recurring lesson we were taught by our parents about money. The debt is bad scenario. Many people, especially those in the 50 and over generation, still view debt as something to be avoided at all costs. I agree. Debt should not be incurred for debt's sake alone. It might break down like this."

Good Debt	Bad Debt
Investment Debt	Credit Card Debt
Mortgage	Car Loans
Appreciating Asset Debt	Depreciating Asset Debt

"So what John is trying to say is that less debt is always a good thing, all things considered, but if you are going to have debt, make sure it is *good* debt."

"But I want to buy a car at some point, I can't wait until I have enough to pay cash for it. I could be 30 years old by that time." James seemed exasperated at the thought of waiting that long.

"I'm not suggesting never taking out a loan to buy a car James. If you do, pay it off as quickly as you can. Cars depreciate, and a good rule of thumb is never buy a depreciating asset on credit. The math looks like this."

Car Loan: $25,000	Car Value
4 Years @ 9%—$622.28/mth	
Total Cost—$29,869.44	$12,500
5 Year @ 9%—$519.09/mth	
Total Cost—$31,145.40	$10,000

"By the time you end up paying off the loan, you've paid over $29,000 for your $25,000 car, which is now worth $12,500, assuming you used the four year option."

"That's right Joyce."

"Well that sucks."

> If you are going to have debt, make sure it is *good* debt.

"Umm, sure James, that's as good an expression as any. But there are many more examples, putting a vacation on your credit card and taking six or eight months to pay it off. By the time you have, you'll have forgotten how much fun the trip was."

"I think financial mismanagement for many stems from the fact that personal finance is not taught as a course in high school or even university and this perpetuates the problem." Richard was now standing which I was assuming meant he was going to rant a little bit.

"It's interesting how we react to the advertising we see around us. Credit card companies bombard us with any number of beautifully created images of the good life, all available at the swipe of their little plastic cards. Somehow buying the item with a blue card makes it more valuable than buying it with the silver card. I've never been able to figure that one out. People get lulled into buying on credit with these cards and somehow feel quite comfortable being in debt to achieve the goal of immediate consumption, paying exorbitantly high, non-tax deductible interest to purchase chud."

"Chud? What's chud?" James was laughing, as he looked sideways at Joyce. She offered up an equally amused glance, as did I, I hadn't heard him use this term before. I was curious about where he was headed.

"Chud stands for Consumable Had-to-have-it Under Delusion. I love the term, but I can't take credit for it. It belongs to Bruce Eaton, author of *Conquering Your Financial Stress*. It describes the things you just *had* to have, that if you really, really thought about it and had the advantage of hindsight, you would give up immediately in order to get your money back. Hey, I'm not immune; do you think I squeezed all this juice myself? No. Bought it already squeezed. So why do I have a $200 juicer under the counter in the kitchen? Because it seemed like a good idea at the time."

"Richard's right, people consume a lot of stuff like this. I can guarantee that you'll do it too—everyone does, even me. The key is to keep it to a minimum if you can. Tax-deductible debt, such as that incurred using leverage or borrowing to invest can be a strategy to help you generate money to buy *chud,* as Richard called it, and not have to use credit to do it. Buying chud on credit is never a good strategy."

"Ok, no chud, credit cards are bad, so why don't people do this?"

"They are impatient for information today, a good sign Richard."

"We never said that credit cards are bad James," Richard was jumping in on this, as I know his thoughts on credit cards. "They are great tools, they are very useful. For example, I use credit cards all the time, not to borrow with it, but to get a detailed account of where I spend my money each month. In a way it is similar to the notebook Joyce has been carrying around. I also get mileage for my frequent flier account. But the key is that I pay the bill in full every month, without exception. Unfortunately, far too many people use them for instantaneous spur of the moment purchases without thinking. Then the bills arrive, and it leaves them paying for last month's spending with next month's income. That's all we're getting at. When you do that often enough, month after month, you'll end up chasing your tail. The amounts on the credit cards grow, you start to make only the minimum payment rather than paying them off in full, and things really start to get out of hand. Let's try this example: if you were to charge $1,800 on a credit card,

Rule of Thumb: Never buy a depreciating asset on credit.

and we'll assume that you are making only the minimum monthly payment, that the interest rate is 18%, which isn't unusual, how long would it take you to pay it off?" Curious stares were being shared between James and Joyce.

"I don't know, maybe two years?"

"I'm thinking longer if you are using this as a teaching example, I'll double Joyce's guess to four years."

"The survey says … 22 years."

"What!?" In unison.

"I know, hard to believe, but you can do the math. Your total payments will amount to close to $5,600 or so, over three times the amount you originally charged to the card. You thought the car loan example was bad James? Sorry to take us off-track John, but this is important to know when people think about spending on credit."

"Agreed. A very good example. So getting back on track, here we go gang. These are what I feel are the myths about why people don't consider borrowing to invest a legitimate strategy. Trust me on this; leverage is not without its critics even within the financial planning industry. As with most things in life—some like it, some don't and usually opinions run deeper than that."

Leverage Myths
1) You have to be rich already
2) Debt = Bad!
3) Way too risky for me
4) Returns must exceed cost to make money

"The fact that you referred to them as myths means that they aren't true—right?"

"Well, I hope I can convince you of that Joyce."

"So, convince me."

"Ok," with a slight laugh, "let's take them one at a time shall we? First, you have to be rich already. There seems to be a commonly held belief in the old phrase 'you have to have money to make money.' Well, where do you think they got that money from in the first place? While it is true that many higher income earners use leverage, it isn't only for them. If you have a decent credit rating, the desire to think long term and be patient, are willing to begin small, anyone can benefit. Many of my clients started small, some have stayed small, some have grown their leverage amounts. We only used an example of $20,000 last time. People often borrow more than that to purchase a car to drive around in, but would be appalled to borrow that much money to turn it into a nest egg of $150,000 in 20 years. I can guarantee you in ten years that you will have long forgotten about that car. So yes, borrowing to invest is open to anyone who would be a decent credit risk to the financial institution issuing the loan. No age requirement, no gender bias. So can we consider this one closed?"

"Closed for me."

"C'est finis pour moi."

"Second, debt is bad. Debt is evil and to be avoided like the plague, or at least like a telemarketer at dinner-time. Good idea, I'm 100% behind that, especially for credit cards, and debt for depreciating assets; most especially debt that is not tax-deductible. If you have debts, pay them off promptly. This type of debt should be avoided. Good debt or constructive borrowing helps to grow assets and increase your net worth. Interest on good debt is usually lower than bad debt. For example, a loan to invest in a leverage program, as we have been discussing, can be had for usually 1% over the prime lending rate or approximately 6% today. A car loan from a bank can be as high as 9%, and credit card interest charges can be as high as 13 to 25% depending on whose card you are using. Case closed?"

> **People often borrow money to buy a car, but would be appalled to borrow the same amount with the potential of turning it into a nest egg worth more than six times the original sum.**

"Closed." In triplicate.

"Third, too risky. Risk is something to consider and I don't want to give a sermon here, but risk can be either financial or emotional. People feel it is a risk to borrow to invest in the stock market, yet they will accept a highly leveraged investment such as a mortgage on a house. I can put down 5% capital to buy a house, the mortgage interest is not tax-deductible and I can own—well, the bank actually owns—an investment that is not liquid enough to sell at a moment's notice. I'm not diversified in any way, it may not grow in value at an appreciable rate, and may not even grow in the long term if you believe the demographics discussed in your Christmas gifts from Richard."

"The current trends seem to indicate that in the future the large houses that we see today may not be terrific investments ten to 15 years down the road." It was obvious James had been doing some reading.

"They might be right James, but that doesn't mean people shouldn't buy houses, everyone needs a place to live, but historically people have viewed houses as good investments and that may or may not be the case as we move ahead. As Richard said earlier, people seem to view non-deductible debt as just a part of life, yet when you get right down to it, it often decreases their wealth or the future potential for wealth. My belief is that you can safely say that borrowing, that is using tax-deductible debt to invest in diversified investments, has less risk than basic consumer debt. As for

Borrowing, using tax-deductible debt to invest in diversified investments, has less risk than basic consumer debt.

emotional risk, that will vary from person to person and I suspect that we'll be discussing that later." I glanced over at Richard, raised an eyebrow in the generic question fashion to see what he thought.

"We just might at that John," he replied, his grin revealed that he knew exactly when, and he would let the rest of us in on it when he was good and ready.

"Ok then, number four, returns must exceed cost in order to make money. I shouldn't have to do too much to convince you of this one. Do you remember the example from last time?" In the off chance that they hadn't, Richard was handing out copies of the chart that I had drawn on the whiteboard.

Age	Opening	Additions	Growth	Closing
22	20,000	0	2,000	22,000
27	37,315	1,000	3,732	42,147
32	66,812	1,000	6,782	74,594
37	114,317	1,000	11,532	126,849
42	190,825	1,000	19,182	211,007
47	314,041	1,000	31,504	346,545
52	512,482	1,000	51,348	564,830
57	832,073	1,000	83,307	916,380
62	1,346,778	1,000	134,777	1,482,555

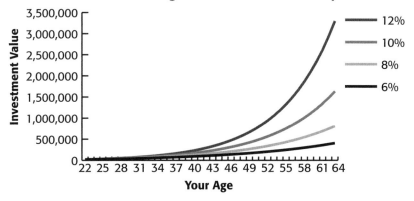

Invest $20,000 at age 22 – add tax refund each year

"In this example, you'll remember that we used borrowing $20,000 at 10% interest and earning 10% on your investments and guess what, you made money. The example made a significant amount of money over the long term. So what do you think happens if we lower the rate of borrowing to something more realistic, say 6%, where to borrow $20,000 your annual payments are now only $1,200 rather than $2,000?" There was a momentary pause as they looked at the example in order to determine what to say.

"You should make more money?" James stated hesitantly.

"Why James?"

"Because your borrowing costs are less, but that means your tax deductibility is less too—right?"

"Right, that has to be factored in as well, so let's use 6% borrowing, with a 10% return for comparison, and that would give us an example that looks like this."

Age	Opening	Additions	Growth	Closing
22	20,000	0	2,000	22,000
27	36,240	600	3,684	40,524
32	62,394	600	6,299	69,293
37	104,515	600	10,511	115,626
42	172,351	600	17,295	190,247
47	281,603	600	28,220	310,423
52	457,554	600	45,815	503,970
57	740,925	600	74,152	815,677
62	1,197,296	600	119,790	1,317,686

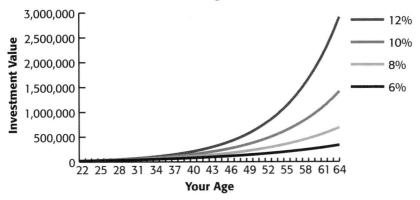

Invest $20,000 at age 22 – add tax refund each year borrowing at 6%

"So from before, where we invested $82,000 over 41 years, adding back the tax refund of $1,000 a year, we generated a future value of close to $1.5

million. Here, we are investing $49,200, adding back a tax refund of $600 a year and we generate a future value of close to $1.3 million. Different? Yep. Lower? Yep. At the same time, you have invested less as well. For an apples to apples comparison, if you are still willing to contribute $2,000 a year to your investment program, and your interest rate is 6% you would be able to borrow approximately $32,500 at a cost of $1,950 a year, giving you a tax refund of $975 a year and if you added that back it looks like this:"

Age	Opening	Additions	Growth	Closing
22	32,500	0	3,250	35,750
32	98,861	975	9,894	109,819
42	273,512	975	27,449	301,936
52	726,512	975	72,749	800,236
62	1,901,479	975	190,245	2,092,699

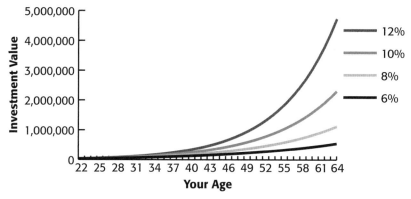

Invest $32,500 at age 22 – add tax refund each year, borrowing at 6%

"Ok, so I think I'm getting this. I can see it makes sense when you are getting a return that is equal to, or higher than your cost to borrow. What happens when you don't? How low can you go before it doesn't make any sense over time?"

"How low can you go? How low can you go?" Richard was now standing, attempting a rather awkward looking limbo move. Apparently, he had learned more during his Christmas vacation in Bermuda than he had let on.

"Well, sorry to have to scare you James, but it's a math thing."

"Sorry I asked."

"It's not that complex, really. It looks something like this."

Interest Rate On Borrowing 9%		Tax Rate Saving 50%		Effective Rate 4.5%
	*		=	

"So if your rate to borrow for the investment is 9% and you are getting a 50% rebate on the tax rate, your effective rate is 4.5%. That means you'd have to earn 4.5% or better in order to stay ahead and make leverage a viable option. The actual math is a little more detailed, and I have leverage software that performs the calculation using a number of variables. I always do a complete set of numbers to show clients who are interested before we make any decisions in order to have full disclosure of information."

Silence.

Perhaps I had thrown too much information at them? Perhaps they were just trying to absorb it all? For two who probably did not have a great deal of investment experience prior to starting this project, they were handling the discussions quite well. Richard was flipping through some notes he had in his folder, so I was expecting him to offer up some insight. I didn't have to wait very long.

"Sorry James, you had a question last time and it was a good one. This might be a good point to talk about it if John is willing." James was looking skyward, as if for some type of guidance when Joyce tapped him on the shoulder and leaned over to whisper something in his ear.

"Do we have to choose between the two? Can't we do both?" He spread his arms, palms up, as if the question had just popped into his head.

"You can certainly do both, many people do. Most people start with an RRSP, and for younger investors I feel that is the way to go. You get the initial tax break, you start putting money away for the future, and you benefit from long-term compounding. I always recommend that people have an RRSP and maximize their contributions before pursuing a leverage program. Once they are doing all that, taking full advantage of the government's generosity, then it is time to examine other options. People typically move to add leverage to their investment programs once they have done all that, and are a little older with a developed asset base to build on. Not that a financial institution wouldn't want you to participate in a leverage program but they'd be more apt to do it once you have established yourself a little bit."

"Ok, so we do both, or you can do both. Are there advantages to one method over the other? You said that from a tax perspective the tax deduction receipts don't make any difference whether from a leverage program or from a contribution to an RRSP."

"Exactly Joyce, it doesn't matter from a tax perspective. That's why this is a good scenario."

RRSP Contribution	Tax Rate	Refund	
$5,000	50%	$2,500	Total Cost
Leverage Loan	Borrow Rate	Loan Cost	Zero
$42,500	6%	$2,500	

"So you build assets within a tax-sheltered investment, you get a rebate from the government for doing it, and you use that money in order to pay the leverage loan in order to build up more assets. Excellent!"

"Excellent indeed James. When we can, it is always a good idea to take advantage of financial situations that work in our favour, especially when the government is willing to help us out. To make it even better, keep in mind that your $2,500 contribution to fund your leverage program will yield you another tax break for the next tax year. It goes, and goes, and goes ..." Richard was motioning with his hands, moving them in a rolling motion like a wave to simulate the ongoing rolling growth.

"The bigger question comes when you look long term, then it becomes a different and somewhat more difficult question. Does an RRSP make a better long-term investment versus a leverage program? That is the dilemma."

"How so? You can build up a substantial amount of money in either plan. Isn't that the point?"

"It is at the start Joyce, but now let's move 30 to 35 years down the road and see what happens when we decide we want to take money out of the plan. For ease of comparison, I'll use the same amount of money in each program and we'll see what the effects might be when we remove some money."

	RRSP/RRIF Value		Leverage Value
	$1.2 Million		$1.2 Million
Take Out	$84,000	Take Out	$84,000
50% Tax	$42,000	Capital Gain	$84,000
You Get	$42,000	Taxable Amount	$42,000
		50% Tax	$21,000
		You Get	$63,000

The difference in your pocket is: $21,000

"Huh?"

"I don't get it either John." James and Joyce both had puzzled looks on their faces. I had seen this before, but I knew they would get it with a little further explanation.

"That's ok, I'll explain. We're assuming that value in the plans is the same at $1.2 million, but the amount in the plan isn't the issue here.

"So we remove $84,000 from the RRSP or RRIF, remembering that it grows tax-sheltered in the plan and at the point we take the money out it becomes taxable income at the highest marginal tax rate you are paying at the time. Assuming a 50% tax rate, you'll pay $42,000 in tax on that $84,000 you took out, leaving you with $42,000 at your disposal. Keep in mind that some of that tax was withheld when you removed the funds. I'm assuming that you haven't forgotten about our with-holding tax discussion from a couple months back? The net result is that you'll take $84,000 out and end up with $42,000. Fair enough?"

Build assets within a tax-sheltered investment; Get a tax refund from the government; Use the refund to pay the leverage loan; Build up more assets!

"Fair enough," in unison.

"So now we remove $84,000 from the leverage plan. It hasn't been growing tax-sheltered in the plan, so it is treated differently than the RRSP withdrawal. When we take $84,000 out, some of that amount will be part of your original investment; some of it will be money you reinvested from any compound growth, dividends or earnings paid to you; the remainder will be capital gains due to growth in the investment. You don't pay tax on your original investment amount, or on the reinvested amounts. You've already paid tax on that money. However, for this example, let's assume that all $84,000 you removed was capital gain. Capital gains are treated differently—remember they are taxed less than regular income."

"I remember that, taxed less, I like this already!"

"I wonder if this is a genetic thing John?" Richard smiled.

"Settle down, it's not a Jarvis family trait, I believe everyone likes the concept of being taxed less."

"You pay tax on only 50% of your capital gain. So we take the $84,000 of capital gain, only 50% of that amount is taxable and that leaves you with $42,000 taxable income from the $84,000 withdrawal. Assuming a 50% tax rate, you'd pay $21,000 in tax on the capital gain. Since you removed $84,000 and paid only $21,000 in tax, that leaves you with $63,000 from your original withdrawal and there are no withholding taxes. In the RRSP example you would have paid $42,000 in tax. Your leverage account is therefore more tax efficient than the RRSP when it comes to withdrawing funds."

"This tax efficiency is a good thing kids," Richard was pacing, a sign we had moved onto a topic that was close to him. "Remember from our discussions on taxes that paying your taxes, or your fair share, is a legal and I believe even a moral obligation. It's part of the cost to live in our society, with all the benefits that we receive from living in Canada. That said, we have no obligation to pay one penny more than our fair share. Given that, using a leverage program can be more tax efficient than using an RRSP for long-term growth. I suspect that John concurs with that."

> When it comes to withdrawing funds, a leverage account is more tax efficient than an RRSP.

"I do. I think the tax situation favours long-term leverage, but not only leverage. You can choose to invest your money in a program with stocks and mutual funds without using a leverage program at all. If a client doesn't feel that leverage fits for them, they can still choose to invest outside an RRSP without using leverage. Many people have successfully grown large investment portfolios using nothing more than their own money, time, compound interest and continual investing. In either of those cases, the same tax efficiency is created outside of the RRSP due to how capital gains are taxed."

Both James and Joyce were writing notes on this concept; I was pretty sure they understood it. I suspected part of their keenness for it was Richard's enthusiasm for paying less tax. He was a stickler on that topic, and I had to agree.

"How about this concept?" Richard tossed me something I hadn't seen in years. About six inches tall, green, made out of a soft pliable plastic material. Yep, it was Gumby. I'm not sure that the kids would even recognize the character, but once I had Gumby in my hands I knew where Richard wanted me to go.

"Yes, our little friend Gumby here can teach us a valuable lesson about the difference between your RRSP program and your leverage program."

"Gumby?"

"Yes James, as in Gumby and Pokey." Joyce obviously knew who they were. I keep forgetting that in the digital age, everything that is old to us gets recycled to be new to the next generation.

"Exactly, same Gumby, but he'll now show us another advantage of a leverage investment program." With that I bent and contorted Gumby into about a dozen different positions, finally depositing his still twisted little frame onto the table.

"That was to explain a concept to us? I don't get it."

"He's a flexible little guy," Joyce had picked him up and was straightening his limbs back to normal.

"Bingo!"

"Ok, before our little mutual admiration society gets out of hand. Gumby is very flexible; your non-RRSP investment program is very flexible as well."

"Flexible how?" James twisting Gumby into a knot.

"Flexible in all of the following ways," I decided this would make a valid list for the whiteboard.

Leverage or 'Open' Plan Advantages over RRSP/RRIF
1) Taxed Less
2) No Contribution Limits
3) No Withholding Taxes on Withdrawals
4) No Minimum Annual Payments to Take Out

"I'll assume we get the taxed less aspect. Capital gains are taxed less than having your RRSP/RRIF withdrawals taxed as 100% income. Next is the contribution limit. Much earlier in this process James, you asked why people didn't put $20,000, $30,000 or $40,000 away each year in their RRSP if they had it. Well, we know why now—because they can't, due to their contribution limits. With a leverage program, there are no such limits. You can invest any amount you choose or, in fact, any amount you can afford in terms of making your loan payments. You can start small, increasing your leverage program whenever you want, no restrictions on the amount you put in. Are we ok with that?" Nods from all.

"You can take out what you want, when you want."

"But that is true for RRSPs as well. You can take money out when you want to. Did I miss something?"

"Nope. You're right, you can take funds from your RRSP at your discretion, no problem there. The differences are more subtle. First there is the withholding tax on the RRSP, so to get $4,000 in your hands, you need to remove approximately $4,500 from the plan, which will affect the future growth. Second, one that only affects people older than you, is the concept of the MAP, if you remember that part of the discussion."

"The minimum annual payment right?"

"Exactly. Let's assume you are 72 years old with an RRSP worth $1.2 million, I think we used something similar to this in our earlier discussion. The MAP for someone who is 72 is about 7.5%, which means you are going to be removing approximately $90,000 from your plan. That's not really a problem in and of itself, but what if you really only needed or wanted $45,000 of income, or even less."

"You have to take the $90,000 out, you have no choice, I remember that. I said it wasn't fair, after all, it was your money."

"You certainly did Joyce and guess what? It hasn't gotten any fairer since you said it. You are stuck removing the funds and will be taxed on that full amount as income in that tax year. From your leverage program, if you only want $45,000 of income in a given year you only take $45,000 out, the choice is yours, take as little or as much as you need."

"You might even add to it as well John."

"Yes, you might even add to it Richard," I nodded an agreement in his direction. "Unlike the RRSP which not only has a limit of how much a year you can contribute, you also have the limitation that you can't contribute past the age of 71, even if you are earning income. Once the RRSP becomes a RRIF, when you turn 71, you can't add any more funds to that plan either. That doesn't apply to your leverage or 'open' investing programs; you can add funds regardless of your age."

"I'm getting the impression you are building quite a case for leverage instead of an RRSP."

"I don't think it is as clear cut as that James, but a leverage program certainly has some benefits that should be examined. The younger you are, the more likely you are to use RRSPs, get the tax benefit, build up your asset base, contribute as much as you can, as early as you can. Once you are accomplishing that you can opt to do some other things, like let your RRSP build your leverage program for you."

"Huh?" Two confused looks from across the room.

"Ok, this isn't as complex as it sounds and this will be a good concept to end the day on. Do you remember when we discussed leverage initially, we used it in order to buy back time we lost or to simply speed time up?" Nods, but not as confident as I would have liked. "Let's assume you've been very diligent with your RRSP contributions since you started working, and you are now 40 years old, which would be *ancient* from your perspective today. Just for fun, we'll assume you are married and between you and your spouse you've done well enough to build an RRSP portfolio worth $250,000, which would be an excellent position to be in by the way."

"Yes, very commendable," Richard added.

"Do we remember the rule of 72?"

"Divide your return on investment into 72, you can calculate approximately when your investments will double."

"Exactly James. Since we've been assuming a 10% return in our example, let's continue to do so here." As I was going to build a large calculation, I erased some writing on the board, and then wrote:

Age	RRSP Value
40	$250,000
45	$402,000
50	$648,000
55	$1,044,000
60	$1,681,000
65	$2,708,000

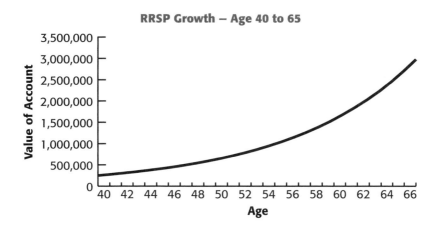

RRSP Growth – Age 40 to 65

"Ok, so here we can see that by accumulating $250,000 by age 40 and adding no more funds to your RRSP, just letting compound interest work for you, by age 65 you could have approximately $2.7 million. Are we ok with that?"

"Who wouldn't be?" James seemed very intrigued by the idea.

"Good point, who wouldn't be? But let's also keep in mind, that with an RRSP worth that much by age 65, we are looking at a very hefty tax bill. Remember, as all that money gets withdrawn via your RRIF, it is 100% taxable and, assuming that tax rates stay similar to today's rates, you'll lose approximately 50% of that amount in tax as you withdraw it."

"Yuck."

"Well said Joyce!" Richard was grinning.

"Ok, so we have another option, and I think it is a good one. We use some of the funds from our RRSP to fund the leverage program. For this example, we'll borrow $250,000 the same amount as we have in our RRSP at that time. For the sake of argument, assume the cost of borrowing is 8%, which means our annual payments would be approximately $20,000. We'll also assume that we continue to get our 10% growth so the examples are consistent. It will look something like this.

RRSP Account		Leverage Account	
Age	Value	Age	Value
40	$230,000	40	$250,000
45	$236,000	45	$402,000
50	$245,000	50	$648,000
55	$261,000	55	$1,044,000
60	$287,000	60	$1,681,000
65	$328,000	65	$2,708,000

Results of using RRSP to Fund a Leverage Program

"So what do we think of this?"

"Let's see if I get this right. We take $22,000 out of our RRSP each year to cover the leverage loan; our RRSP, because the money is still invested, continues to grow, but at a slower rate than if we just left the RRSP alone. Our leverage program grows from $250,000 to approximately $2.7 million, the same amount as the RRSP would have grown, except now we have an asset that is more tax efficient due to capital gains. Then we get to remove the money when we want, not according to the MAP schedule. We still have an RRSP worth over $300,000, for a grand total of close to $3 million, but we are in a much better tax position. Am I close?"

"You've got it. Even though we have to declare the RRSP withdrawals as taxable income, that amount is offset by the tax deductibility of the leverage interest for the amount we borrowed. We used money we had accumulated already, we grew it to a larger amount and we made it more tax efficient. So for me, a good answer to the question, 'To RRSP or Not to RRSP' would be do both."

"It is a pretty good deal in my books. Of course, it is contingent on you doing the work to grow your RRSPs up front, making the most of the government's generosity while you are younger and letting time and compound interest work for you. I concur with John's thought, this would be a great place to end the day as we've had a full morning."

"Whew, that's for sure."

"I'm all for that, but I'm intrigued by this last example, using your own money to make more money."

"Keep in mind James, money isn't everything, ok? But if you want to start somewhere, start by building your RRSP. It was one of your goals wasn't it? Once you have done that, an entire world of options will open up for you."

> **Another Option: Use some RRSP funds to support the leverage program.**

The room was suddenly quiet; I think we were all lost in thought, thoughts about this morning, perhaps thoughts about what we were going to do with the rest of the day. After several moments, James broke the silence.

"There is a lot of information on that board. It makes me wonder where we are going to be heading next. We are heading somewhere, are we not Richard?"

"By any chance do you mean these? I'm glad to see that someone actually looks forward to my little creations. I'd hate to think that I do them for nothing." As was the ritual, Richard produced four 5" × 7" cards, but this time they were taped to brown manila envelopes. I noticed as he handed them out, our initials were on the corner.

"What's this?" James was tentatively opening his.

"Argh!" Joyce had beaten him to it.

"They're not that bad." It became obvious that each envelope contained an 8 × 10 picture of us taken at the last meeting at Richard's, when he went crazy and started taking pictures. There was a solo shot of each of us and a group shot of the three of us. Interesting group—James had the big grin on his face, Joyce was turning away, I had my back to the camera. Richard had written, "To my advisory team, Richard" in marker at the bottom.

"We do look quite pitiful, don't we?"

"Speak for yourself Joyce, I'm quite photogenic."

"And ever so humble too James!"

Our laughter starting to subside, we turned our attention to the 5"× 7" card taped to the envelopes we were holding. Now this was certainly different.

"What is this?"

"Nope. No hints. No clues. Nothing. I made it too easy last time. I'm out to stump you this time. Is anyone up for a return to the cabin for the next meeting?"

"Sure!" in unison.

"Hey, what's wrong with my office?"

"It's not your office John, nothing personal. It's just that the cabin is more … ummm … more …" James seemed lost for the right word.

"Fun?"

"Well I didn't mean it like that."

"That's ok, I'm for the cabin too."

"Great then, April 28th if that's ok. I have to run, I hope that's not a problem. If it is, call me. I gotta run." Richard quickly packed up his basket and leftovers and was gone in a flash. For Richard, this was a most unusual exit. That left the three of us sitting in silence.

"So what do you make of this?"

"His leaving so quickly or the card?"

"Either."

"I have no idea."

"You're a big help John!"

"Sorry James," I shrugged my shoulders. "I'm sure we'll find out in due time, but I think we should get out there and enjoy the sun while it lasts. The next sunny day could be summer." There was no time to waste while the sun was shining.

■12

Risky Business

To get profit without risk, experience without danger, and reward without work, is as impossible as it is to live without being born.
A. P. Gouthey

Wind.

I heard it before the alarm went off, a strong steady wind blowing from the east. The wind in the trees was a rather eerie sound, yet comforting at the same time. Since it seemed that I wasn't going back to sleep I turned on the bedside light and opened the folder containing the project material that was sitting there.

I had been reviewing the material last night. Richard had talked about a blueprint that day in the park—it seemed so long ago—and I was going to have to talk to him about that. I needed to know what his intentions were, and how he intended to achieve them.

I picked up the card that Richard handed out at the last session. Richard had acquired an interest in the eastern cultures during his time in Vietnam and I knew what the symbol was. I was curious to see what strategy the kids would take to uncover the message.

As I pulled into Richard's driveway, I noticed the rocking chairs were back on the front porch—a sure sign that winter was over. Not only that, Richard and James were each occupying one, holding what must have been a humorous discussion given their smiles.

"Good morning guys!"

"John!"

"Where's Joyce?"

"I told her that I'd bike out, I needed the exercise. Besides, it's spring, better take advantage of it since we've been waiting so long."

"More power to you James; I'm too old to bike that far."

"Too old, bah! Too lazy is more like it."

"Say Richard, remind me again why you are my friend?" We both broke into a short laugh, as James seemed to watch with amusement.

I joined them in the third chair, but hadn't yet settled into a comfortable position when Joyce pulled into the driveway. She came to a skidding halt on the gravel.

"Hey lead foot, nice stop!"

"Sorry Richard, guess I didn't realize my speed."

"Never be that impatient to get where you are going Joyce."

Never be so impatient to get where you are going that you endanger yourself or others.

We stayed on the porch for a few minutes, I offered my chair to Joyce, and I found a nice warm spot in the sun leaning up against one of the posts. Richard rose and ushered us inside. The great room was already set up for us to start. The whiteboard was in place and a tray of assorted fruit, surrounding a mound of Oreos, was on the table. I noticed that there was a selection of bagels there as well. Perhaps this was Richard's attempt to strike a balance between healthy food and my passion for donut holes. We had only started to dig into breakfast when Richard started the session. "So before we get too side-tracked, did we have any luck with this?" Richard was twirling the card in his right hand, looking at James and Joyce.

"I didn't and I did look. I tried tracking down several books on symbols and lots of places on the Internet, but I couldn't make any connection."

"Well, after my defeat last month, I was determined not to be shut out this month," Joyce seemed excited at the prospect that James had not been successful. "I think I have it." In a repeat of last month's opening of the meeting, Joyce rose and wrote the following on the whiteboard:

"How did I do?" She appeared anxious to be right.

"Your thoughts John?" Joyce appeared dismayed at the thought she may have failed. The confirmation that she expected wasn't forthcoming, but I must admit I knew better and he was just testing her resolve.

"I like it, don't you?"

"I do. Well done, Joyce. How did you arrive at that?"

"Well, like James a few months ago, I had a little help," she smiled an acknowledgement to him.

"I figured it was an eastern symbol, perhaps Chinese or Japanese, so I started there and before I went too far I just asked a friend if he recognized it. He didn't, but suggested I speak to one of the professors in linguistics. So I found one and she took a look and said 'risk.' She explained how it was made up of two symbols, one for crisis and the other for opportunity."

"Nice to see you using resources and being diligent. The answer to every question you probably will ever have is out there; all you have to do is find the person with the answer. So why is risk important?"

"Important? I thought it was to be avoided?"

"Really James? Why?

"Risk implies danger, as in risky, no?"

"At times, certainly in a physical sense. How about financially?"

"The risk of making a bad investment perhaps?" Joyce added.

"What would make an investment risky?"

"Not making any money, no return on your investment."

"Does risk apply to your return only? What about your capital? Any risk there?"

> **Remember: If it sounds too good to be true, it probably is.**

"Well, you could lose all your money. That would be risky."

"Ultimately that is the largest risk. To invest money in something, and not only to not make any money, but to lose all that you have invested and be left with nothing."

"Does that ever happen?"

"Certainly, companies can go bankrupt, but there are all types of wacky investment schemes, pyramid schemes, penny stocks, even some that appear to be truly legitimate. Remember the scandal that surrounded a Canadian mining company several years back. It became what many called a gigantic fraud in which some people made out exceptionally well, many more lost their entire investment, including some professional money managers who were taken in, right John?"

"It happens to professionals as well. They are not immune to making a bad investment decision, but we hope it's the exception rather than the rule. It is still a safe bet to apply the common wisdom: 'if it sounds too good to be true, it probably is.' You'd do well to consider that anytime you are making an investment decision, and I suspect that will be our topic for today."

"Precisely John, investment decisions and the impact of risk on them. This will be a good place to start tying the pieces of this puzzle together. To be honest, I'm surprised that this topic hasn't reared its ugly head before now, but that's ok."

"Have we missed something somewhere?" Joyce was anxiously looking around the room, as if she had somehow failed.

"Not at all, but when John and I explained the concept of RRSPs and leverage programs, usually one of the first questions that gets asked, and one that you have asked before James is, 'So, what do we invest in?'"

"That is an important question, to be sure, but it should never take the place of the question, 'Why are we doing this in the first place?'"

Why are we investing in the first place?

"Well said James, goals come first. Until you set some goals and plans for where you want to be or what you want to accomplish, then there is no sense trying to determine what to invest in."

"Ok, so let's assume we buy into this, we have a plan and we hope that we are going to stick to it, what then?" A short shrug of her shoulders indicated to me that Joyce wasn't sure about the question.

"Then we need to talk about types of investments, what you can expect to receive in return and how they may affect your plans. Take it away John."

"We are gathered here today, to join together these two concepts, risk and reward, in matrimony. If there is anyone present today who has knowledge of why these two should not be joined together, let them speak now or …"

"What are you talking about John?"

"Well, I was just trying to have a little fun. In a more serious vein the concept of risk and reward is closely linked and you shouldn't think of one without factoring in the other."

"Like nothing ventured, nothing gained?" James asked.

"Exactly. There are several issues to examine when we start to look at risk from an investment perspective. You have many options to invest in. Here is a relatively broad snapshot." With that I opened my folder and produced a sheet containing the following chart. I had created it in paper form only because I was too lazy to write it out by hand, also because I like to hand it out to prospective clients when we talk about investing.

Investment Type	Degree of Liquidity	Safety of Capital	Type of Return you Receive
Bank Accounts	Highest	Highest	Interest
Canada Savings Bonds	Highest	Highest	Interest
Money Market Funds	Highest	High	Interest
Treasury Bills	Highest	Highest	Interest
Balanced Funds	High	Medium	Dividend/Cap.Gain
Bond Funds	High	Medium	Interest/Cap.Gain
Mortgage Funds	High	Medium	Interest/Cap.Gain
Preferred Stock	High	Medium	Dividend/Cap.Gain
Canadian Stock Funds	High	Medium/Low	Dividend/Cap.Gain
Exchange Traded Funds	High	Medium/Low	Dividend/Cap.Gain
Foreign Stock Funds	High	Medium/Low	Dividend/Cap.Gain
Precious Metals Funds	High	Medium/Low	Dividend/Cap.Gain
Common Stock	Medium/Low	Medium	Dividend/Cap.Gain
Corporate Bonds	Medium/Low	Medium	Interest
GICs/Term Deposits	Medium/Low	Highest	Interest

There was a period of silence while everyone looked at the chart; I was interested to know how the kids were going to react to the data contained there. Until this point in time we had not yet discussed actual investment vehicles. I was pretty sure that this wouldn't overwhelm them. After all, they were a pretty savvy pair. As they were doing that, I wrote the following on the whiteboard:

Key Investment Concepts
1) Liquidity
2) Safety
3) Return—Type of Return & Average Rate

"So how much of that sheet makes sense?"

"I think it's pretty straightforward."

"Ok Joyce, pop quiz, what does 'liquidity' mean?"

"How easy it is to get your money back out or from an investment. Cash is very liquid, real estate is not."

"How about 'safety' James?"

"The amount of risk you are exposing yourself to?"

"Well done, and while I think that is important, there are other elements at play as well in terms of risk. Such as these," Richard added the following:

The Real Risks
1) The risk of low returns
2) The risk of a bear market
3) The risk of losing capital
4) The risk of outliving your money

"How do we feel about these?"

"Why is there a risk to low returns? Aren't any returns a good thing? As long as you are getting better than zero, that is a good thing isn't it?"

"Not necessarily Joyce. Remember our discussion about inflation? While I'd rather make 2% on my investments as opposed to 0%, if inflation is 3.5% we will be running behind. Our money doesn't grow in real terms and our purchasing power falls backwards. We saw in the example of James purchasing his new bike that by putting his money in a shoebox it was very safe, earning 0% interest, but his $400 wouldn't buy him the $500 bike two years later."

"That said Richard, we must also be wary of the investment that promises 17% a year guaranteed on our money—if it sounds too good to be true, it probably is. There will always be exceptions. For example, you could have taken out a bond or GIC earning 17%, perhaps more in 1981. Inflation was almost 14% at the time as well. We have to be wary of investments that expose us to far more risk, not just of not producing 17%, but of exposing capital to complete loss."

"What's a 'bear market'?"

"Those people who follow the market James use the expressions 'bull market' or 'bear market' to describe the long-term trends in equities. A bull market is a rising market, positive growth, signified by a bull, charging forward. A bear market is considered to be in retreat, falling stock prices, generally accepted to be in effect when prices have fallen greater than 20% in any given period of time. The bear signifies a snarling, angry mar-

> **Bull markets are rising markets, positive growth, charging forward. Bear markets are in retreat, falling stock prices, snarling, angry markets.**

ket, one in decline, and if you can avoid investing your money in this type of market, then you should try to. While prolonged bull markets can do great things to your investment portfolio due to growth, a prolonged bear market can not only wipe out your growth, it can have a devastating effect on your capital, all of which affects the long-term financial health of your plan."

"Don't bear markets scare people? Scare them a lot?"

"Certainly. But they don't occur in a vacuum James?"

"What does that mean?"

"You have to take them in consideration of the big picture. Richard's example from 1987, he picked what might be considered the worst time to invest money. Nobody saw that market drop coming. If we had, I would have had Richard wait 25 days. Had he invested his $100,000 on the day after the crash, or significant correction as I prefer to call it, then his returns would have been far more significant than the almost $500,000 value we talked about two months ago. Does that make sense?"

"So the fears Richard outlined are very real. Numbers 2 and 3 are linked together and are real. Ultimately as you look to your future, and as your parents look to theirs, the biggest risk is probably number 4."

"Outliving your money, as if money has a life? I don't get it."

"Unfortunately, most people, especially those in the older generation don't understand this fear either Joyce, and it is a very real concern. For many, it will affect their "golden years" in a severe way. The example I'll show is based on a couple who retired at age 60, who had created a store of wealth valued at $850,000. They have done very well for themselves. Prior to retirement, their combined income was $100,000 per year and I will use 70% of that amount for a desired retirement income. Some planners like to use 70%, some use 80%, others are fine with 55%, and the amount is subjective and will change for every situation. The key here is the rate of return on the investments. Somewhere, some scaremonger has convinced people that the investments they used to create their wealth before they retire are suddenly too risky to hold once they retire. This is why you may have read or heard about older investors switching from being in the stock or equity market, to bonds, GICs, money market accounts, or even bank accounts. Well, let's take a look and see what happens. When you start to receive those lower returns, you are withdrawing more funds now in order to maintain your existing lifestyle. Notice the potential to run out of money by age 74." I started writing.

Age	Opening	3% Growth	Withdrawal	Balance
60	$850,000	$25,500	$70,000	$805,500
62	759,665	22,790	"	712,454
64	663,829	19,950	"	613,743
66	562,156	16,865	"	509,020
68	454,291	13,629	"	397,919
70	339,857	10,196	"	280,053
72	218,455	6,554	"	155,008
74	89,659	2,690	"	22,348
76	−46,981	1,409	"	−118,390

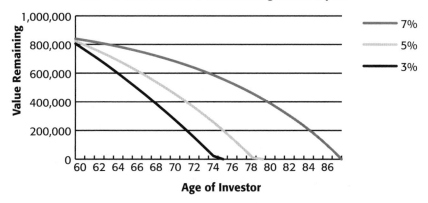

Retired with $850,000, withdrawing $70,000/year

"My own personal bias is that this is a very unsettling picture, especially if I happened to be 60 years old."

"So even though your investments are making money, you can still run out of money?"

"Certainly. Not only can you, it's pretty much guaranteed that you will under certain investing conditions. Your culprits are time, taxes and inflation. The reason we create this store of wealth is to stop working at some point in the future. At the point that we are no longer generating income from our employment, we start drawing on the investment pool that we have. That is what the chart signifies. If you'd like to see something really scary, try this out. Let's use the same example I just showed you, but we will allow for 3% inflation. Let's see if it makes any difference." I changed the board to reflect the revised numbers and when I turned to see what they thought of the changes, their expression showed me—they didn't like it.

Age	Opening	3% Growth	Withdrawal (3% Inflation)	Balance
60	$850,000	$25,500	$70,000	$805,500
62	757,565	22,727	74,263	706,029
64	650,719	19,522	78,786	591,455
66	528,049	15,841	83,584	460,307
68	388,025	11,641	88,674	310,992
70	228,988	6,870	94,074	141,783
72	49,140	1,474	99,803	–0–

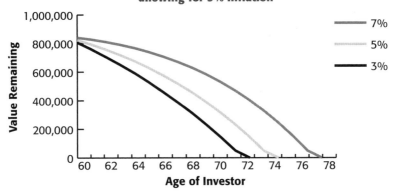

"So what do we think now?"

"Ugh!"

"Well said Joyce. Ugh. So can we now agree that a large risk that we have to fear is running out of money or of outliving our money?"

"Yes, but that doesn't tell the whole story. I don't think it does anyway. You would like to think that people bright enough to amass $850,000 would be bright enough not to spend themselves into the poor house?" James looked puzzled.

"You're probably right. People that bright would be looking forward, running projections on future growth versus withdrawals and their financial planner would be looking out for this as well, right John?"

"Right. That is part of what I do for my clients. First I help them build it. Then I help them hang onto it as long as they can so they don't run out. The couple in this example would have many options—draw less out of the plan or switch to investments that have the opportunity to produce higher returns. They may also have the opportunity to receive some form of government assistance as well, Canada Pension or Old Age Security—all of these will affect their income mix."

"I've been doing some reading on the topic, especially since we started this project, and I've seen articles that say financial planners who use 70% or 80% in retirement calculations are just trying to scare people. Instead of needing millions of dollars, you could actually get by on 35% or 45% of your pre-retirement income. Is that true?"

When you choose to retire, your employment income stops but your living expenses do not.

"It's a valid question Joyce. My belief has always been that when you choose to retire, your employment income stops but your living expenses do not. Sure, your house is probably paid off, and if you have children, hopefully they are out on their own and independent. But you still have to eat, drive a car, pay property taxes, maintain your home, see some movies, take care of health issues, go on vacation, buy Christmas presents for the grandkids, etc., etc. In short, life is an expensive proposition; just ask your parents, they'd be happy to tell you I'm sure. I haven't had a client yet tell me they retired with too much money.

"So the question that led us to this point in the discussion was 'What is Risk?'"

"That was the question?"

"In a manner of speaking, yes. That is why I chose the symbol on the last card. The symbol was for the word 'risk,' but what does it signify?"

"Crisis," from Joyce.

"Opportunity," from James.

"If I didn't know any better, I'd have thought that you rehearsed that," Richard was grinning as he erased the whiteboard. I wasn't sure that I knew where he was headed, so I was content to just sit back and watch for a while.

"The marriage of crisis and opportunity is very interesting. For what one person sees in the word risk, can be completely different from what the other sees. Nowhere is this clearer than in the case of investing and strategies about where to put your money to work for you."

"But investments don't have to be risky to be good, do they?"

"Not at all James, but there is a balance to be struck somewhere along a curve that looks something like this."

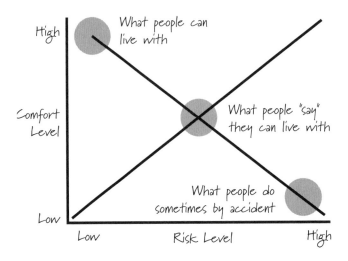

"At the end of the day, all investors, myself included, want to get a good night's sleep. Our ability to do that is affected by the level of risk we feel we are taking with our investments, the level of risk that we are prepared to take with our investments, and what the real world is doing to affect our perception of those risks."

"Aren't the first two the same?"

"How so?"

"The level of risk we feel we are taking, and the level we are prepared to take—they have to be the same, or you wouldn't choose whatever investment you have made."

"I like your logic James, but, there is this neat little thing called investor psychology that we all have to deal with. Care to jump in John?"

"Sure. Investor psychology is what causes people to buy investments when they shouldn't, sell them when they shouldn't, not invest in markets when they are ripe for a substantial gain, and hang on to an investment that should have been sold a long time ago."

"So it sounds like just a bunch of contradictions to me."

"In a way it is Joyce. There is a motto in investing that I am sure you have heard before, 'buy low, sell high.' A very simple wisdom. So simple that it is deceiving. The problem with that motto in the real world is that we know neither how low is low, nor how high is high. Somewhere in the middle the investor stands to get burned." I had a pair of puzzled faces staring at me, and I wasn't sure why.

"Ok, let's try this as an example; you've both bought 100 shares of Linden Corp. at the price of $10, a $1,000 investment. Fast-forward six months; the price is now $12.25. What do you do?"

"Hold it." Joyce jumped in first.

"Umm, hold it I guess." James seemed content to follow Joyce.

"Why the hesitation James?"

"I've made $225, over 22% in six months, which is a significant gain. Things don't go up forever."

"Right you are, so let's assume that you both hold and we fast-forward another six months, now the price is $11.25."

"So the adage is right then, what goes up must come down," Richard tossed this out. My impression was that he was trying to muddy the waters a little and get them to think.

"So now I've lost $100, great." James seemed exasperated at the thought.

"Not at all, you're still up $125 from where you started; a 12% gain in a year is a good thing James."

"So what you are trying to say is that investor psychology causes people to be irrational when it comes to investments and do the wrong things at the wrong times, thus compounding everything else that is happening around them at any given point in time?"

> **The Advice: Buy low, sell high.**
> **The Problem: How low is low? How high is high?**

"Very well said Joyce!" Richard's voice took everyone a little by surprise I think—not the comment, but the volume. It certainly got our attention.

"Ok, so we make mistakes. Mistakes cost us money, but how does this relate to risk and sleeping at night?"

"Thanks for bringing us back on track, I'm glad you're paying attention. The point is that the vast majority of people are risk adverse. They talk like they aren't, but deep down inside they are. They crave safety and would like to just leave their money in a bank account. In this way they feel market forces wouldn't affect their holdings and most people consider a bank account to be safe."

"You aren't going to tell us that banks aren't safe?"

"Not at all, I have bank accounts. Banks are a safe place. I never worry about them going under or failing as some did during the Depression years of the 1930s. That said, if they pay you 1% on your money in interest, but inflation is 3%, what happens?" I was interested to see what they retained from the session regarding inflation and its effect on your ability to generate or preserve wealth. While I was awaiting a reply, I figured this example would offer something more visual for them.

Year	Opening	1% Growth	3% Inflation	Value
1	$100,000	$1,000	$-3,030	$97,970
2	97,970	980	-2,968	95,981
3	95,981	960	-2,908	94,032
4	94,033	940	-2,849	92,123
5	92,124	921	-2,791	90,253
10	83,145	831	-2,519	81,457
15	75,042	750	-2,273	73,518
20	67,728	677	-2,052	66,353
25	61,127	611	-1,852	59,886

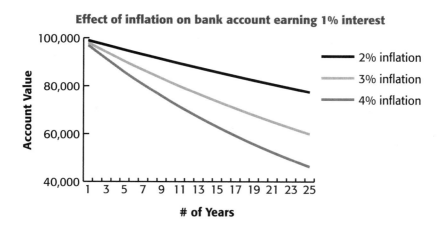

Effect of inflation on bank account earning 1% interest

"So, our money is safely locked away in the bank, earning interest, and what happens?"

"Because you aren't earning in excess of the inflation rate, your real dollar value is declining and your purchasing power declines along with it as well."

"Excellent. But it is safe—right?"

"Only in the sense that your capital is preserved. You'll never have less in terms of the actual dollar amount, but the value of that money will be worth less in the future."

"Exactly. But since banks are considered safe, people put money there, seemingly unaware of what they are doing to their future earning potential. Since we are aware, what is it that we have to do to avoid the risk of a safe investment?"

"Find an investment that earns more than the rate of inflation, as that is the only way our money can truly grow."

"That would be?"

"An investment in equities or related equity items like a mutual fund." Richard was jumping in again, which was always welcomed by the group. There are times that I felt he stayed quiet desiring not to interrupt whatever flow was happening.

"Hey, stocks, stock markets, mutual funds, I've read about those things, it's like gambling. I'm not putting my money there—no way!" I think I took the kids by surprise with my impassioned little speech. Both were looking at me funny. After all, wasn't I the financial planner who now looked afraid of actually putting money into the market?

"Why not?" James looked puzzled.

"Risky. The stock market is synonymous with risk. Too risky."

"But low returns are risky too, even when they are guaranteed—risky to your long-term growth and your ability to build a store of wealth for the future."

"Ok, I'll give you that one. Convince me a little more." I was getting that blank stare again, the one that generally meant that Richard and I were going to have to jump in to keep it moving. I was pondering which direction to take the discussion, assuming that Richard was thinking the same thing, when from out of nowhere, James went to the whiteboard and wrote:

People feel stocks are too risky when the
real risk is not owning them

James finished writing and returned to his seat on the couch, and not a word had been spoken. We were all looking at each other and I wasn't sure who wanted to speak. It was as if we were all afraid to break the silence.

"Superb James!" It was Richard.

"Thank you."

"But why?"

"Why what?"

"Why is that the truth? How did you stumble onto that?"

"It has to be where we are headed, the mix of crisis and opportunity. Where one sees crisis, the risk is too high to own stocks, the assumption being that you might lose money. The opportunity is that by owning stocks you are avoiding the certainty of having less money by investing in safe interest based investments."

Joyce was staring at James. She wasn't sure how to react to what he just said. It was interesting that only eight months ago he was perhaps the most excited about the project, albeit the most skeptical. Yet he had unearthed perhaps the most fundamental truth to the psychology of the investor. The thing they fear most—the loss of their money or assuming risk—is overrated when compared to their fear of being unable to generate long-term wealth and growth by avoiding the risk associated with investing in the market. I'm not sure how long this pause really lasted, probably only a few seconds.

What is the fundamental truth of investor psychology? The fear of losing their money.

"Proof. I demand proof James." Joyce was tapping with her pen.

"What do you mean?"

"It's like an exam, getting the right answer is only half the battle and doesn't get you full marks. You have to show that you know how to arrive at the answer and didn't just guess. So prove it to me." James was looking at Richard and me for a little help. Sometimes you are sure that you stumbled upon the answer, you just can't prove it. Fortunately for James, I thought I could. Hopefully this would provide some of the proof that Joyce wanted to see.

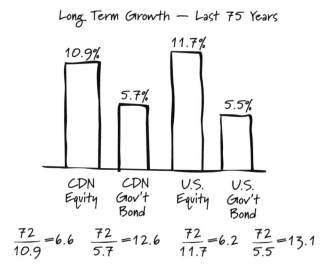

Long Term Growth — Last 75 Years

$$\frac{72}{10.9}=6.6 \qquad \frac{72}{5.7}=12.6 \qquad \frac{72}{11.7}=6.2 \qquad \frac{72}{5.5}=13.1$$

"You've heard Richard and me talk about long term in terms of investing and planning for the future—not gambling, market timing, or jumping in and out of the market on a whim. This data represents averages from a variety of sources, a long-term view, 75 years to be exact, so I think we can agree that is 'long term.' Over that period of time and keeping in mind everything that transpired in that timeframe—depression, WWII, recessions, assassinations, inventions, elections, etc., etc.—equity market investors received almost double the return over fixed interest investors. To make things just a little easier, the data has been grouped into two areas. Canadian and U.S. equities represent the average returns from the TSX for Canada and the S&P Index for the U.S. Canadian and U.S. government bonds represent the average returns for bonds or interest-based investments offered by the respective federal governments. Looking at both Canadian and American history will give us a broader perspective.

"But what about inflation? You keep bringing up the fact that inflation is our enemy too."

"Good point Joyce, so let's look at that. The best data we have is that during the same time period, inflation averaged about 3.1%, so let's break that out to look at the real return, because that is very important."

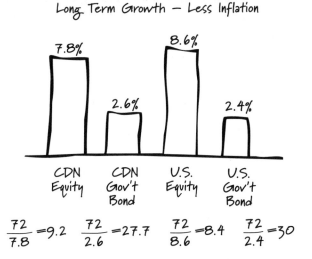

Long Term Growth – Less Inflation

$$\frac{72}{7.8}=9.2 \quad \frac{72}{2.6}=27.7 \quad \frac{72}{8.6}=8.4 \quad \frac{72}{2.4}=30$$

"Notice anything interesting in these numbers?" Richard was motioning at the board making weird little circles with his hands. Then it hit me—he had a laser pointer in his hand, on his key chain to be exact, and he was drawing little circles around the 2.6% and 2.4% rates of return.

"They're lower than the figures for investing in equities?"

"Ok James, I'll give you that one. What else?"

"The rate of difference I think. Before inflation, the equities outperformed the interest-based investments by about two times, after inflation, the factor is closer to three times."

"Good observation. What does that difference mean to us as investors?"

"More growth after inflation is the key to building wealth. The higher percentage growth you can get, the better off you will be."

"Precisely. So what are we missing?"

"Missing?"

"Think about it."

"Think. Think. Think. Is that all you and Richard do?"

"No. But it helps."

"Taxes!"

"Bingo! See James, you just had to think about it. That changes our chart to something like this."

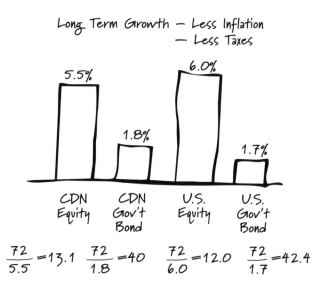

"Now I'm using assumptions that some might not agree with, but that I feel justified in using—there isn't great data to be had concerning long-term tax rates. The best data seems to put the long-term rate factored in at approximately 30%, and that is what was used here. After seeing this, what do you think of the differential now Joyce?"

"They are up again, from around three to almost four, and that just kills the rule of 72 doesn't it?"

"Kill is harsh, but it certainly affects the time to double. That in turn affects our long-term growth, our ability to build a store of wealth, and our ability to become rich in whatever form that may be."

"Caveat time."

"What time?"

"Caveat time. I think the dictionary defines it as: an explanation to prevent misinterpretation."

"Oh, much clearer now, thanks, I think."

"Ok, here we go. I don't suggest I have any inside information that the returns shown in these examples will repeat themselves in the future. The example showed approximately 11% stock market growth, 5 to 6% interest rate returns, and 3% inflation. Will these figures hold for the next three, five, ten, 25, or 50 years? I have no control over that, I can't predict it, and those who tell you they can are lying to you. The point then? That the perceived risk of being in the market is not a risk at all, but an opportunity cost that is lost to the investor if they remain out of it."

"What my esteemed colleague is trying to say, I think, is that all things go up, all things go down, but the market as a whole does not stay down. This chart might help make some sense of that."

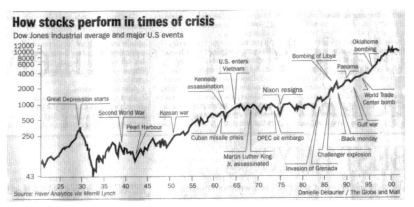

Source: Reprinted with permission from the *Globe and Mail*.

With that comment, Richard handed out a chart of the markets rise and fall from 1925 to 2000, a slow but relatively progressive advance upward and to the right, peaks and valleys, dips and troughs, short-term volatility, but long-term growth.

"I think I see the point John, but there are lots of dips and drops on this chart. There have been many from 2000 until today. I'll just assume that there will be more dips and drops to come in the future. Is part of that investor psychology you were talking about our ability to deal with these?"

> **All things go up, all things go down, but the market as a whole does not stay down.**

"You bet. I'll let you in on a little secret. This psychology applies to everyone. Richard and I aren't immune to it. We really aren't any wiser than anyone else you know."

"Speak for yourself!" Richard laughed.

"Ok, so I'm not any wiser. Those dips you see scare people, bear markets scare people, the thought of losing money scares people. You said from an example earlier today, James, that you had lost $100 on your Linden Corp. investment when in reality you were up $125 in less than a year. It all stems from that fear concept we spoke about many months ago. People have much pent up emotion surrounding money issues and this emotion will cause us to act irrationally rather than rationally. Perhaps this will help show the psychology of the investor, as it relates to psychology and risk."

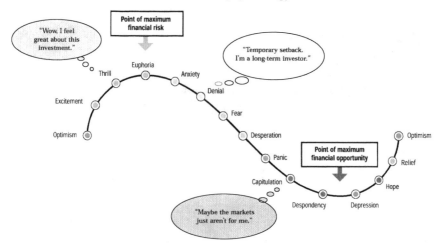

Source: Westcore Funds/Denver Investment Advisers LLC, © September 1998, Denver Investment Advisors, all rights reserved.

"That's cool!"

"But what does it mean?"

"I don't know, I just like it."

"Unfortunately James, understanding what is happening in the chart requires more thought than that. It starts with optimism on the left, the point at which we make an investment. It doesn't matter what the investment was, we have decided to invest money and we are optimistic that our investment will do well for us. It does well, and we get excited about that. The price is rising, we have some gains, on paper at least, and at the point of euphoria something critical happens."

"What?"

"We feel that we can do no wrong Joyce. The gods, whichever ones we choose to worship, are with us; our $10 stock, which might be up to $18 or

$28, is on the way to $50, and probably by next Friday. That is why it is the point of maximum financial risk."

"Why is that risk? Things are going great."

"It's risk James because that is precisely the point where the investor begins to think that they have outsmarted the market. The idea that 'I'm up 100%, I'd better buy more before it goes higher.' The point at which we tell our friends how brilliant we are, when the business press is telling people to get in before it is too late, don't miss the boat, the sky's the limit."

"Reality check!" Richard was making a 'T' symbol with his hands.

"Exactly. Reality check. Time out. There is an old adage that fits very well right here." I went over to the whiteboard and wrote:

Never confuse brains with a bull market

"That doesn't mean you aren't brilliant, just that it is more likely that the stock didn't move from $10 to $28 because you are. As with all things, normalcy shall return. The price starts to fall back, perhaps earnings are off, perhaps some new hot stock has everyone's attention. The value of your stock starts to fall, $16, $14, $10, $8, now it's worth less than you paid for it and you have slid down the enthusiasm scale from euphoria through panic to despondency and perhaps even depression as it hits a new low of $4.75. I mean, how stupid could you have been? Didn't you see this coming? What were you thinking?"

"October 19th, 1987. I know what I was thinking and I won't repeat it here. You might actually remember that phone call John."

"I remember it well. Yours wasn't the only call that day, and thanks for not repeating what you said. We touched upon this once before, the largest single day percentage drop in market history occurred on that day. People moved from euphoria to depression in less than a day, and many of them bailed out of the market, selling everything they had, knowing it was going to get worse."

What goes up, goes down. What goes down, also goes back up.

"So why is that the point of maximum opportunity?"

"Because James, that is precisely the point where people who didn't panic and didn't sell started to invest more money back into the market. What goes up, goes down. What goes down, also goes back up. The market upswing that began only days after October 19th returned 15% to investors within six months of that day and less than 14 months after the event, the markets were back to the point just before the correction. The people who stayed and didn't panic watched their investments come back. People who added new money into the market saw 15% gains quickly, and then ultimately 34% gains within two years. As the market starts back up we regain our hope, we're relieved and, yes, we even get back to the point where we feel optimistic again."

"So how long does this cycle last?"

"You never know, that's the fun part."

"Fun? What a warped sense of humour you have."

"Not at all Joyce. It's fun; it's an exciting business, and certainly not boring. Sometimes though it makes absolutely no sense at all. The cycle you see on that chart might last six months from start to finish. It might last 14 months, it might even last five years. Sometimes depending on the event, it could be less than a week. Here is a chart with a sampling of selected major crisis events, the type of events that cause large swings of anxiety and fear." I passed the chart to the group and we spent several minutes trying to digest the information and make some sense of it.

"So map this chart against the one that Richard handed out earlier and you can see some of the dips on that chart map exactly to these crisis points. Yet the long-term trend is up and to the right, signifying growth in the overall market."

"So why don't people just get out when they know this is happening? As you said, it is not always a defined event, sometimes it is just a general slide, so get out at the point of maximum risk, then get back in at the point of maximum opportunity. That's what I'm going to do."

"More power to you James. Richard and I also have another piece of advice for you," I glanced quickly to Richard, who nodded his head.

"GOOD LUCK!" in unison from the both of us. Richard who was standing behind James at this point simply patted him firmly on the back, before slipping back into his chair with a huge grin on his face.

"Ok, so what am I missing then?"

"You didn't miss anything James. Richard and I are just trying to temper your enthusiasm a little. The point is that what you are suggesting is called 'market timing' and more books and seminars have been presented on this topic than perhaps any other."

"The long and the short of it is that market timing is a myth, practiced by many, successfully attained by few, but it makes for a wonderful theory." Richard was pacing now. "Jumping in, jumping out, out and in, in and out, will make only one person relatively wealthy and that will be your broker or fund company handling all of these transactions."

CRISIS EVENTS, DJIA DECLINES AND SUBSEQUENT PERFORMANCE

Event	Reaction Dates	Reaction Date %Gain/Loss	DJIA Percentage Gain Days After Reaction Dates			
		22	63	126	253
Germany Invades France	05/09/1940 – 06/22/1940	-17.1	-0.5	8.4	7.0	-5.2
Pearl Harbor	12/06/1941 – 12/10/1941	-6.5	3.8	-2.9	-9.6	5.4
Korean War	06/23/1950 – 07/13/1950	-12.0	9.1	15.3	19.2	26.3
Eisenhower Heart Attack	09/23/1955 – 09/26/1955	-6.5	0.0	6.6	11.7	5.7
Sputnik	10/03/1957 – 10/22/1957	-9.9	5.5	6.7	7.2	29.2
Cuban Missile Crisis	10/19/1962 – 10/27/1962	1.1	12.1	17.1	24.2	30.4
JFK Assassinated	11/21/1963 – 11/22/1963	-2.9	7.2	12.4	15.1	24.0
U.S. Bombs Cambodia	04/29/1970 – 05/26/1970	-14.4	9.9	20.3	20.7	43.7
Kent State Shootings	05/01/1970 – 05/14/1970	-6.7	0.4	3.8	13.5	36.7
Arab Oil Embargo	10/16/1973 – 12/05/1973	-18.5	9.3	10.2	7.2	-25.5
Nixon Resigns	08/07/1974 – 08/29/1974	-17.6	-7.9	-5.7	12.5	27.2
Iranian Hostage Crisis	11/02/1979 – 11/07/1979	-2.7	4.7	11.1	2.3	17.0
U.S.S.R. in Afghanistan	12/24/1979 – 01/03/1980	-2.2	6.7	-4.0	6.8	21.0
Hunt Silver Crash	02/13/1980 – 03/27/1980	-15.9	6.7	16.2	25.8	30.6
Falkland Islands War	04/01/1982 – 05/07/1982	4.3	-8.5	-9.8	20.8	41.8
U.S. Invades Grenada	10/24/1983 – 11/07/1983	-2.7	3.9	-2.8	-3.2	2.4
U.S. Bombs Libya	04/14/1986 – 04/21/1986	2.8	-4.3	-4.1	-1.0	25.9
Financial Panic '87	10/02/1987 – 10/19/1987	-34.2	11.5	11.4	15.0	24.2
Invasion of Panama	12/15/1989 – 12/20/1989	-1.9	-2.7	0.3	8.0	-2.2
Iraq invades Kuwait	08/02/1990 – 08/23/1990	-13.3	0.1	2.3	16.3	22.4
Gulf War	01/16/1991 – 01/17/1991	4.6	11.8	14.3	15.0	24.5
ERM U.K. Currency Crisis	09/15/1992 – 10/16/1992	-4.6	0.6	3.2	9.2	14.7
World Trade Center Bombing	02/25/1993 – 02/27/1993	-0.3	2.4	5.1	8.5	14.2
Asian Stock Market Crisis	10/07/1997 – 10/27/1997	-12.4	8.8	10.5	25.0	16.9
U.S. Embassy Bombings Africa	08/06/1998 – 08/14/1998	-1.8	-4.0	4.8	10.4	32.0
WTC & Pentagon Terrorist Attacks	09/10/2001 – 09/21/2001	-14.3	13.4	21.2	24.8	-6.7
War in Afghanistan	10/05/2001 – 10/09/2001	-0.7	5.9	11.5	12.4	-16.8
Iraq War	03/19/2003 – 05/01/2003	2.3	5.5	9.2	15.6	22.0
Madrid Terrorist Attacks	03/10/2004 – 03/24/2004	-2.4	3.9	3.9	-0.1	4.4
London Train Bombing	07/06/2005 – 07/07/2005	0.3	2.3	0.1	5.6	7.8
India Israel & Lebanon Bombings	07/11/2006 – 07/18/2006	-3.0	5.0	10.9	16.4	28.3
Bear Sterns Collapse	03/14/2008 – 03/14/2008	0.0	5.6	3.0	-4.4	-38.1
Lehman Brothers Collapse	09/16/2008 – 09/16/2008	0.0	-18.8	-22.6	-32.3	N/A

"The nature of the market would appear to be logical, but it's filled with too much emotion to be purely logical. Logic and emotion seldom work together as a team over the long run. Let's look at the history on both sides of the border for data about recent market timing. In this example we'll be looking at data from the period of mid-2002 to mid-2008. Let's start with the Canadian experience."

S&P/TSX 2002–2008
Total Days Out	Avg. Annual Return
0	14.8%
10 Best	9.5%
20 Best	6.5%
30 Best	3.6%
40 Best	0.9%

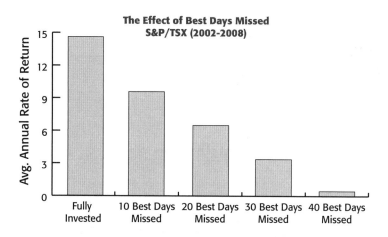

The Effect of Best Days Missed
S&P/TSX (2002-2008)

"Do you see what Richard was talking about so passionately? Let's assume that by trying to time the market over that 6-year period, you missed just the 20 best days, less than 2% of all the available days. Your average annual rate of return drops from 14.8% to 6.5% because you think you can outguess the market. Let's look at this numerically."

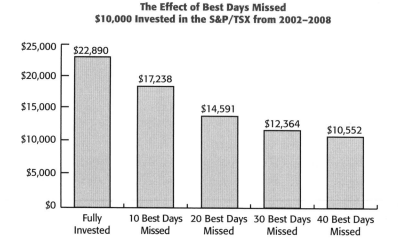

The Effect of Best Days Missed
$10,000 Invested in the S&P/TSX from 2002–2008

"Because you are smart enough to time improperly, as most do, your investment of $10,000 over that 6-year period falls from a potential value of $22,890 to $14,591 by missing out on just 20 days. How smart do you feel now?"

"Ok, not so smart. But you're going to tell me that it gets worse, right?"

"I'm sorry James, I'm not picking on you, really I'm not, neither is Richard. We're just trying to apply some time proven principles to an emotional endeavour. But since you asked, let's look at the U.S. example."

S&P 500 2002–2008

Total Days Out	Avg. Annual Return
0	3.1%
10 Best	−4.0%
20 Best	−7.5%
30 Best	−11.0%
40 Best	−13.5%

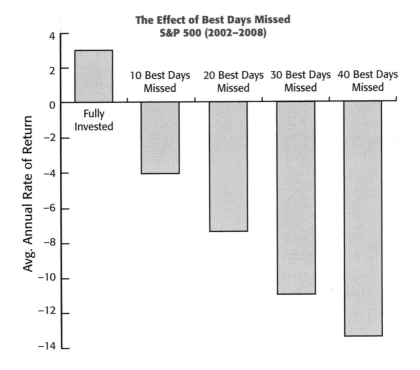

The Effect of Best Days Missed
S&P 500 (2002–2008)

"In this example, we look at the same period. If you missed just the 20 best days, less than 2% of the available days, your average annual return drops from 3.1% to –7.5% which makes a substantial difference in your assets as you can see here."

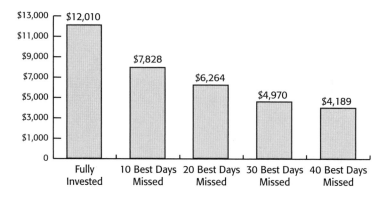

The Effect of Best Days Missed
$10,000 Invested in the S&P 500 from 2002–2008

"What John and I are trying to get across to you is that it is *time in* the market that is much more important than *timing* the market."

"Exactly, but you know what? You just might be different. I think Richard and I will give you the benefit of the doubt on this one. You are different and you might just have what it takes to successfully time the in and out of the market, not just closely, but with stunning accuracy, picking the very best time to get in, year after year. Are you up to the challenge?"

"Sure!"

"We'll put you up against your arch nemesis, Joyce. Unlike you, she's a 'Ms. Can't get it Right' and picks the worst possible day to invest year after year after year."

"Hey!"

"It's just an example, Joyce, we're not implying anything. So here's the story, we're talking long-term investing here. Each of you had invested $2,000 per year every year for 20 years using the Standard & Poor's 500 Index as your investment tool. James invested on the S&P lowest day of the year, the best day of the year. Joyce invested on the S&P highest day of the year, the worst day of the year. Let's assume all dividends or earnings are reinvested in your account. Are we ready? Drum roll please."

Richard was drumming on the table with his fingers; James and Joyce eventually caught on and joined in. While they were doing that I wrote the following on the board:

James: Mr. Perfect $207,537
Joyce: Ms. Imperfect $180,655
            Difference $26,882

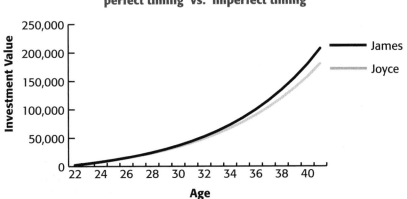

Difference after 20 years of 'perfect timing' vs. 'imperfect timing'

"That's it, that's all the difference?"

"Yes. That's all you get for your hard work. Keep in mind that if you had messed up anywhere on your timing during the last 20 years, that your results would have been different."

"But I've been paying more attention to this topic since we started the project and I know James has too. There are so many articles out there that talk about timing, so many theories about it, buy now, sell now, what are you supposed to believe? In short, everything looks risky."

"You're right Joyce. In short, everything looks risky. But when it comes right down to it, we aren't looking short term, we are looking long term. We have time on our side and time to work with. Especially in the case of yourself and James, you have a 30 to 40 year horizon to work with and time alleviates short-term risk."

"So when exactly are you supposed to invest?" James had a puzzled, slightly desperate look.

"When you have the money." In unison from Richard and I.

"And you take the money out at what point?" Joyce was looking much like James right now.

"When you need the money." In unison from Richard and I.

"That's it?"

"That's it."

"Invest when I have it, take it out when I need it. That is all I need to know?"

"Not exactly Joyce."

"I knew you were holding something back."

"No. That would be mean. The 'not exactly' pertains to the how and when you'll need the money. If you remember back to our earlier discussion on savings we talked about core and opportunity savings. Your core savings are here for the long term, the big picture type of future, the money you don't touch. Your opportunity savings are for the ski trips, a new car, perhaps a down payment on a house. The timing is much different on those funds."

"Different how?"

"When we are looking at the long-term picture, we are looking at a minimum of ten years out, often longer, sometimes much longer than ten years. That is how we eliminate the short-term fluctuations of the market and grow money to secure your future. The short-term picture is different; your approach has to be different as well. We don't put that money at risk unnecessarily by exposing it to the market. After all, we can be relatively confident of our predictions over a 20-year horizon based upon the historical past, but the potential for severe short-term fluctuations make putting your opportunity money there risky."

"Remember," Richard was heading for the whiteboard, "we have always talked about a targeted growth of 10% for the long term. Looking 18 to 36 months out, while I'm sure it seems like a long time to you, is actually quite short in terms of an investing horizon. The things for which you are saving money and hope to acquire in a shorter timeframe than that, the market is not the place to be. Yes, you could guess right and look like a hero, scoring a 50% gain in 13 months. Then again, you could look like a doofus, scoring a 42% drop in 11 weeks. I'm pretty sure you don't want to be explaining to your spouse that you won't be going on vacation, or be able to purchase your first house because you exposed your savings to too much risk by trying to time the market. Enough said?"

"So with all this panic that seems to be happening, major events that create turmoil in the markets, how do you handle all of the stress of trying to figure out when not to panic and jump out of the market Richard?"

"I don't figure it out actually."

"You don't? Who does?"

"John does." With that, both sets of eyes trained in on me momentarily, then back to Richard.

"John does?"

"Yes, and to be honest, he provides the best value for me when he brings me back to earth and prevents me from panicking and running at the worst possible time. I know they call John a financial planner, but perhaps a better word would simply be *advisor*."

"Thank you Richard."

"Kids, having John on my side is a large reason why I am where I am today. He's had faith and patience with me. On many occasions he has acted as a sounding board for any number of wacky investment ideas I have had. He has acted as a buffer when I was going to panic and get out of the market. As an investor you will eventually encounter an emotional battle between fear and faith."

"Fear of what?" Joyce looked up from where she was writing.

"The future."

"Faith in what?" It was James' turn to ask.

"The future."

"Huh?" In unison.

"We've spent time today talking about the risks associated with investing, bad investments, low returns, market crashes and market corrections. In short, all things that will occur in the future. We are afraid of what's coming; yet we must have faith in what we can't see. One of the hardest concepts that you'll ever have to come to grips with is this," Richard went to the board and wrote the following:

All we have to fear is fear itself

"It's not my line, I think it belongs to Franklin D. Roosevelt actually, and he wasn't talking about investing, but he could have been. We've talked about investing and finance creating fear and angst in people. Watch the value of your investments during a 20% market correction if you'd like to feel fear. Watch your hard earned retirement funds decline in value for 12 straight months. That will inspire fear too. That is exactly when John is at his best. He can't tell me if Mutual Fund Doodad will outperform Mutual Fund Foobar next year and that's ok. Anyone who says they can isn't telling you the truth. The greatest function John performs for me is convincing me not to lose faith, not to panic, to stick to the plan. That doesn't mean that I've never sold anything. We've moved investments around on many occasions, bought and sold a number of times. But it is the times John has helped me to determine that the panic is unfounded, not to sell at the wrong time, that is the key to the advisor's role. Feel free to jump in here John."

> **The greatest service your financial planner can perform: convincing you not to lose faith, not to panic, to stick to the plan.**

I couldn't help but smile, "I don't know that I'm as bright as Richard portrays me. When it comes to risk, we all try to do the right thing at the right time. My role is to help prevent you from doing the wrong thing at exactly the wrong time. There is so much *logical* stuff to deal with in the world of finance and investing, and invariably it all gets side swiped by the *emotional* aspects of human nature. A quick example you ask? Richard lived through and prospered past the Crash of 1987. We've talked about that event. But what about the Meltdown of '98? The Asian Contagion? The Wall Street Meltdown? The Subprime Crisis? While they don't all have the historical significance, they were scary just the same." I tossed a couple of headlines from August and September 1998 on the table. James and Joyce picked them up with some interest.

"They are almost the same headlines as those in 1987, the ones Richard shared with us a while back."

"Exactly Joyce. You know what? They'll be the same as the headlines from

sometime in 2010, 2013 and 2018 as well. I can't tell you the month and the exact date, but I can tell you this, they'll draw all the comparisons back to 2001, 1998, 1987, 1975, 1963, or 1929—pick whatever year's headlines you prefer. Once they do the analysis they'll tack on the following four words that strike fear into everyone." To ensure they got the next point, I added it to our already crowded board.

This time it's different!

"How does that scare anyone?" James looked up from his notes rather puzzled, but wrote it down anyway.

"Simply because if it wasn't different, the press would have nothing to write about. They'd say, 'yep, just like 1998, just like 1987, sit tight, remember how the market bounced back, don't panic, keep the faith.'"

"So why don't they say that?"

"At the risk of being rude and interrupting, it's because it makes great press and for interesting headlines. It sells papers and it makes people buy the paper again tomorrow to see what is different."

"Your uncle is making a good point. The fear aspect about the future is 'what if it really is different?' If it is, we won't know how to deal with it, and trust me; the unknown generates plenty of fear. What we know for sure can do enough damage. What we don't know takes it to the next level. As I've told Richard, and many clients with respect to screaming market headlines is this," I was hoping this would be the last entry on the board for today, I was running out of space to write.

If what you are reading scares you—stop reading!

"Does that actually work?"

"It usually does, at least until the next crisis du jour comes along and starts it all over again. Clients call me, we talk it over, do a sanity check to make sure it really isn't different, then we move ahead."

"So given everything that you've heard this morning, how do you feel about the concepts of risk, crisis and opportunity right now?" Richard was sitting back in his seat, looking pretty pleased with both his comment, and the path the discussion had taken over the preceding two hours.

James and Joyce were pretty quiet. I knew by the expression on their faces that they were pondering the concept. While they were doing so, I thought I would proceed with a gentle prod in the right direction.

"Everything can be a risk. Risks have to be calculated and accepted, and once they are, you can begin to realize the largest risk outweighs all of the other risks we talked about. That would be?"

"The biggest risk is not to invest at all. Fearing investment and equities as too risky can help guarantee that we'll outlive our money and never be able to save enough for the future."

"Well said Joyce."

"Does that make sense James?"

"Yep. Not that there are no risks, but the risks of doing nothing outweigh the risks of making the occasional mistake by trying to pursue a financially independent future."

"You got all that from today?"

"No, not just from today, but by trying to put all the pieces together from the past lessons and doing some research and reading on my own, as well as the *Boom, Bust & Echo* book you gave me. It appears that the future is going to be a scary place."

"I think that's a little harsh, James."

"Actually, he might be right to a degree, Richard. The future will be a scary place for those who don't plan for their future. This is not anything new; it has always been that way. After all, you were the one who told me about the three types of people." I figured this was worthy of adding to the board, so I wrote the following:

Three types of people
1) Those who make things happen
2) Those who watch things happen
3) Those who wonder what happened

Richard was smiling when I turned from the board. It was always gratifying to see people remember things that you told them or to put into practice suggestions you have offered. For Richard and me the feeling was common. One of the keys to our friendship was the fact that we respected each other and gave heed to each other's suggestions.

"That is great! It covers a whole bunch of the people that I go to school with, especially number two."

"I can see people I work with in there, but mostly number three." James let out a small laugh, seemingly amused with himself.

"Ok, so as we move toward the future, you'll strive to be?"

"Number one." From both James and Joyce.

"I'm sliding to number three. I'm tired of being number one." This drew a hearty laugh from the three of them.

"Ok, so with the exception of John, we're all striving to make things happen. While that doesn't mean just financially, for the purposes of our project, that brings us to this." Richard produced four new 5"× 7" cards from somewhere as he had wandered around the room. I was going to have to start paying more attention to how he did this. He passed them to us and gave us a moment to ponder.

"Ok, the Chinese character card was one thing. What is this all about?"

"Our next lesson of course!" Richard was grinning ear-to-ear. "This is how I know when I've designed a good card John—when nobody protests, I haven't done my job properly."

"Well this certainly appears to be a challenge tossed our way James. Just because we managed to figure out the last two. Geez."

"So how long do we have to figure it out?"

"How about three weeks? That would take us to May 19th, is that ok with everyone? I know that's shorter than our usual four weeks, but it can't be helped." There was a momentary pause while everyone checked whatever scheduling system they used.

"Sure. Sure. Yep." Three confirmations.

"Are you sure we don't get any hints?"

"Zip. Zilch. Nada. Well, maybe just one."

"That would be?"

"It's the answer that you've wanted for a long time and have been very patient about James."

"What answer?"

"Well I can't help you if you don't remember," Richard was grinning again. "I guess we'll just have to wait for next time."

"But …"

"No buts. No dice."

"That's not fair!"

"Fair? My dear cousin, who told you life was going to be fair?"

"Hey, that's my line."

"Sorry Richard, I just beat you to it."

James gave up his quest for a hint and we spent our last 20 minutes of the morning discussing the next month, and who had plans to do what, and with whom. Everyone was glad to see that winter's grip had been released and that spring was on the way. By the next meeting James would be working full-time at the bike courier company, Joyce will have completed her current semester at school, and Richard was going to be off speaking at several venues across Canada, which accounted for the need to shorten the time gap between this session and the next one. As for me, tax season was now officially over, and I could get back to doing what I liked to do best, working one-on-one with my clients and continuing to develop new ones. Goodbyes were exchanged on the porch, and we were all on our way.

Investment **Allocation**

To explode a myth is accordingly not to deny the facts but to re-allocate them.
Gilbert Ryle

Fresh.

There is something about an early spring morning that just lets you know that it's spring. While summer and winter have no discernable smell to them, spring and fall do. As I stepped outside, it was obvious, even with my eyes closed, it was spring. It could have been the freshly cut lawns or gardens with their freshly turned soil. As they say—spring has sprung.

The drive out to Richard's was uneventful and before I knew it I was coming to a stop on the gravel. He was sitting in his favourite rocking chair, a steaming cup of coffee on the small table beside him, contentedly enjoying the sunshine.

"Morning John!"

"Richard."

Before I could get up onto the porch to join in the 'rock and talk' as we called it, the distinctive sound of tires on gravel came from behind me. I wasn't startled, but probably appeared that way as I turned around. I took a second to realize what was different—James was driving. Now this was certainly a first.

"What gives? I've never seen you drive." James was slowly unfolding himself from the front seat; it was obvious that he'd prefer to be jumping off his bike.

"Just trying something different for a change. It is for the experiences after all, is it not?" Richard raised his still steaming mug in James' direction, a large grin on his face.

"I don't know, I think he should stick to cycling," Joyce had already bounded up onto the porch and taken up the chair to the right of Richard.

"Well, it's nice to have everyone back in good spirits. So before we let the nice weather distract us from our appointed duties, perhaps we can get started? If we finish early enough, we can get back out here and commune with nature for a little while. Fair enough?"

Try something different— Life is for the experiences after all.

We didn't need much prodding, I held the door open for everyone and I entered last. Everyone loaded up with breakfast from the assortment on the table and we jumped into our usual discussion of the events of the past month.

The biggest change was for Joyce. She had returned to Bradley Jarvis for another work term after a successful semester at school. James was continually prowling the streets masquerading as a bike courier, although he preferred the term 'urban mobile commando.' Richard's speaking engagements had been a success, including some repeat business, which was always welcome. Me? I had taken a long weekend and flown to Banff to get in some final days of spring skiing in the Rockies. Very enjoyable. I spent some time on double black diamond runs, by design this time. We had all reloaded our plates when the inevitable question was offered up.

"So, what did we think of this?" Richard was twirling the checkerboard 5"× 7" card in his fingers.

"Quilting."

"Excuse me James?"

"Quilting. It looks like a quilt, squares of colour all stitched together in a random pattern. Just a thought."

"No. Not quilting. Besides, what does that have to do with what we have been talking about?"

"That's easy—comfort."

"Care to explain?"

"Quilts are comfortable, they're warm, people like them. By setting up our financial lives and investment futures properly we are trying to be comfortable, setting ourselves up to stay warm and enjoy life."

"James, you're scaring me a little on this one. But, you do have a point about the comfort aspect, we are trying to create a comfortable future. Joyce?"

"I told you James," she rolled her eyes at him; it was obvious this must have been a discussion topic in the car on the way up here this morning.

"Yours isn't much better, Ms. 3.78 GPA."

"You may be right, so here goes. I guess I tried to look at it logically, which doesn't always seem to fit with relation to 'art' as we'll call it. I couldn't see any discernable pattern in the colours except that if you look at the columns, there are five colours in each. It's almost as if they were randomly generated."

"Randomly generated—that's a good one!"

"You're right James, it is. Well done Joyce." She cast a rather amused look at James.

"What?" James appeared very surprised.

"Hold on a second, let me finish. Well done to Joyce on finding some randomness in the pattern and to you James too on determining a sense of comfort. That was something I frankly hadn't thought of when I created the card. But I did say last time that it was the question that you had wanted answered for a long time James."

"I know. I went back through all of the stuff I had ever asked about, all my notes, and the only thing that kept coming up was 'where do we put the money that we are saving?'"

"Bingo!"

"Really?"

"Yes. That is exactly what the card represents, and on two different levels—distinctly different ones at that."

"You're losing me here."

"Never fear Joyce. With the help of my trusty sidekick John, we will reveal the mysteries surrounding that mysterious concept known as," he paused while he walked over to the whiteboard and wrote:

Asset Allocation

"I asked about asset allocation? I don't even know what that means."

"You did James, you just didn't realize it. For some time you have been wondering where we were going to invest the money that you're saving, or what you might do with the money in a leverage program."

"Ok, that sounds familiar."

"It should, you've mentioned it several times."

"But what does that have to do with this?" James held the card up, showing it to us all.

There was a pause in the discussion as Richard decided to take the opportunity to pace a little bit. I think that it served two purposes: first, to make them think a little bit, and second, to let him compose his thoughts.

"Interesting you should ask that question James. What do you think the relationship might be?"

Joyce jumped in, "It might have to do with those blocks of colour, that would be my guess. The blocks of colour are different things that we invest in, different things at different times, which is why all the combinations are different. Am I close?"

"As close as I would expect you to be at this point, but I'd hate to leave John out of the conversation. So enlighten us John. Explain the concept of asset allocation."

I was silent as I got up to speak. In contrast to Richard I had no idea what I wanted to say. Not that there was any shortage of material to draw upon, it was the sequence and the examples I was struggling with. I picked up the 5"× 7" card, twirled it around for several seconds, then I began.

"Asset allocation means different things to different people, and what I'm about to tell you will be only my version of the definition. Can we live with that?" I was getting skeptical looks from James and Joyce, an amused grin from Richard.

"In short, we have four different, inter-related scenarios to deal with, not complex to understand, but interesting enough that they create no shortage of material for financial writers and the financial press to argue about. So we'll begin with the first basic form." I walked over to the board, and wrote the following:

Scenario #1
Own vs. Loan

"Back when we were discussing the concept of risk, I handed out this sheet. It didn't draw many questions then, but it might now." I handed out copies of the sheet showing different types of investments, their liquidity and capital safety. I gave them a moment to scan the sheet to refresh their memory.

"I remember this, but I have a question. If we make an investment, regardless of what it is on this sheet, don't we own the investment? I'm not sure I get the concept of loan that you are referring to."

"Point taken Joyce, you will own the investment regardless of what it is. The 'own vs. loan' comes into play with what that underlying investment is comprised of. If you are receiving interest from an investment, such as a mortgage, bond, GIC, term deposit or bank account, you are, in fact, *loaning* money to that institution in return for a fixed or known rate of return. You know what return or income you are going to have, and when you'll get your money back from the investment."

"You say that like it is a bad thing," James looked up from his writing in time to give me a puzzled look.

"Not at all, but it does bring up a couple of questions. First, who benefits the most from this? Second, could you do better? Let's look at a bank for example. You have a savings account there, you are accumulating funds in that account and in return they pay you interest. What does the bank do with the money? They loan it out to other people in the form of mortgages, car loans, small business loans, etc. For them to make money, they must earn more on the money they loan out than they are paying you in interest. That should be a fairly easy concept to understand. With a company, you typically have two ways to invest. You can buy a corporate bond, or you can buy their stock. With a bond you are loaning them money that they are going to use to invest in their operations and with the purchase of stock you are buying a piece of that company, and your return will be tied to the performance of that company in the marketplace."

"But not guaranteed, right?" James still looked puzzled.

"Absolutely, no guarantee."

"Guarantees are good."

"Sometimes they are."

"Only sometimes?"

"Let's take the bank example again. I could invest $1,000 in a term deposit with them, or I could buy $1,000 of their stock. With the term deposit I know exactly what I'll be earning, say 3.5% for a year, so I get back $35 at the end of the year. With the $1,000 you could have purchased 20 shares of stock at $50 per share. At the end of the year, let's assume they are worth $51.75 or a gain of 3.5%."

"Ok, so in each case you made $35."

"True."

"But we are ahead in the stock scenario."

"Why Joyce?"

"Because interest is taxed at the highest marginal tax rate. The gain from the stock is a capital gain and you pay tax only on 50% of that gain. So in the term deposit scenario you would be left with $17.50 and in the stock scenario, you would be left with about $21 or so."

"Well done!" Richard's voice from the corner of the room caught us by surprise. "Now don't let that example fool you with its simplicity; there is a time to loan. For example, if that term deposit is inside your RRSP, your interest is not taxed, you keep the full $35. That said, own versus loan is more of a personal philosophy, is it not John?"

"I think so. Perhaps key to the concept is the understanding that when you invest by loaning, you are a loaner to the business, not an owner in the business. If you trust them enough to follow through on the generation of income or wealth in order to pay back your loan and the appreciable interest, why would you not trust them enough to grow their business and make your ownership stake in it more valuable as well?"

"Remember back to our discussion about risk? Over the long term there can be a risk associated with being in interest-based investments. Not that interest-based investments are risky, but that the real risk, the one that hinders your ability to create wealth, is playing it safe in the interest game. Especially considering how interest is taxed."

Richard and I were enjoying this back and forth bantering; I hope that James and Joyce were getting something out of it as well. From the amount of writing that was occurring on both their parts, I assumed that they were.

"I don't know if it is common sense or not, but it would appear to make sense that owners of good businesses should make more money than the people who loan money to them. This is deserved because they take more risk than the person loaning the money. When we look at the long term, investment return is higher to owners by a factor of almost two in gross terms, almost three after inflation, and almost five after inflation and taxes." I walked to the board and redrew for them the chart I used during the discussion on risk in order to reinforce the point from that session.

> **Owners of good businesses should make more money than the people who loan money to them.**

"Ok, we get the point, we want to own not loan," James appeared to be writing that down as he spoke.

"Mostly."

"What do you mean *mostly*? You can't change your mind that quickly. Pick a side."

"Can so change my mind!" Richard struck a defiant pose. "All I'm suggesting James is that as an idea, I very much like the concept of own over the concept of loan, but it is not an absolute law. There are issues to consider, such as liquidity, short- or long-term horizons and the risk level you are willing to be exposed to."

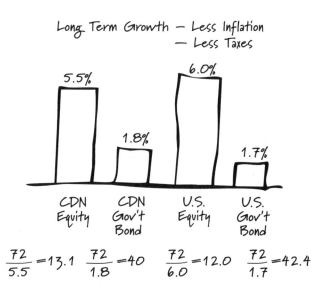

Long Term Growth — Less Inflation
— Less Taxes

$$\frac{72}{5.5} = 13.1 \quad \frac{72}{1.8} = 40 \quad \frac{72}{6.0} = 12.0 \quad \frac{72}{1.7} = 42.4$$

"Your uncle is right," Richard gave me an appreciative nod. "Keep in mind the one thing we have seemingly overlooked here as part of this discussion—which is?" I was getting blank stares from both James and Joyce, but I wasn't going to cave in as I might have in the past.

"New bike, Tour de France, 3.5 grade point average, singing lessons ..." Richard's voice was just above a whisper, his hand clasped over his mouth.

"Goals?"

"Certainly, our goals. Remember those pesky little things? They certainly come into play here. Not just from the own/loan discussion, but in all forms of asset allocation. Why, you might ask?"

"Ok, why?"

"Thanks James. We aren't just choosing to allocate our money based on some random whim, or just to satisfy our desire to have more. Rather, we are trying to help ourselves accomplish and attain our goals. Both long and short-term goals. If, for example, you can accomplish what you need financially with a 6% return on your money and you have the opportunity to earn 6% in a loan investment—do that. This isn't about saying that own is the only way to invest; you have to make sure that you can live with what you are doing as well. If you can't sleep at night knowing that you don't have the guarantee of a loan investment—there is a lot to be said for that. Now, I think we can safely move on to the next scenario. Are we ok with that?"

It appeared that we were. Both James and Joyce nodded in agreement and had flipped to new pages. Richard had pushed the button to print the page, saving what had already been written on the board.

"Ok, scenario number two."

Scenario #2
How much own,
        How much loan?

"Wait a second, you just told us, well—you didn't tell us, but tried to explain that own was the way to go over loan. Did we miss something?"

"No. You didn't miss anything. Generally speaking you are correct. But, remember the comment about goals? There are no absolutes. Additionally, we are going to introduce another variable into the equation."

"Another variable?"

"You're getting good at this James. Yes, another variable. This variable, which defines each investor, is different for each of us in this room today. Any thoughts?"

"Age?" Joyce broke the short silence.

"Why?"

"Here we go again, answering questions with questions. Because age is different for each of us in this room and it will be different for each investor."

"I can buy that."

"Good—that's all I have." Joyce appeared relieved.

"The new variable is age, and that will account for some potential differences—perhaps in how we examine scenario number two."

"It's sort of an unseen factor, don't you think?" Richard tossed this out like it wouldn't have a large impact, when in fact it did.

"I think so. Age might be the unseen factor in number two, the way that risk might be unseen in number one. Before we go too much further, let me offer up the following ideas," I proceeded to the board, figuring that I might lose James and Joyce if I didn't get something up there for them to think about.

"Here are some examples of how to split the own/loan scenarios. Which do you prefer?"

"There isn't any split there, this is all or nothing from what I can see." James looked puzzled.

"True. But a split nonetheless—if I give you $20 James, and tell you to split it with Joyce however you prefer, and you prefer to give her none; you've still split the money. You simply gave her 0%, right?"

"But you're playing games here."

"Yes, in reality, that is all we are talking about," Richard got up and moved to the board where he added the following:

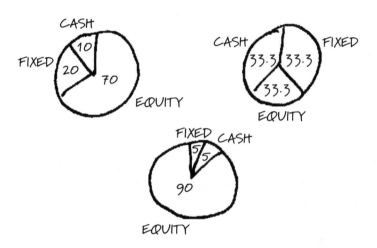

"Perhaps these are more appealing to you? What I suspect John is trying to get at is since own versus loan is probably not an absolute for everyone, we split the money we have to invest according to what we want to accomplish. Is this any better?" By the way James and Joyce were examining the board I wasn't sure where the jury of two was at this point.

"So we have to mix, if I get this at all, our goals, our risk tolerance, our personal thoughts on own versus loan and our age in order to come up with the split. So while I might want 25% cash, 25% fixed and 50% equity, James might want 5% cash, 10% fixed and 85% equity."

"Bingo!"

"So what is the right mix?"

"There isn't one."

"Huh?"

"There will be a right mix for each individual based on all of their personal variables, including several we haven't mentioned yet, but that would be getting ahead of ourselves."

"What about—Regle de bas?"

"You didn't actually think you could sneak that one by me did you Richard?"

"Not at all Joyce. I was hoping you'd catch that."

"He asked about…."

"Rule of thumb. I'm not completely unilingual Joyce," James made a quick tapping motion of his finger to the side of his head.

"Richard raises a good point. Rules of thumb are just meant to be guidelines, not actual rules per se. That said, it is not uncommon for financial planners to use the age to 100 rule to determine the split. Your age, subtracted from 100 would tell you how much to have in fixed income investments and how much in equity. At age 21, Joyce would have 21% fixed, 79% equity, I would be 45:55, Richard would be …"

"I think we all get the point quite clearly John. Don't we?" Rather amused grins from James and Joyce.

"So from all of this, it is an individual decision, what one is comfortable with, what meets their needs and helps to accomplish their goals."

"Well said. It can and will vary by time, age, need, want, the economy, taxation, etc."

"We're not trying to make this more complicated than it appears. We're just trying to give you the nuts and bolts, or the variables that John goes through in trying to determine with a client how best to meet their needs given all of these ever-changing variables."

"I think we are getting this. Bring on number three!"

"Careful what you ask for James, you might just get it." Having said that, in conjunction with a large grin, I went and added the following to the board:

Scenario #3
Sectors & Geography

"Sectors? This isn't math stuff is it?"

"I suspect you are thinking of vectors, James."

"Whew! I was getting the shakes just thinking about it."

"All right you two comedians, let's see if we can carry on from this point, shall we?"

"So what is a sector? What do we mean by geography?"

"Pick me! Pick me!" James was thrusting his hand into the air.

"Ok James, you're on."

"Geography deals with maps and countries, I know that much," he appeared to be quite pleased with himself.

"What about sectors?"

"No ideas at all. Try Joyce."

"Thanks, you're a big help," Joyce seemed exasperated to be put on the spot. "I don't know why, but I'm thinking something like a logical segment, a grouping of something. The only thing that is popping into my mind is from Star Trek or something—'Captain Kirk, we have a problem in the Romulan sector.'" Joyce had put on a deep husky voice to impersonate the character, and we all seemed to find it quite amusing.

"Well, you are closer than you think, on both counts. As it relates to financial management, what we are concerned with from a sector perspective is what type of industry would I like to invest in? What type of investment in general do I want?" While I had been handling the more descriptive chores, Richard had been busy drawing on the board; I turned around to see what James and Joyce were looking at behind me.

Corporate Debt Financial GICs Minerals Stocks Large Cap
Industrial Mutual Funds Technology Gov't Bonds Healthcare Transportation Oil & Gas

"Well done Richard, thanks for the help."

"What does all that mean?" Joyce had stopped writing; Richard was printing a page for each of them.

"What it means is that you have options. People often complain about not having enough options. Well kids, when it comes to investing your hard earned money, you have more options than you can imagine."

"So imagine if you will that you can now do something like this, should you so desire," Richard had been drawing behind me again, and he presented to us the following:

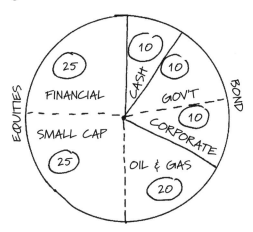

"This is starting to get more and more complex. I liked this better when I had to think a little less."

"Easy James, thinking is good. Even your brain needs a little exercise now and then," Richard was grinning as he walked behind James, took his head in his hands and gave it a gentle shake from side-to-side.

"I get this. We're building on each scenario from the previous one. Had we decided that 100% loan was the way to go, we'd still have the option of creating a chart like that. It might be split into government bonds, corporate bonds, treasury bills and GICs with no equity component. Right?"

"Exactly!"

Not to be outdone, James rose from the couch and added the following to the board:

"That too would be an allocation James, a very narrow and probably very risky one, but I do appreciate your faith in my fictional little company."

Joyce was next; she completed her commentary before I had a chance to finish complimenting James on his decision and artwork.

DIVERSIFICATION!

"But if we don't do this," pointing at the word she had just written, "we are increasing the risk of having all our eggs in one basket. Richard used that term at some point, but I can't remember when."

Diversification: Decreases the risk of having all your eggs in one basket.

"I'm sure I did and you are 100% correct. We use asset allocation to spread our investments across a number of different sectors in order to reduce the risk associated with being in only one—living and dying by the performance of a single investment. That is what the point of the card was all about. The colours represent the different things you can invest in, the columns represent year to year returns, what performs well one year, won't necessarily perform well the next year. Therefore we allocate our investments across a spectrum so that we maximize our return and minimize our risk."

"But what if you have a *sure-thing* Richard?"

"Well, if you think you have a sure-thing, think again, because you don't. There are no sure-things. These so-called sure-things, hot tips, gut feelings, psychic hotlines, guaranteed winners, have nothing to do with investing and planning. What you are talking about falls into the area known as speculation and gambling." James was sinking a little lower into the couch. "Now I didn't say *never* James, there is certainly a time to toss some money at a speculative investment. You might want to allocate a tiny slice of your investment portfolio for that purpose solely, as long as you are prepared to lose your entire investment and not gripe about it afterwards. For now however, I think you should be spending your time creating a solid basic platform for investing. You ok with that?"

> **Our goals, our risk tolerance, our personal thoughts on own versus loan and our age are factors in determining the split.**

"Sure," but it didn't seem to be entirely enthusiastic.

This seemed to be a natural break in the flow and it seemed that everyone was in the process of refilling their drinks. I waited until we settled back in before hitting my next point.

"Which country has approximately 4% of the world's available stock market for investing?" I began humming the tune from *Jeopardy* for effect.

"Canada!" An enthusiastic reply from Joyce. I simulated an incorrect buzzer sound.

"What is Canada?" James still didn't seem that enthusiastic.

"Yes. Well done. Sorry Joyce, but answers must be in the form of a question."

"Picky, picky, picky."

"Sorry. But why did I even bring this up? I'm sure that is the question you have, but aren't asking."

"Well, since Canada has only 4% of the available stuff in the world to invest in, it would make sense to seek out investments in other countries."

"Ok, but why?"

"To diversify our portfolios?"

"Exactly. That type of diversification might lead us to this." Once again, Richard was busy behind me, drawing more circles on the whiteboard in order to produce the following:

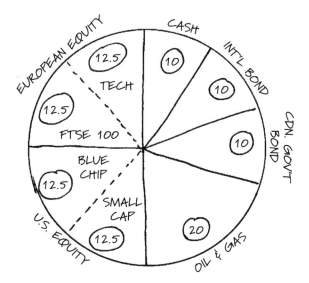

"Every time you change this it gets more complicated Richard. How do people stay on top of everything?"

"You couldn't ask for a better set-up than that John."

Richard was right, I probably couldn't ask for a better segue into the final scenario on asset allocation, so I decided to take it while it was there. Confidently striding to the whiteboard, I wrote:

Scenario #4
Advisor or D.I.Y.

"What is DIY?" I guessed Joyce hadn't been in too many hardware or home supply stores based on the question.

"Short for do-it–yourself, Joyce."

"Somebody actually wants to figure out all this stuff for themselves? Yuck."

"Not really 'yuck' Joyce. There are plenty of people who actually like the work that goes into planning investments, researching the markets, determining a strategy, creating an investment style, handling the transactions, calculating the risks, keeping track of the percentages …" Just when I was on a roll, Richard interjected.

"Then there are the rest of us. People who have better things to do, at least in our own minds, and who don't want to spend their time doing all of this stuff when we can have other competent people do it for us. I mentioned previously how valuable I have found John's advice and guidance in the past during times of market turmoil. That same advice and guidance applies to the creation of investment portfolios as well. John suggests a mix of investments that meets your needs after considering all of the variables that we have been discussing over the past few months. I'm not saying that you can't do it yourself; I'm not suggesting that you can't be successful if you chose to; I'm not saying you have to have John as your advisor. There are plenty of other competent advisors to be found out there. In short it is all about personality, choice, experience, comfort level, confidence and a bunch of other variables including something we haven't talked about in months—feelings. How does it feel? Are you comfortable with this person? Are you confident they are advising you specifically and not simply offering the same advice to every person? Are they excited and interested in what you want to accomplish in your life? I could go on, bail me out here John."

Initially I simply sat on the edge of the couch, shaking my head, but then I decided to assist.

> **Are you confident your financial planner is advising you specifically and not simply offering the same advice to every person?**

"There is a comfort level to be certain. I would hope that my clients feel that way and they are happy with the work I do, the suggestions and recommendations I make for them. At the end of the day, all I can do is suggest and recommend. The final decision on anything we discuss always belongs to the client. That doesn't mean that clients don't come to me with ideas based on things they have read or because they are experts in a particular field and want to examine an investment that I might not be familiar with. Getting back to the fourth scenario, I believe there is a place for do-it-yourself in certain instances, with a certain percentage of your money. Why not? It can be fun and rewarding to try to beat the professionals at their own game. It also gives people a certain sense of accomplishment that they are doing it on their own. Does that make sense?"

I left the question hanging as I sat down to refresh myself with a glass of Diet Coke that was sitting on the table. I knew my mother would be appalled at my dietary habits, especially if she saw the spread on the table in front of us. The thought did remind me to keep following up on one of my goals for the year, which was to keep in more consistent contact with my parents.

While that thought was cycling through the back of my mind, I was looking over at Richard, who was looking at James and Joyce, and then he returned my glance with a smile. I was pretty sure he was happy with the progress they were making, and the impact that he was having on them.

"I have a question for you." James had sat up, he was tapping his pen on his notebook. "I think what we have covered in the four scenarios goes a long way to answering my basic question of what do we invest our money in? At the same time, it still leaves me with the question of *how*? Do we simply stop by John's office, toss $20 on his desk with a note attached that says 'invest me wisely.'"

"That is certainly an interesting method and you make a good point James. This would be a good place for us to examine one final point for today and another aspect of allocation that we haven't seen yet. One of the best ways to allocate your investment funds lies within this principle." Once again, I was writing on the whiteboard, drawing in large letters.

D.C.A.

"Not more TLAs." Joyce rolled her eyes.

"TLAs?"

"Three letter acronyms—come on John, stick with the program will you?" Joyce was quite amused, as were James and Richard.

"You got me. So figure out DCA for yourself then." I was getting what I suspected was her best sad face. I decided to help them out by adding more to the board:

D.C.A.
Dollar Cost
Averaging

"DCA is the TLA for Dollar Cost Averaging—a powerful tool not just for allocating, but for investing in general," perhaps Richard had seen Joyce's 'help me' face before. He jumped right in as soon as she made it, which surprised me. Usually he'd let them suffer a little.

"Richard's right. Dollar cost averaging is a powerful tool and someone starting their investing program from a position such as yours can take full advantage of it. Care to hear more?" I wanted to see what their level of interest was. After all, we had been covering a lot of ground today.

"Tell us more John!" With some enthusiasm.

"I'll try to keep this brief and to the point. To start the answer for James, we would begin by opening an investment account. It could be an RRSP account, but it could also be non-registered, or what some people call an open account. That done, we would select the investment that we are going to use. It could be one, it might be several depending on your need, your goals, and the amount of money to be invested. For purposes of this example let's pick a fictional mutual fund called 'Doodad,' a fund that invests in Canadian companies, focused on the TSX 300, not sector specific. Are you with me so far?" Two quick nods.

"Let's assume that the fund has an initial require-ment of a $500 investment and after that you can invest monthly, quarterly, annually, or whenever you feel like it, with a minimum additional $50 investment. Remember way, way back to our discussion about compound inter-est. This is really where we begin to see it in action. We used examples at that time showing investments of $2,000 a year. On a monthly basis, that works out to about $165 per month. So once the account is set up, $165 each month will be withdrawn from your bank account automatically and that money will go into your investment account. In addition to everything else I've asked you to remember, add this to the list—our discussion about market timing. Dollar cost averaging might just be considered the antidote for the rest of us who couldn't care about market timing."

> **Dollar cost averaging might be considered the antidote for market timing.**

"Examples please, examples!" Richard tossed me a marker and motioned to the board. He was probably right; this would have more impact visually.

Month	Investment	Price	Purchased	Owned		
January	$165	$10.00	16.50	16.50		
February	"	9.80	16.84	33.34		
March	"	9.50	17.37	50.71	Invested	
April	"	9.25	17.84	68.54	$1,980	
May	"	9.05	18.23	86.78		
June	"	8.85	18.64	105.42	Value	
July	"	8.60	19.19	124.61	$2,149.71	
August	"	8.55	19.30	143.90		
September	"	8.65	19.08	162.98	R.O.I.	
October	"	9.15	18.03	181.01	8.57%	
November	"	9.45	17.46	198.47		
December	"	10.00	16.50	214.97		
	$1,980		214.97			

"As we can see from the example, the concept of DCA is relatively simple. We invest the same dollar value each month. We are able to buy more of the investment when it has a lower price and less of it when the price is rising. Remember that chart about the cycles of investor psychology? We purchase fewer of them near the euphoria of market highs. This helps us offset what many investors do. They buy all their shares when the market says they are worth the most, and then refuse to buy them when the market says they are *on sale*." I decided to give a brief pause to my monologue, as both James and Joyce were looking at the chart and making some notes.

"This process helps to keep our average cost lower than it might be if we bought in a lump sum. And the lower your costs to purchase, the higher your returns are going to be. In short, by investing the same number of dollars month after month, your timing of the markets is not an issue at all. Check the example. Your $1,980 investment is worth $2,149.70 at the end of the year, a return of 8.57% on your money, yet the value of each share is exactly the same as it was at the start of the year. Markets have a tendency to do one of three basic things, and this will be the last picture for today I promise."

THREE MARKET TENDENCIES

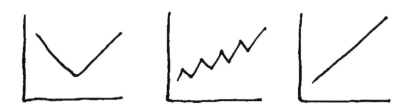

"Now just to save both my hands and our time today, here are three tables that correspond to each of the examples I just drew on the board." From my briefcase I took out three stapled sheets with a single chart on each. The first was the one that was already on the board.

Month	Investment	Price	Purchased	Owned	
January	$165	$10.00	16.50	16.50	
February	"	10.25	16.10	32.60	
March	"	10.05	16.42	49.02	Invested
April	"	9.80	16.84	65.85	$1,980
May	"	9.25	17.84	83.69	

Month	Investment	Price	Purchased	Owned		
June	"	8.85	18.64	102.33	Value	
July	"	9.15	18.03	120.37	$2,155.58	
August	"	8.55	19.30	139.67		
September	"	8.65	19.08	158.74	R.O.I.	
October	"	9.15	18.03	176.77	8.88%	
November	"	9.45	17.46	194.23		
December	"	10.25	16.10	210.33		
	$1,980			210.33		

Month	Investment	Price	Purchased	Owned		
January	$165	$10.00	16.50	16.50		
February	"	10.05	16.42	32.92		
March	"	10.10	16.34	49.25	Invested	
April	"	10.15	16.26	65.51	$1,980	
May	"	10.20	16.18	81.69		
June	"	10.25	16.10	97.78	Value	
July	"	10.50	15.71	113.50	$2,088.91	
August	"	10.60	15.57	129.07		
September	"	10.70	15.42	144.49	R.O.I.	
October	"	10.80	15.28	159.76	5.50%	
November	"	10.90	15.14	174.90		
December	"	11.00	15.00	189.90		
	$1,980			189.90		

"This is pretty impressive, making money by investing a little bit at a time."

"It's actually pretty simple James. Many people think they have to have a large sum of money in order to invest. You can actually create large sums of money, a little bit at a time, as long as you are diligent and stick to the plan that you have created for yourself. But only you can do that. I can help people create the plan and make the suggestions, but I can't make them execute the plan. Only they can do that."

"Wait a minute. Why did I make less in the third scenario? The first two have me with a return on investment of over 8%, the last example has me with 5.5%, yet the market went straight up—well, it looks like straight up. What gives?" Joyce appeared to be puzzled at this turn of events.

"Excellent point, I'm glad you caught that. Fortunately, there is a relatively simple explanation." I decided to pause, just to see how long I could get away with it.

"The explanation is ..."

"The example given is not a real reflection of what happens in the markets in the real world," I punctuated my comments with hand gestures. "The first two are. In the first the market goes down, then the market comes back up. In the second, the market shows some upward mobility long term, but plenty of fluctuation in the short term."

"In the last example, you'd have made more money, almost double if you had put all your money in during January. You'd have earned 10% instead of 5.5%. Doesn't that dispel the dollar cost averaging theory?" Joyce was tapping her pen rather emphatically on her notebook.

"Yes, but …" time to try the pause again.

"But what?" No such luck this time.

"But you didn't have all the money in January. That is the key to dollar cost averaging; it allows you to consistently fund your investment strategy on a timely and consistent basis, regardless of what is happening in the market. It eliminates the concept of trying to time the market and determine when the right time to invest is and it avoids making you dependent on saving a lump sum of money. The problem with lump sum saving is that just around the time you have reached your target amount, something neat that you've wanted for a long time will go on sale. Remember our discussion about CHUD—the consumable had-to-have-it under delusion purchases? If it isn't that, then perhaps the market will be in turmoil or you simply decide, nah, I'd rather be doing something else with this money."

> Dollar cost averaging is potentially one of your most powerful allies in the investing game, perhaps second only to compound interest.

"John's right," Richard was beginning to pace. "Dollar cost averaging is potentially one of your most powerful allies in the investing game, perhaps second only to compound interest. It's easy, it's consistent, it takes all the guesswork out and it builds wealth slowly and effectively. I know you both want to be rich by your 30th birthday. I did too. Heck, I'd like to be rich now for that matter. Investing for the long term is a game won by the determined and consistent, applying proven principles in a systematic fashion. No fancy stuff, no undue risks—there are enough books written on that to fill my library. Investing in commodities futures, trading derivatives, day trading technology stocks, foreign currency swaps—it is all really sexy, cool stuff. It gets headlines and press and the small percentage of the people who make money at it get plenty of publicity. The rest of the people who are generating wealth for themselves are doing it the old fashioned, boring way."

"Boring?"

"Certainly. There isn't much excitement to this. Remember the early charts we looked at, save $2,000 per year from age 22 to 32, then you sit and wait—use compounding to your advantage. Then voila, at age 62 you had close to $650,000. How hard was that?"

"It doesn't seem that hard." James shrugged his shoulders.

"Because it really isn't. The biggest fallacy that people have about money is that it is some sort of sophisticated, magical process, which takes years of study in order to understand. I'm not suggesting that you don't learn about investing—there are some great books on the subject which make for interesting reading—but the keys will always remain," Richard cleared some space on the board for the following:

Keys to Investing
- Start as early as possible
- Stay consistent to your plan
- Use D.C.A. to beat market timing

"Ok, this is starting to make sense to me. I'm still left with a question. Well several actually, but one that seems to stand out from the rest."

"Fire away James."

"But what do we invest the money in? I understand the allocation concept, not all the eggs in one basket; I understand the geographic splits, fixed versus equity; but I'm still struggling with 'What am I investing my money in?' Does that make any sense?"

"Certainly, and I think it will be a great place to finish the session for today. Where do you put the money you are investing? For relatively new investors such as yourself and even for more experienced investors as well, investing small lump sums using dollar cost averaging is most easily done via this route." I felt it was worth adding to the board:

> The biggest fallacy about money is that it is some sort of sophisticated, magical process, which takes years of study in order to understand.

Managed Money

"What exactly is managed money?"

"It's worth explaining James. When you invest using managed money, you are looking at investing in financial vehicles such as mutual funds, wrap accounts, pooled funds, or pension funds to name a few. You are putting your money together with many other people and asking a professional money manager to invest it on your behalf. The manager invests it for the whole group into a variety of investments, which suit the specific investment objectives. The easiest to explain would be a mutual fund. Each mutual fund has its own objectives. Funds can invest in stocks, bonds, cash or other securities or combinations of these types of securities.

Mutual funds cover just about every investment scenario you could invest in or imagine.

If the fund manager's investments make a profit, which would be the goal, then you share that profit along with everyone else in the group. If the investments lose money, everyone shares in the loss."

"But how do you know what your investment is worth at any point if it is lumped with all the other investments from other people?"

"When you put money into a fund, you receive in exchange, units or shares of that fund. A mutual fund's unit value is described as the net asset value per share —NAVPS. The NAVPS is calculated by taking the total value of the fund if everything was sold on that day, less any outstanding debts, and dividing by the number of units held by all the fund's investors. For example, if a fund is worth $10 million (value less what it owes) and has one million units outstanding, the NAVPS will be $10. If you own ten units your investment is worth $100. You can pick up the business section of the paper any day and find the worth of your particular fund, or look at any number of Web sites that cater to people with an interest in finance."

"Ok, that seems to make sense."

"There are some advantages, and some disadvantages to using them. The basics are these," I turned around and added:

Managed Money
Advantages   Disadvantages
- Diversification   - Buried Costs
- Professional Management   - No control over investments
- Systematic Investment &
  Withdrawal plans

"There are mutual funds out there to cover just about every investment scenario you could invest in or imagine and they are perhaps the best vehicle for covering geographic diversification. They make it easy to diversify in any given sector, you can dribble amounts in a little at a time, you get professional money management and you have the ability to track historic returns with proven companies to invest in."

"But you listed some disadvantages as well." Joyce looked up from her notes.

"I listed them as disadvantages, but I don't necessarily see them that way. For example—costs. It costs money to get professional management of the funds; they get paid out of the money in the fund. Mutual fund costs are often referred to as an MER—sorry Joyce—or Management Expense Ratio, expressed as a percentage. A typical MER for a Canadian equity fund can range from 0.5% to 3.5%."

"So lower cost is better, right?"

"Yes and no. You should be concerned about cost but not single-mindedly focused on it. It is your after-cost return that is the most important issue. If a fund has an MER of 1% and a return of 8.5%, your after-cost return is 7.5%. If a different fund has an MER of 3.5% and returns 12%, your after-cost return is 8.5%. You paid more, but you made more. Much like the tax discussion from months back—it's not about what you make, it's about how much you get to keep."

"What about the other disadvantage?"

"I feel it is more of a personal issue than an investment issue, but that is simply my opinion. A manager may choose to invest in a company that you don't like, or that does business in a country that you have concerns about. In short, you don't get to pick the underlying investments. Conversely, if you want to own a particular stock, perhaps you work for a publicly traded company or have an interest in a certain industry, then by all means, purchase that stock if it fits your plan. That can be part of your DIY strategy."

"So why don't we just invest in the fund with the best performance or return. That sounds like the easiest way to do it, no?" James was waving around today's business section where a company was trumpeting its one-year return.

"Keep in mind that past performance is not an indicator of any future performance. Just because a fund has returned 9% a year for seven years doesn't mean that it will do it this year or the year after or the year after that." I was glad that Richard brought up this point. It's a key point people need to understand—that the past is not a predictor of the future.

"Richard is right. You cannot guarantee future behaviour from past performance. Does anyone remember what the three guarantees were?"

"Death, taxes …"

"And inflation!"

"Hey, I was going to say that."

"Sorry Joyce, I didn't want you getting all the credit."

"Ok, settle down, you both have that clear. Did you notice that consistent investment returns is not one of life's guarantees? Good." I was glad to have Richard make that point. As a financial planner, one of the hardest things to do at times is convince people that their money won't be doubling in three years. Setting and dealing with expectations is a large part of my job, one made easier with people like Richard who have a realistic view of the world and how it operates.

"Ok, I grasp the mutual fund concept. I've been doing some reading; there are over 180 mutual fund companies in Canada, offering up close to 3,500 funds to invest in. How do I wade through all of that?"

It was obvious that Joyce had been doing some homework, James too for that matter. The questions were getting better each month.

"You don't. I do. Well, to be more precise—we do. There are a number of tools at my disposal for analyzing all of the data produced by all of those funds. I'll match that data up with the goals of your investment strategy, then I'll create some recommendations. Once that is done, we sit down together, I present what I feel are the best options available at that time, but the final selection and choices are always made by the client—it's your money after all."

"I've made the comment before, but it is worth repeating. John's strength is the professionalism and pride he brings to being an advisor. Helping you to select the right investment options and creating, not just a short-term path, but a long-term investing strategy."

I sat down, and Richard did the same. We had been at it for quite some time this morning and we had covered a lot of ground. I think that James and Joyce had figured we'd reached the end of the session as well; both had closed their notebooks and were picking at the remains of the breakfast spread.

"Well gang, how do we feel? We've covered a lot of ground today, this has been a good session."

"A little overwhelmed actually, sorry John."

"Why? No need to be sorry. We tossed a pile of information at you. Let it sink in for a bit. If there are still any questions when we get to the next session, bring them up and we'll address them. You are always free to call me anytime. Don't feel you have to wait. Fair enough?"

"Fair enough."

"How about you Joyce?"

"I'm ok—lots of information. It's starting to make sense, a bigger picture is starting to emerge, but I still feel we are a few pieces short."

"Interesting that you mentioned a bigger picture Joyce. We might just be heading in the direction you are looking for. Why don't we take a look at these," Richard had produced the requisite four 5"×7" cards, at least we had a picture to deal with this time.

"Interesting, a sports metaphor perhaps? I didn't think you were much of a fan Richard."

"I'm a fan James. I like sports metaphors as much as the next guy."

"Ok, before the male testosterone gets too intense in here, when is the next meeting?"

"Ever the scheduler Joyce. Where would we be without you?"

"Off time, off schedule and probably off topic," she grinned.

"Well, I hate to disappoint you, but I have some upcoming personal commitments so we'll be off our somewhat regular schedule, if that's ok? I'm actually thinking of June 3rd, but we'll switch to John's office, if that works for everyone. If we don't meet then, it may have to be put off a while." There was some silence as everyone checked whatever time management system they used.

"Sure."

"Good"

"I'm in for June 3rd."

"Great, that's settled."

"No hints on the card Richard?"

"Nope. You guys are getting too good at this, even without the hints, and this one certainly isn't that tough. I don't know about the rest of you, but it's time to rock."

"Ok, we get the point."

"I'm afraid you don't James." Richard's voice trailed off as he headed out the door, the wooden screen door snapped shut with a loud smack. I just grinned at James and Joyce, who were looking at me slightly amused and slightly puzzled. I wasn't going to say anything, although I knew exactly what Richard was getting at.

"Oh! I get it," with that Joyce bolted for the door herself, James in close pursuit. I was content to let them get there first. I caught the screen door thrown open by James, to find the three of them rocking gently in the sunshine. I sat down on my own piece of the porch and leaned back against one of the posts, closing my eyes for a moment to enjoy a gorgeous springtime morning.

The discussion centered on plans for the summer, and everyone had something in mind. Joyce was going to be on another work term at Bradley Jarvis, continuing the practical side of her education. James would be biking around town, not just for work, but also in preparation to enter some road races. Richard and I had already drawn up some plans to do a little fly-fishing on the Grand River, a favourite spot of ours.

I'm not sure how long we sat there enjoying the sunshine; I didn't even bother to look at my watch. I knew Richard didn't, he never wore a watch unless absolutely necessary. Sharing a Saturday morning 'rock and talk' with his niece and nephew certainly wasn't one of those times.

Creating the
Game Plan

Create a definite plan for carrying out your desire and begin at once, whether you are ready or not, to put this plan into action.
Napoleon Hill

Mist.

There wasn't enough moisture to call it rain, but it was certainly damp outside. Not dense enough to be called fog, just a pervasive mist that seemed to hang on everything. There was enough of it to need the wipers, but not enough to leave it on the lowest setting—very annoying. The last six weeks, the last two months actually, had been exceptionally busy. Finally it got to the point where I had actually hired a second assistant to help cope with the volume of paperwork the business was generating.

On the seat beside me were some examples of client plans that I had brought along for today's meeting. The questions that had been asked at the last meeting and the focus of Richard's last card were leading in the direction of creating a plan, and how you take all of the information that we had been discussing and merge it into something more concrete.

I had selected three distinct sample plans for purposes of showing James and Joyce the process that I undertake in order to create a plan that is comprehensive and flexible, but most importantly, a plan that fits the needs of the client. Not only does it have to fit where they are today, but it has to be flexible enough to allow for changes in the future as their needs inevitably change.

My office clock had just finished chiming 8:30 a.m. as I opened the door. I was just about finished cleaning the whiteboard when Joyce strolled into the office.

"Morning John! Nice to see you."

"Likewise Joyce," I turned to see her tossing her green nylon rain suit onto the coat rack.

"Biking it today. Not so bad as long as this mist doesn't turn into rain. Guess I'm the first one here?"

"Yep. Which doesn't surprise me actually, you're quite good at the punctuality aspect of the project."

"Hey! I'm trying!" James must have heard us from the hall, seconds later he appeared in the doorway, covered in a similar rain suit, only blue.

"I know, I know, you're both doing well, except for your uncle who seems to be the one holding us up today." Given that he was still 15 minutes away from being officially late, I decided to cut Richard a little slack.

I got the distinct impression that James and Joyce hadn't spoken much since the last meeting, as they were having a very animated discussion about the events of the past two weeks, with some interjected 'shut up!' and 'no way!' comments punctuating the conversation. I liked to see people enjoying each other's company this much and session after session I was watching the bond grow between the two of them.

"Greetings all!"

Now there was a sight—a grown man, slightly past middle age, standing in my office doorway covered head to toe in fluorescent orange nylon, wearing a yellow headband, a green backpack, and a purple iPod nano hanging off his belt.

"Nice look. What are you up to Richard?"

"Cycling. Isn't it obvious?"

"Obvious for these two. It's not what I expect from you. You aren't serious are you?"

"I most certainly am; it was James' idea. He wanted to show me his new bike, well, his soon-to-be new bike, and the next thing I knew I was buying a bike for myself. It's great, you should try it John."

Richard ditched the rain gear and proceeded to set up the table with the usual array of breakfast essentials taken from his pack. While Richard had his back turned, I casually positioned a box of donut holes in the middle of his display of healthier breakfast alternatives.

"So did I miss anything?"

"Nothing," in triplicate.

"Good, so what have we been up to? Especially you John, you've been hard to get hold of recently."

We launched into our ritual 'who has done what' discussion, filling our faces with food as we talked. With the news exhausted, everyone's plates refilled and a small glimpse of sunlight breaking through the clouds, Richard pulled last month's card from his folder.

"So, what do we make of this?" Richard was spinning the card around lazily in his hands.

"A plan obviously. I thought the words 'Plan A,' 'Plan B,' sort of gave that away," James seemed quite surprised that Richard was asking.

"Anything else?"

"Nope."

"Anything else?"

"The clipboard, something about the clipboard. I have been thinking about that," Joyce was looking in her notebook, the card was taped to the page, but there wasn't much writing underneath, which was unusual for her.

"I've got it! It's a play, not just a play, a play is part of a game—it's a game plan—right?"

"Exactly Joyce. A game plan. But why a game plan?"

"Because when coaches create game plans, they always have multiple scenarios, alternatives, and contingencies. They start with a basic plan to begin the game and expand it once the action starts and everything around the original plan starts to change." James jumped in before Joyce could speak.

"Well done, both of you. You make a good team."

"I knew that 15 years of watching televised sports would benefit me at some point in the future. I guess the future is now."

"It certainly is. The interesting thing about the future is that it will arrive faster than any of us expect it to. As such, it is important that we set up our personal game plans well in advance."

Game plans get revised, revisited and altered as things and situations change.

"Richard is right. While hindsight is always 20/20 we have to move forward with our planning even though we don't necessarily know what the future will bring. It isn't just a static event though. You don't just create the game plan and then let it sit. It gets revised, revisited and altered as things and situations change. Your reference to multiple scenarios and alternatives couldn't be more insightful James."

James had as large a smile as I had ever seen during all of our time together and it was matched by Richard's large grin. I think that Joyce was trying to stay reserved, but she relented a little and playfully punched James in the shoulder.

"That's quite enough," Richard said in a faux stern voice. "Let's try to stay on track here. So I'm assuming that you have brought some sample game plans for us to take a look at John?"

"Indeed," I opened the folder containing three plans I had selected and tossed them onto the table.

James and Joyce each immediately picked one up and started to thumb through them. Richard sat back, sipping his coffee. When I opened my business 25 years ago, a detailed plan might have consisted of a three to five page report, probably typed, perhaps a hand-drawn chart, and some rough tables. Today a 20 to 50 page game plan in full colour, graphics, bound nicely was the norm for each of my clients.

"So everybody gets one of these? Also, can't we save some trees?"

"All my clients do get one and yes, electronic formats are available for the clients—I like to save trees when I can. Prospective clients get one as well, when we get to the point of actually creating a sample plan. There are many times that I'll meet with a prospect and we mutually decide not to go any further with the discussions."

"They decide they don't want to do business with you or you decide not to take them on as a client?" Joyce put the plan she was holding back on the table and picked up her notebook.

"Either, or both. It depends."

"What does that mean—either or both?" James asked.

"Well, sometimes I meet with a prospective client and they choose not to use me. It could be personality reasons, investing style, or personal comfort level. Whatever the reason, I respect that. When people's finances are involved, finding the right fit is extremely important. Sometimes I meet with a prospective client and I decide not to take them on as a client because what they tell me they want to achieve is unrealistic. Perhaps they don't seem like they have the discipline required to stick to a plan. They prefer to gamble rather than invest, etc. Sometimes, the two of us, or three if it is a couple, don't have any common ground at all. So it can be either or both. Does that make sense?" Nods from both.

"Ok, that makes more sense now. So where do you start when trying to create a game plan?" Joyce looked like she was ready to take some notes.

Before I could even attempt to reply, the sound of a twanging guitar could be heard coming from Richard's location in the room. He was holding his iPod nano in his hands and lifted it up as the vocals kicked in— "Hello out there, we're on the air, it's hockey night tonight!"

"What is that?" James and Joyce had expressions on their faces akin to hearing fingernails scraping on a chalkboard.

"That, my good friends, is Stompin' Tom Connors, a Canadian icon if ever there was one, with his signature piece, *The Hockey Song*." Richard had turned the volume down, but the music could still be heard as he put the iPod gently on the table.

"You're subjecting us to this in June for what reason?"

"Two actually. First, because the National Hockey League playoffs are not over yet, even though it's technically summer. Second, well perhaps John is in a better position to work on that one." Both turned to me for an explanation.

"What your uncle is attempting to say, I think …"

"And he uses that term loosely," Richard grinned.

"Since I like to use the term game plan to discuss creating a financial planning model, the appropriate music should be Canadian and refer to hockey. I feel one can make the case for some distinct parallels between the two."

"How so?" James certainly seemed intrigued by this; he was sitting up, ready to take notes.

"Well, let's start with these three sample plans. We have Sample 1—the fictional couple known as The Lindseys, a young couple in their early 30s with two children. Sample 2—the fictional Ms. Deborah Morley, she recently turned 40, single with no dependants. Sample 3—the fictional couple, The Taynacs, both having reached their early 60s, their kids moved out years ago, both are still working but looking forward to joining the ranks of the happily retired in the not too distant future."

"Ok. I got that from flipping through these," Joyce had picked up one of the plans and tossed it back on the table, "but where does Stompin' Tom and his Hockey Song fit into this?"

"In keeping with our game plan analogy, and it is simply that, an analogy, I like to view the creation of a financial plan as a coach of a hockey team might. In that sense, you have three periods in each game. Sort of like this." The whiteboard was completely empty, so this was as good a time as any to start writing.

The Game Plan
1st Period—Age 20-35
2nd Period—Age 35-50
3rd Period—Age 50-65
Post-game

"Cool. I like it. I guess Joyce and I are still in the first period, while Richard is somewhere …"

"Easy hotshot! Suffice it to say I'm still in the game, and we'll leave it at that," Richard pointed a decidedly non-threatening finger at James. "Please continue John."

"Keep in mind that what you see here is pretty arbitrary and merely something I like. Some planners like to use decades, others have their own unique breakdown, this has always worked fine for me. I guess being a hockey fan helps a little."

"Ok, I guess boys will be boys. So what is the goal of each of these periods?"

"Nice pun Joyce. She shoots, she scores!" Richard had his hands raised in mock celebration.

"Well, I'm certainly glad to hear you bring up the concept of goals, not only because of the hockey analogy, but because they are the foundation for much of what happens here in the planning process. In fact, I can't even help someone start to create a plan without them."

"Really? I remember talking about them months ago, but I didn't think that they were really this important."

"Then commit this to memory," Richard was up and pacing now, not surprising at least to me, knowing how he felt about the subject. He went to the board and added the following:

"Your accomplishments will be a reflection of your plan, your plan a reflection of your goals. So take away the goals at the core of it all and it collapses. Does that make sense?" Nods from both.

"I'm not simply referring to financial accomplishments here either. This model goes to all aspects of your life, from me learning to play piano, James participating in cycling events, Joyce graduating from university, and John continuing to develop and build his business."

"Richard is right, and while I know his passion for this subject might seem overstated to you, it really isn't. When it comes to creating a game plan for a couple or an individual, the more they have a clear and well-defined set of goals they would like to accomplish, the easier it is for me. I can't create goals for people and I certainly don't want to be in the position of suggesting them. They have to come from the client."

"Ok, we get it. Well, I get it at least," Joyce cast a quick glance at James who nodded in agreement.

"Good. The sample plans on the table are merely that, samples. Fictional creations to show you how the pieces we've talked about fit into place. Not just that, but to set the groundwork for some of the things left to discuss in the future. Since we're not going to pore over the details of each plan with a fine-toothed comb, let's look at what generally happens, the characteristics of each period of our investment game." Pen already in hand, it was time to start really filling up the board:

> **Your accomplishments will be a reflection of your plan, your plan a reflection of your goals. Take away the goals and it collapses.**

First Period

Life	Financial
- Start working	- RRSP/RESP/TFSA
- Create goals for the future	- Regular Savings
- Kids/no kids?	- Wills
- Marriage/no marriage?	- Insurance

I hadn't quite finished writing when Richard took the opening and started to talk.

"So here is where the game starts. No score. Some of the truly dedicated might start before this, especially if exposed to it from their families— remember those early discussions about learning about money at home? Typically however, it is after school is completed and one enters the workforce that thoughts about money enter into the picture. You're making some money finally, eventually you are out on your own, and this period is characterized by all the *big* questions in life—marriage, children, more schooling, career choices, etc. While all of this is happening, perhaps you've started to build some assets, perhaps only in the form of a bank account, but it's a start. Remember 'Pay yourself first?' Those habits that, once started, just simply continue without you having to think about them? Implementing those habits now, at this time, will go a long way to creating a solid base for the future." Having someone like Richard to carry the ball for this discussion made this a little easier for me, but now it was my turn.

"Financially, this period is typically where RRSPs and TFSAs get opened and start being funded, RESPs for educational savings if you have children, the habits of continual savings are solidified, and we start to examine the role of wills and insurance as part of the financial planning process. We won't be going into detail about that today however."

"A will, at my age?" Joyce seemed very surprised at the comment.

"A will is useful at any age, only because it would help in the event of something unfortunate happening. For a single person your age with minimal assets, it is not an absolute requirement. For anyone who is married, living common-law, has children or dependants, a will is a must."

"But what would I insure at my age?"

"Nothing basically."

"Thanks a lot!"

"I didn't mean it like that James. What I meant is you don't have assets to insure. As for life insurance, unless you wanted a small policy to cover expenses in the event of something unfortunate, or you wanted to leave Joyce or someone else money if that happened, you probably don't need any. I would be surprised if the basic insurance provided by your employer, and the same applies to you Joyce, wouldn't be sufficient to cover that."

"That said, once you have a spouse or dependants to consider, life insurance is a must in order to help protect the family from unfortunate circumstance, in terms of disability or death. But that is a topic for a different day," Richard resumed sipping his coffee.

"Ok, so in keeping with our analogy, in the first period we try to take a quick lead if we can, we start the basics of saving and planning for the future. Remember from our compound interest discussion we don't have to start big at this point in time, but it certainly helps to start. RRSPs and TFSAs are key to the plan. Wills and insurance are required to make sure we get out of the period without any undue injuries. That brings us to intermission, where we get snacks and drinks before the game continues," I think they were taken by surprise at this turn of events. I sat down, grabbed a full glass of Diet Coke, and started to munch on a donut hole when the group decided to join in. After a moment or two, I jumped up, startling both James and Joyce.

"Game on! It's time for the second period sports fans." My enthusiasm carried me directly to the board, where I added the second period notes.

Second Period
Life   Financial
- Major earning period   - Build asset base
- Raise family—education   - Broaden asset base
- Travel/Cottage/Sabbatical   - Focus on tax reduction
- Caught between generations   - Financing education

"You might call this prime time for lack of a better description—you're loosened up, warmed up from the first period, you've checked out the opposition, otherwise known as life, to see what you are up against. Now the game begins in earnest. Most are solidly in a career, this period generally comprises the peak earning years for most people. Kids are being raised, and educating them is a concern. Many have the desire to get away occasionally and travel or to have a cottage to escape to. But as people move up in age through this period, an interesting thing happens. People get caught in a bind between being parents and the fact that they are still someone's children themselves."

"That sandwich generation."

"Exactly."

"The what?"

"The sandwich generation Joyce. They talked about it in *Boom, Bust & Echo*. Sort of what would happen to our parents if their parents were still with us. Getting torn between the demands of taking care of aging parents while still having dependent children at home."

"I'm very impressed James," Richard's smile said more than his words did.

"Financially, this is the prime period for building the asset base, starting to use more asset allocation to diversify the investment portfolio, continuing the asset building started in the first period. Typical assets during this period are houses, cars, a cottage or vacation property, RRSPs, TFSAs, investments outside the RRSP/TFSAs and, depending on the situation, some form of inheritance from either grandparents or parents who have left them."

The Sandwich Generation: Those torn between the demands of taking care of aging parents while still having dependent children at home.

"This may or may not be the case. But let me assure you of one thing," Richard's voice had taken on a deeper, sterner tone than I had heard in quite some time, "do not—I repeat—do not be basing your financial future and well-being on the presumed arrival of an inheritance. Much has been made of the so-called 'trillion dollar transfer' that will be occurring between the parents of the boomer generation and the boomers themselves. For some it may come, for others it won't due to taxation and insurance issues. I suspect that many people in the second period are letting good planning slide due to the expectation that their future will be taken care of by the assets of the generation preceding it."

"Well said Richard, I'm in complete agreement with you. If something comes your way, be very thankful, enjoy it and use it wisely to help both yourself and your family—just don't expect it to be there to bail you out from your own poor planning and execution. Speaking of game plan execution, as incomes for this period rise, and remembering that this tends to be a peak earning time for most people, tax reduction strategies are often a focus during period two. Any thoughts about how we do that?" It was time for a little brainteaser to see what they remembered.

"Use RRSPs for sure," from James.

"Use interest expenses from borrowing to invest—the idea of a leverage investment program," from Joyce.

"Or simply make less money!"

"Yeah, but who would want to do that Richard?" James seemed dismayed at the thought.

"More people than you might think James. A popular activity for many would be a short sabbatical from work, either to spend time with their families or to celebrate being empty nesters if they started young. They may have accumulated RRSP assets to the point that taking some time off would mean more to them than just adding more assets to the pile."

"If they tap into their RRSP during a low earning period they'll pay less tax when they remove the funds than they might by removing them via a RRIF when they get older. Right?"

"Well done Joyce," again Richard's smile gave away his true feelings. I must admit I was very impressed at the level of knowledge they had built up to this point.

"The key to having built up the assets in order to take that type of sabbatical would be?"

"Start early, let compound interest be your friend," in unison.

"So keep in mind that as your assets grow during this timeframe, so do your options. We talked about asset allocation and the need to diversify; this is also a time when options that require a larger investment might become more desirable. Some choose to invest in real estate, others into small businesses, some drop out of the corporate rat race to start their own business. When people at this stage have built their asset base properly, there usually aren't many restrictions on the things they can choose to do."

"But what about those who haven't done that? What happens to them?"

"I'm sure if you can get people at our age John, you can set up a plan for them. If they stick to that plan for 20 years, they'll hit age 40 and be well on their way to achieving the freedom that Richard talked about when we discussed the concept of rich. But I'm sure you meet people all the time who haven't done any planning by age 40 or even 50. Now they show up in your office asking for help. So what do you say to them?"

"First, I thank them for coming to talk to me. Realizing they need to talk to someone to start accomplishing their personal goals is a great start. Second, I ask about their goals and long-term objectives, where do they want to be, what do they want to achieve? Third, and this is a little different than starting with younger prospects, I find out exactly what they have managed to accomplish up to this point. Most people have accomplished more than they suspect, they've never really added it all up. Then, once we have the present reality sorted out, we look at the difference between where they are and where they want to be. The *gap*, if you will, becomes the focus of the game plan that would be created to help them move in the direction of their goals. Remember back to our discussion about compound interest—starting early is great and had many benefits, but you can start later and still accomplish a substantial amount. The key is to get started. Remember this chart?" I thought that this might be a good time to reinforce some earlier learning:

Age	Monthly	Yearly	Total	Return	Value: Age 65
20	95.83	1,150	52,190	10%	1,001,621
30	253.33	3,040	109,440	10%	1,000,280
40	694.17	8,330	216,580	10%	1,000,433
50	2,108.00	25,300	404,800	10%	1,000,481

"If their goal was to amass a million dollars, it is still easy to do—ok, it's not easy—but it can be accomplished. You would simply have to raise, and in many cases dramatically raise, the level of saving they currently have. Conversely, that larger saving amount might be used to fund a leveraged investment program which may help make up for time lost in the planning process. That strategy also comes with some additional tax benefits as well."

"The key, and both John and I tell this to people all the time, is start early, start late, just make sure you start."

"I like that, sort of like Nike's 'Just do it' campaign."

"Very much so. I like the link between personal fitness and financial fitness," Richard took the opportunity to roll up his sleeve and flex a respectable bicep to us. "So where do we go from here John?"

"Well, we've reached the intermission between the second and third periods. We've taken a quick break, we've refreshed ourselves, perhaps we've changed our outlook or our game plan, and we are now hitting the ice for the third period." While Richard had been flexing for his audience, I had been getting us ready for the next step.

Third Period

Life	Financial
– Retirement in sight	– Review wills
– More family time	– Review Insurance
– Travel/Hobbies	– Plan for estate/trust
– Help younger generation	– Taxation Issues
	– Giving/Gifting

"In deference to Richard, you could also label this prime time as well. In fact, your definition of prime time will change substantially as you age. I know that mine has." Richard simply grinned.

"Retirement in sight. Only in sight?"

"Somewhere during this period it not only comes into sight, retirement also comes into play, for those who want it to, but I'm getting ahead of myself. Life's priorities change during this period. For the vast majority of people, the pursuit of the corporate ladder has a tendency to wane. They also find that family becomes a large part of life, kids tend to be grown and raising their own families, which means that grandchildren start to make an appearance. For many in this period, extended vacation time comes into play. It's not uncommon for people who've worked for 20 to 30 years to have four to six weeks of vacation. Since they've earned it, you'll see people exercising their right to take the time, either by traveling, spending time with their families or simply enjoying time away from work in some form or another. Some even take periods of unpaid leave. All of this enjoyment comes with a price tag, hence the desire to have done some proper planning in advance." Both James and Joyce were looking at me like I had two heads, but that was ok. I knew the concepts I was talking about for the 50 and older audience were as foreign to them as they were to me when I was their age. I decided to move ahead.

"Financially, new topics enter the game, a review of wills, power of attorney and insurance is undertaken to make sure all the bases are covered. As uncomfortable as it may be to talk about, eventually we all die."

"It was a guarantee after all."

"I'm not sure which one is worse, death or taxes," Joyce stopped taking notes just long enough to toss that into the mix.

"I complain about taxes all the time, so I'll let you in on a little secret. The thought of paying taxes is far more pleasurable than the alternative."

"Enough on that topic. Other things that enter the game during the third period are planning for your estate, perhaps a family trust to leave things to people close to you, or to fund charitable causes that you care about. The concept of giving or gifting starts to enter people's minds. Often, people want to give back to an organization, school or charity that has had an impact on their lives."

"The other concerns from the previous periods don't go away do they?"

"That's a great point James. Financial planning and the game plan are very much cumulative things. Everything from the first and second period combines into the third, at least it should. You continue to build your asset base, focus on tax reduction, allocate assets properly to achieve your goals. You must also ensure that you are not exposed to any more risk than desired, and continue to build savings if you are still working."

"Imagine if you will kids that some people get to the third period and haven't even laced up their skates yet. That means all of the things that we have been dealing with all along get compressed into a much shorter timeframe. That doesn't mean they can't be accomplished—but the effort will have to be that much greater to reach the same goal."

"But the goals will be different for everyone, right?"

"Like snowflakes James."

"Like what?"

"Snowflakes. Each one individual, no two the same. Goals are like snowflakes. John's job is to get people to examine them, be able to voice them, quantify them, then to help people focus on the direction they are headed in order to meet their goals. The goals for some people focus on financial amounts, some want time, others like me ..."

"There is no one like you Richard!"

"Despite what you say John, others like me want a mix of financial, time and life experiences."

"Your uncle is making a good point here. These sample plans I brought in today are merely examples that reflect some of the realities for these fictional people. Every game plan I do reflects the real situation for an individual, couple or family who want to create a plan together. So what's missing?"

"Missing?"

"The questions that haven't been asked yet. At this time, usually during the third period, some serious thought starts to be given to the concept of …" this point was worth adding to the board.

When do I want to retire?
When can I retire?

"Same thing aren't they?"

"I understand your point about why they appear the same, but the reality is there are often widely different answers to those two questions."

"How so?"

"Well, some perspective is required here. Once you have slogged it out in the work world for 20 years, perhaps raised a family, did the home ownership thing, paid your taxes, funded your RRSP, neglected your health a little bit, you'll wake up one morning at age 45, or 38, or 32, or 53, pick any age, and ask yourself the following question: So when do I want to retire? Trust me, regardless of your age, the answer will be one of the following—today, this week, this month, this year. That will be the emotional side of your brain talking, and then the logical side will kick in—so when can I retire? You close your eyes, start number crunching, your financial snapshot being processed, the odds are you'll come up with the following—not today, not this week, not this month, not this year—not ever? Argh!" Richard buried his face in his hands at this point and shook his head violently back and forth.

"Yes kids, you are witnessing Richard in the middle of a very bad dream, thinking that he'll never be able to retire, wondering what he did wrong, and how can he get himself out of this mess. It's not really that uncommon a dream and for many in the second period, what Richard has acted out so convincingly, will be their reality."

"So how do you know when you can retire?"

"Yeah, there has to be some sort of formula or something. We've had one for just about everything else."

"Ok, I'll try to satisfy your curiosity as best I can with this," I flipped open one of the sample plans to a page containing a worksheet showing a retirement analysis for The Lindseys, the fictional couple with two kids.

The Lindsey's Retirement Worksheet Analysis			
Present Age:	35		
Present Gross Annual Income:	$80,000		
Annual Retirement Income Goal:	$80,000		
Current Average Tax Rate (Ont):	49.6%		
Estimated Marginal Tax Rate:	52.3%		
	Option 1	Option 2	Option 3
Proposed Retirement Age:	55	60	65
Years to Retirement:	20	25	30
Average Investment Return:	10.0%	10.0%	10.0%
Life Expectancy After Retirement:	27.4 Years	23.2 Years	19.1 Years
Estimated Annual CPP Benefits at Retirement:	Not Selected	Not Selected	Not Selected
Estimated Annual Pensions (Entered in Today's Dollars):	$0	$0	$0
Estimated Annual Pension Accumulation at Retirement:	$0	$0	$0
Total Estimated Pensions at Retirement:	$0	$0	$0
Compared to the Amount Needed (Retirement $):	$118,876	$131,248	$144,909
Amount of Annual Income Still Required (Retirement $):	$118,876	$131,248	$144,909
Capital Needed at Retirement for Annual Income Desired:	$1,981,263	$2,187,475	$2,415,149
(Assuming Specified Annual Withdrawal Rate of 6%)			
Current Value of Capital:	$67,000	$67,000	$67,000
Estimated Value of Capital at Retirement:	$450,742	$725,926	$1,169,110
Amount of Additional Savings Required at Retirement:	$1,530,521	$1,461,549	$1,246,039
RESULTS:			
	Retire at Age 55	Retire at Age 60	Retire at Age 65
Scenario 1			
Save the following each year:			
- RRSP	$13,500	$13,500	$7,575
- Open savings (before taxes)	$13,222	$1,361	$0
- Total annual savings required	$26,722	$14,861	$7,575
- Net after-tax payments	$19,662	$7,801	$3,613
- Monthly net after-tax payments	$1,638	$650	$301
Scenario 2			
Or, Borrow to Invest: (Interest Only Payments @ 8%)	$267,223	$148,611	$75,750
- Annual payments	$12,025	$6,688	$3,409
- Annual tax Savings	$6,289	$3,498	$1,783
- Net after-tax payment	$5,736	$3,190	$1,626
- Monthly net after-tax payment	$478	$266	$135
Scenario 3			
Or, Maximize RRSP and Borrow to Invest:	$112,569	$12,355	$0
- Annual RRSP contributions	$13,500	$13,500	$7,575
- Annual loan payments	$5,066	$566	$0
- Annual tax savings	$9,710	$7,351	$3,962
- Net after-tax payment	$8,856	$6,705	$3,613
- Monthly net after-tax payment	$738	$559	$301
E.&O.E. **For Discussion only**		Prepared:	9/17/08

Both James and Joyce were silent for a minute as they looked over the sheet.

"That's a lot of numbers."

"Not really James. Break it down into the logical groups, most of it is simply repetition," it didn't appear that I'd have to do too much, at least at this point. I was going to let Joyce run with this one.

"Ok Joyce, you seem to have a handle on this. Walk us through the example."

"Umm, ok. Current Age—how old they are—currently 35. Present Gross Annual Income—what they make combined for the couple—$80,000. Desired Retirement Income—what they want as income once retired—$80,000. Tax Rate—49.6%. Estimated Marginal Tax—52.3%. Then we have three options each looking at a different retirement age, 55, 60 or 65 years of age. Years to Retirement—subtract the current age from the proposed to show how many years they have left to build assets. Average Investment Return—expected rate of return from their investments—10%. Life Expectancy after Retirement—probably an actuarial table of some sort showing how long you might be expected to live based on when you retire—retire earlier, the assumption is that you will live longer. At least I think you will."

"You're doing great Joyce, keep going."

"There are options for payments from the Canada Pension Plan and I'm assuming some sort of pension plan contribution if their employer has a pension plan. I'm guessing here."

"Good guess, keep going."

"But why are they zero? You said you didn't think CPP would be broke when we talked about it several months ago."

"No, the government will be there in some form or another, be assured that they will be there. In this example I'm also factoring in neither the wife nor husband working for a company with a pension plan."

"What John is trying to show here by using zero as the Estimated Pension at Retirement is what it would take for them to be self-sufficient at retirement, not dependent on either the government or a former employer to keep them in retirement. If in fact they do receive anything from either source it will simply be a bonus. The goal is to be self-sufficient. You're doing a great job Joyce, keep going."

"Ok," she didn't look quite as confident as she did when she started. "Amount Needed at Retirement—assuming an inflation factor has been applied, so that the desired $80,000 income is actually $118,876 in 20 years, even more when looking at 25 or 30 years. Since there is no contribution from CPP or an employer pension, the Amount Still Required is the same as the Amount Needed. The Capital Needed at Retirement for Income Desired is the amount of assets that you would need to allow a withdrawal of 6% in order to hit the target income. Feel free to stop me anytime now."

"You're doing fine Joyce."

"Current Value of Capital—this is the amount of assets you already have—I'm assuming bank accounts, RRSPs, any other investing assets that you have. Estimated Value of Capital at Retirement—what those assets could be worth in the number of years to retirement in the future, using the assumed average investment return. Amount of Additional Savings—the difference between your Capital Needed and your Estimated Value at Retirement. Somehow, and I'm not sure how, we—or they—would need to find a way to amass that value of assets in order to retire by the date in that scenario. The other scenarios are exactly the same in format, only the numbers change due to the change in the number of years. Ta da!"

"Right you are Joyce, we need to find a way to amass the value in the Amount of Additional Savings field on the worksheet in order to accomplish retirement by that particular date. Now please keep in mind, on paper this looks pretty static, but this is merely a printed copy of a worksheet. When I am working with clients and prospects, we have the ability to change any and all of these numbers to come up with the exact retirement scenario that the client wants. In fact, you'll see in the plans that there are multiple pages, with several scenarios to compare. Ok James, do you want to take a stab at the second part of the worksheet?" He didn't seem to be expressing the same confidence that Joyce had shown.

"We have three scenarios, retire at 55, 60 or 65, with a similar set of numbers under each, so let's look at the retire by age 55 scenario as our example. We're trying to reach the value of the number for Amount of Additional Savings Required at Retirement from the top portion of the worksheet. Each Retirement Age has three scenarios associated with it. Scenario One is the Savings scenario, consisting of RRSP savings, plus regular savings outside the RRSP, total them together, factor in your after tax cost—because you are getting a tax refund for your RRSP contribution, this leaves an after tax value, which when divided by 12 months leaves you with the Monthly Net After Tax Savings value. In this example, to retire at age 55, all other things being relative, a monthly saving of $1,638 would be required."

"Excellent, continue."

"Scenario Two appears to be an example using leverage to help build up the assets. It shows the amount borrowed, what the interest payments would be at 8% borrowing cost, subtract the tax savings to arrive at a net after tax payment, divide that by 12 months to arrive at a Monthly Net After Tax Savings amount of $478."

"You're almost done."

"Scenario Three combines RRSP and leverage as part of the program, a smaller leverage loan amount, combined with the RRSP contributions, less the annual tax savings, yielding a Monthly Net After Tax Saving requirement of $738."

"There doesn't seem to be a large difference between the scenario of borrowing to invest and the maximizing RRSP and borrowing to invest, only $260 in this example."

"Very observant Joyce. It is there to show people that there are different ways to arrive at the same goal, some people might not be as comfortable borrowing to invest, other people like the taxation and flexibility issues of having their investments outside of an RRSP or RRIF."

"I remember that discussion, I was surprised at the difference in income tax you pay once you start to withdraw the funds from your investments depending if they were inside or outside an RRSP or RRIF."

"That's true James, but before you get too excited, keep in mind that one size does not fit all, especially in the personal finance or investing game. That is why we have three options to be presented, pick one, the other, or you can mix and match. Also keep in mind that these are not the only possible scenarios, many more could be created, the ones presented here are simply a couple of most likely scenarios. You can also start with one option today and change to something else at a later date when it is more appropriate."

"I'm very impressed with both of you; you've come a long way in not such a long period of time. I really am impressed." The impact that had on James and Joyce was clear; they did little to hide their smiles, but at the same time seemed a little embarrassed. James, especially, looked for a way to change the topic and to break what was becoming an awkward silence.

"So what is post-game?"

"I would think that would be after the game James."

"Very good Joyce," James said with obvious sarcasm.

One size does not fit all in the personal finance or investing game.

"Post-game is life and all the interesting things that go with it James. That concept of freedom that you mentioned earlier, the ability to be in a position to accomplish the things you want to do, see what you want to see, spend time with the people you want to spend time with. For some, the post-game will be like an overtime period, where they may still be trying to build the assets to get to where they want to be. It will depend on the situation. The rewards of a game well played, for lack of a better description, are my impressions of post-game." Richard hadn't left his seat for this dialogue, which surprised me a little.

"We've covered quite a bit of ground today, and I think we have been able to get a good handle on the game plan. At the risk of stealing one of Richard's favourite questions—I have to ask. How does that make us feel?"

"Feelings, nothing more than feelings ..." Richard's wobbly singing voice was way out of tune.

"Stop it please. You're killing us."

"Ok, then just tell me how you are feeling."

"Tired. Overwhelmed. Confused."

"About?"

"About this whole concept of a game plan. I get it, I just didn't think that there were so many different concepts that needed to be brought together."

> **The financial plan brings many different concepts together.**

"Everyone's situation is different Joyce. All we tried to present today is a fundamental approach to show that your plans will change as you change, as your life changes. That's all."

"I'm not sure I'm ready for that much change, thank you."

"Nobody is Joyce," Richard was standing behind her and he messed up her hair with his right hand.

"I guess that is why I find it hard to believe that people want to do all of this by themselves. Didn't you call it DIY or something like that?"

"Exactly. DIY—do-it-yourself. It's not for everyone, but it is for some. It's a personal choice, just as it is with finding an advisor to help you draw up a game plan."

"I've done my own thing at times kids, sometimes successful, sometimes not, but I never took my eye off the complete picture that John and I established."

"I get it, I really do. Do I say that too much?"

"Yes!"

"I wasn't asking you James."

"I get it, but it just seems like a lot of work and you mentioned earlier today that we haven't even got to all of the pieces of the game plan yet."

"Nope, there are a couple of pieces we haven't investigated yet, but all in due time. I like their impatience John, don't you?"

"Quite refreshing."

"I guess it just seems like work, that's all. Lots of work." Joyce had her head down. This was perhaps the first time I'd seen her lose her enthusiasm for this project.

"It can be if you choose to do it yourself, and keep in mind having an advisor doesn't eliminate all of the work. You are still expected to be a participant in the process, but it's like having a tour guide in a country you aren't familiar with. You can tour without a guide and you'll find and discover lots of interesting stuff. You might also waste a great deal of time and money going down paths that you wouldn't have had you known in advance where they led. I guess the whole point that we've been trying to get across to you is that we wished we had someone to explain this to us when we were younger. That doesn't mean we would have done everything differently, but it is always to your advantage to know what your options are, even if you choose not to use them. John?"

"The last point I want to address today would be this—the comment that it seems like a lot of work. I'd ask where the work really is Joyce, the biggest part of the work from your perspective comes in two parts." I thought I'd reinforce the point by adding it to the board.

> **A financial planner is like having a tour guide in a country you aren't familiar with.**

How much work is involved?
1) Decide you want a better future
2) Decide to start saving money

"Those are the two hardest parts to the whole plan and they are totally within your control. Realize that you don't have to do anything at all if you don't want to. Richard and I aren't here to convince you, cajole you, force you, or any other such thing. It's all about teaching, to some degree that is all I do. I teach. I advise. I might nag a little. Hopefully encourage and inspire if I am truly lucky. I know it seems like work from where you're sitting. I've been your age, hard as that might be to believe. Let me leave you with one final thought for today and it is something we talked about last December. It's worth examining again." I cleared a space off on the board and redrew a chart that I committed to memory a long time ago.

Men @ 65
1—Rich
8—Lifestyle = Work
14—Working
24—Dead
53—On Assistance

Women @ 65
1— Rich
2—Lifestyle = Work
4—Dead
11—Working
82—On Assistance

"This isn't intended to be a scare tactic Joyce," Richard had decided to take the floor, "and I'm including you in this too James. But the figures are there to be seen. Where do you want to be when you get to age 65? That doesn't mean you have to start today, or next week, or even next month. But at some point you will have to start. When you decide to, at whatever time you feel is appropriate, I'll be here to help. John will be here to help too. Life, when you boil it down to its basic concepts, is really all about choices."

"Well said Richard."

"Thank you."

"So is it any clearer now Joyce?"

"I think so, but I'll still have to give it some more thought if that is ok."

"100% ok with me. How about you James?"

"More thought for me too. Just don't start singing again Richard."

"I'm crushed. My fragile ego is shattered." Richard hung his head as he stood at the board.

"Ok, I'm better now," Richard was back with us. "So if you think my singing is bad, wait until you see these." With a flourish he produced what we all knew was coming at some point this morning—the next four cards. "Here are the remaining pieces of the preliminary puzzle," Richard passed the cards to us, and then sat down, an amused grin on his face.

"Friends, Romans, Countrymen, we come not to praise Caesar, but to bury him." James assumed a very Shakespearean pose.

"Not Shakespeare from James." Joyce rolled her eyes.

"Et tu Joyce?" James appeared to be on a roll.

"What does this mean Richard?" Joyce chose to change the subject.

"Whatever you'd like it to mean. But actually James, it was 'we came to praise Caesar, not to bury him.'"

"Whose tombstones?"

"Nobody in particular—did you have someone in mind?"

"No!" A quick reply in unison.

"We talked about death very briefly when we talked about life's guarantees a long time ago, did we not?"

"But why do we have to talk about it at all, it's so far away."

"Not as far as you think, unfortunately."

"Are you trying to tell us something Richard?"

"Not at all, just that when the time comes, the grim reaper won't check in with you first to see if you are ready. He'll just decide to show up and that will be it. That said, we have some things to talk about and examine and as we might find out next time, some of these pieces are more important than anything else we've talked about to date, right John."

"Exactly. The plans you put in place while you are here will certainly make dealing for the time you aren't here much easier."

"Ask not for whom the bell tolls, it tolls for thee! Ha, ha, ha!" James was doing his best Boris Karloff impersonation. He'd obviously seen too many late night horror film extravaganzas on television.

"Well said James, bravo."

"You guys are scaring me; I think it's time to go."

"Next time, do we have a next time?"

"Suggestion if I can," Richard was packing up his belongings, but stopped long enough to make sure that he had our attention. "I'm heading to Alaska for a few weeks for a little R & R, and to work on that goal of finding a little fly-fishing place. Given that, I'd like to take a summer vacation if you will. I think we've all been quite dedicated to the process for the past 11 months—we deserve it, don't you think?"

James, Joyce and I were exchanging curious glances. Certainly I was all for a summer vacation, a little break might do us good and give us a chance to reflect on things. No time like the present to voice my opinion.

"I'm game. Count me in."

"Me too!" In unison.

"Ok, it's agreed then. Class is officially out of session."

"Returning when?" Joyce had her BlackBerry® at the ready.

"First Saturday after Labour Day, whenever that is."

"That would be September 9th."

"September 9th it is. Should we return to the cabin?"

"Sure. So tell us more about this Alaskan adventure Richard."

We spent the next 20 minutes pouring over some brochures that Richard had brought in, some absolutely gorgeous scenery, as well as his plans for doing a fly-in bear viewing in Katmai National Park. Richard seemed truly excited about the trip, who could blame him? It made me a little jealous to be honest. However, I didn't bring it up because I knew he'd simply tell me to add it to my goal list and start pursuing it. I hated it when he was right.

We finished up our discussion talking about our plans for our self-imposed break. While the rest of us had nothing definitive, I knew that we'd all find more than enough things to fill the time. It was nice to see the morning mist had given way to a bright, if not completely, sunny day. If nothing else, it would give our intrepid biking crew a drier ride home. I had ushered everyone out to the front door and watched as they peddled away in single file, Richard leading the team away. Once I lost sight of them, I returned to play catch up with some paperwork.

Of course, once I actually got there, the urge had passed. I was flipping through the brochure Richard had left behind—a not so subtle hint—and the beam of sunlight crossing my desk was beckoning me to head outside. Before I did that, there was one thing left to accomplish. I pulled my goal list from the file folder in my desk and added to the bottom: Plan trip to Alaska.

15

Where There's a Will

A man can do all things if he but wills them.
Leon Battista Alberti

Fog.

A grey shadowy mist covered everything in sight as I drove into the office this morning. I'd always been fascinated by fog—how could you get that much moisture in the air and not have rain? That was just one of the many questions I had on my mind this morning. The biggest question was 'why'—why did this happen to Richard and why now.

That thought occupied my entire drive into the office. Today would be the first day I had been at my desk in five days—hard to believe what had transpired in less than a week. My desk was a mess, albeit an organized mess, with neat piles of papers. I was accomplishing little. I stopped. I struggled to come to grips with what I was feeling. I simply felt lost.

Lost in thought. A familiar place for me the past week or so. A yellow file folder sat open on my desk, labelled: JARVIS, Richard. I flipped it open to reveal a cream-coloured document, expensive paper to be sure, the lettering seemed to jump off the page:

LAST WILL AND TESTAMENT
OF
RICHARD JARVIS

I had read it several times since last week, it was clear and concise. Brian, who had spoken so eloquently at the funeral, had done a good job at creating a comprehensive document that would leave no loopholes or room for uncertainty. As executor of the will, my job would be easy compared to what happens when someone dies without a will, intestate. When this is the case it is simply a crapshoot, you have no idea where your estate or belongings will go, who will get what. It has been the cause of more than one family fight. The government will be guaranteed to get their hands on more of your estate than they are entitled to. In short this is why I encouraged Richard, and all my clients, and friends, to prepare a will in the first place. His first will was drafted close to 25 years ago when we broached the subject after our initial meeting. There had been several revisions over the years. Wills were never designed to be static. Wills change as you change, as your life situation changes, and Richard's changed as he changed.

My view has always been that you are showing disrespect for those you hold dear by not having a legal and binding will because you never really know what is going to happen tomorrow. It takes the pressure off the people who are left behind, not having to interpret what you 'might' have wanted done once you were gone. But there was more to Richard's planning than just a will, the other documents, filed underneath became equally important the moment he fell off the horse. I was lost in thought as I held Richard's will in my hands, flipping through it as if reading. I didn't hear my door open and I was startled by, "John? Are you ok?"

James and Joyce were standing in the doorway to my office. I had forgotten all about inviting them here when we were at Richard's funeral only five days ago. "Hi guys!" It was a long time ago that we had officially agreed on 'guys' as the combined moniker when I was speaking to them both—it got me around the awkwardness of using both names; it got them away from being referred to as 'kids.'

Joyce placed a backpack on the table near the window and was busy removing sandwiches and drinks.

> **Wills were never designed to be static. Wills change as you change, as your life situation changes.**

"Let's eat. I'm starving!" James was always the first to jump into the food.

We all sat around the table, eating and not talking. This felt pretty weird. This was the first time that we were meeting without Richard. It was something that we were going to have to get over due to last week's events. I guess we had always looked to Richard as the initiator and to keep us focused—now I think it was assumed that I would enter into that capacity. I'm not sure I was ready for this.

"So what do we do now?" Joyce asked tentatively.

"You said at the funeral that we'd finish the project—how do we do that?" James' voice was quiet too.

"Yes James, I did say that. I think we should."

"Me too. What would Richard have wanted us to do? He said that day in the park that he wanted to give something back to the family, but he never defined what he meant."

"I'm pretty sure that has been accomplished guys. Look at all you've learned in the past year—the discussions, the ideas that we've all shared. That certainly gets left behind, we haven't lost it, and all we have to do is remember it."

We were quiet for several minutes. I think we were all trying to remember everything that we had shared in the past year, how we'd all grown from the process, and what we'd learned—as much from each other, as about ourselves. Richard was a huge proponent of self-discovery.

I felt bad on one level because I was holding out on James and Joyce. I did know what Richard wanted to leave behind—a book—a written account of our discussions over the past year; something tangible to leave behind; something to be considered a legacy; something that might even be read and used by others.

In fact, it was the last thing we talked about on the morning he died. When he asked me to honour the promise, it was the promise that I would bring the book to completion, not just for the four of us, but also for the rest of the family.

I had been to Richard's cabin on Sunday. When I agreed to honour the promise, he told me that I would find everything I would need in a folder on his desk, aptly labelled 'The Project.' Once I got over the initial unease about being in his space for the first time since his passing, the file was easy to locate—exactly where he said it would be. The folder was several inches thick and I could hardly believe what I saw when I opened it—close to 150 pages of typed and formatted material, which seemed to capture the essence of each meeting, all the 5"× 7" cards, anything he had handed out to read, his notes and highlighting on his copies, as well as several micro-cassettes of his thoughts. In short, it was definitely a file he was compiling to develop a book.

The question remained what to do with it? I spent several hours with the material, reading his notes, listening to his oral accounts of the meetings and observations about what we were learning. But the question remained —how do we take that to a book form? I would deal with that question in due time, at the present we actually had a topic to cover.

"So what do we think of this?" I had taken the liberty of borrowing Richard's standard opening as I tossed the 5"× 7" card from the last meeting onto the table. The card spun around in a lazy circle a few times before coming to a stop.

"Does the fact that it is pointing at me mean I have to start?" Joyce slowly opened her notebook, and at the top of the page was the card from the last meeting taped neatly in place, but for the first time, there was nothing in her stylish script written beneath it. "I'm sorry guys; I guess that I've really dropped the ball on this one. I haven't had the time—well, I've had the time, but not the ambition to think about this."

"Me neither, this just came out of the blue without warning." James' book reflected that of Joyce's, the card in place at the top of an empty page.

To be honest, I wasn't really surprised. They had been mid-teens when their grandmother Beth had passed, so this was probably their first experience with death as adults. I have lost a few people close to me in my time and it doesn't get any easier. It is a brand new experience every time.

"That's ok. I would have been really surprised had you been prepared. I'm not that prepared myself. Nobody could have foreseen the events of the past seven days and I feel there is an eerie link between today's topic and the events of the past week." When Richard had passed out the cards at our last meeting there was some snickering and laughing about what Richard had been trying to tell us in the card. I felt a little guilty as I looked at the card on the table; I could only imagine how James and Joyce were feeling.

"Do you think he knew?"

"Knew what?"

"I don't know—that his time was coming?"

"What are you talking about Joyce?" James had a tinge of annoyance to his voice that I didn't want to carry on any further.

"Ok. This isn't going to be easy." I wanted to make sure that such an emotional time as this didn't get the better of us.

"It's just at one point that Richard remarked that there are no such things as coincidences, then he hands out this card, and now here we are meeting without him." Joyce's voice was cracking as she finished, and in a show of genuine compassion, James leaned over and put both his arms around her.

"I remember that well Joyce, it was a favourite line of Richard's. I can assure you that he didn't know. I say that because I had knowledge of his plans for the future, of the goals that he had planned to accomplish. When people know the end is near, they don't start planning ten, 15 or 20-year goals. You remember back to the meeting about goals when we shared ours with each other? None of his goals were within a one-year horizon. I suspect that his goal with this card was to get us to think a little about the concept; we talked briefly about it when we discussed the three guarantees. I'm not sure which of you remarked that death seemed out of place when discussing financial planning for the future, compound interest and leverage."

"That was me," Joyce tentatively raised a hand.

"Now we have a chance to examine firsthand why Richard and I both said that death would play an important part in the planning process. This is probably as good a place as any to start. Agreed?" Nods from both.

"I've been doing this for over 25 years, and few topics surround themselves with as much emotion as wills, estates, and planning for the inevitable. Lump insurance in with that group as well, because it is a fundamental piece of this puzzle. I'm probably going to talk, or seem like I am talking a lot today. Are you ok with that?" Again, nods from both.

"Some disclaimers. Having been in this position before doesn't make this any easier. The stories of what can happen within families upon the death of a family member can range from the horrendous, to a simple 'everything was taken care of.' Why the variance? Most people see death, wills, and estate planning as extremely difficult subjects to talk about, let alone develop a plan for. In short, we all seem to be in a massive state of denial about it. Richard would have told us that it was not an *if*, but merely a *when*. It was one of his three guarantees after all and, even with all of the advances we have made in the medical field, death is still inevitable. As we have seen firsthand, we don't know when and we don't get any advance warning.

"I suspect that the easiest place to start this discussion would be with the topic of insurance. While there are many types—home, auto, health, disability, critical illness, long-term care, travel and the like—for purposes of this discussion we are going to limit ourselves to looking at life insurance. This brings us to the first question—why. Why would we want life insurance in the first place?"

There was a very quiet moment, I was sure that they were actually thinking about the question, but I was also sure that parts of their thoughts were elsewhere. Perhaps it was just too soon to try to carry on with this exercise?

"To leave something for the people close to you?" It was more of a question than a statement. Joyce seemed quite tentative at offering up this opinion.

"Certainly, to leave something behind, definitely a valid reason."

"How about to pay for bills you might have outstanding."

"Valid as well James. There are several reasons to use life insurance as part of a valid financial planning model. Here are a few key ones in my opinion." The board was completely clean.

Why have insurance?
- Maintain value of estate
- Cash to pay bills
- Tax-free component
- As a savings/investment tool
- Income replacement
- Pay children's education
- Pay off mortgage

"Life insurance, like most of the topics we'll cover today, strikes some fear into people, especially when they are younger because it is thought of as something you do when you are older. Perhaps they see the process as self-fulfilling—if you spend time thinking about the things that need to be done once you are no longer here, you somehow hasten the arrival. It isn't so. But to some degree it is like winning a negative lottery."

"What's a negative lottery?"

"One you don't want to win. Life insurance is like that; you win by getting to collect the money or the policy. That's the good news. The bad news? You're no longer here to enjoy it. Now what I am going to tell you is being told with the following caveat. I am not an insurance broker, but I do feel I know enough about the process and role of insurance in financial planning to guide us along the right path. So let's examine each one of these points on the board a little bit. Sound like a plan?" Nods from both.

> **Life Insurance is like winning a negative lottery.**

"First, maintenance of wealth for the estate. Certainly it should be easy to understand that having life insurance can help maintain the value of an estate upon the passing of the policyholder. The question sometimes is why. Why insure? Each situation is different, but the goal of most insurance policies is to leave a family in a financially secure position after the death of a spouse, or for the children in the family—to help take care of their needs in future years should either or both parents not be there.

"Second, ready cash. People tend to own a lot of things, especially as they get older, but there can be issues of liquidity. Certainly, someone might own a house, with no mortgage on it, but that won't help you much if you need cash in three weeks. You may have investments, after all you've been contributing and building that asset pool, but you may not want to or may not be in a position to sell. In addition, there may be capital gains taxes to take into consideration. The death of a spouse or family member is a traumatic time, the last thing you want to be worried about are bills—bills which won't stop coming just because you aren't there. The tax people in Ottawa aren't too patient if you owe them money, and even the incidental bills that come from dealing with a funeral are not cheap. So using insurance proceeds as a form of immediate cash to help pay off expenses or debt outstanding is an excellent use of insurance.

"Third, tax free. Now you know that Richard had to love this," both James and Joyce managed a slight smile, which I was happy to see. Mostly I was glad they were still paying attention. "When you designate a beneficiary for your insurance policy, the proceeds or payout from the policy are received tax free. If you happen to be a business owner and had creditors who were owed money upon your passing, the creditors cannot claim this money. That said, if you do not designate a beneficiary on your policy, or choose to simply make the estate a beneficiary, then the proceeds are subject to all applicable taxation.

"Finally, a saving tool. In a couple of different situations you can use insurance policies that split your premiums into two parts. One part is used to pay for the insurance coverage; the other part is a savings component to allow you to build up a pool of investment money. We'll see more of this in a moment."

"Question John." Both were busy taking notes, it was nice to see them getting engaged in the process again.

"Fire away."

"How much insurance do you need?"

"Great question. I have no idea."

"What?"

"There is no magic number James. The right answer could be $100,000, $250,000 or $1,000,000; it could be zero in certain instances. There are however some rules of thumb to help us."

"I knew you were holding out on us."

"Ok, maybe a little, here's a basic formula, I know you seem to like these."

How much insurance?
Debt + Income Replacement = Total Insurance Amount

"Huh?" In unison.

"Ok, let's break this down a little. First, how much do you owe people? What is your total accumulated debt? For a couple it might be the mortgage on the home, car loans, lines of credit, credit card balances, etc. Add these up to arrive at a number. Next, figure out how much you earn, which isn't hard for most people. Then to determine the replacement amount, divide that by an expected rate of return if you were to invest the proceeds of the policy. Here are a couple of examples."

Required Income	Rate of Return	Policy Value
$75,000	10%	$750,000
$60,000	5%	$1,200,000
$45,000	8.1%	$560,000

"Ok. So now that we have that number, we can complete the first formula, again perhaps easier to see visually with a couple of examples."

	Bill & Ara	Robert & Mary	Brenda
Total Debt	$150,000	$0	$225,000
Income Replacement	$750,000	$500,000	$1,200,000
Total	$900,000	$500,000	$1,425,000

"Wow. That's a lot of insurance, or at least it seems like it."

"It is perhaps less about the bottom figure James, than it is about getting to the right number. I'm showing some fairly simplistic formulas here. Other variables certainly come into play such as the age of the people involved, how many dependants they have, if they have other insurance coverage through their employer, if they have assets already that might be used to offset the drop in income due to a spouse passing. My personal belief is that at a minimum, you should ensure that the remaining partner, or your family, is left without any debt. We know from our earlier discussions that debt is an insidious problem and a leading cause of why people don't grow wealth for themselves is because they are slaves to paying off debt. So we must make sure we remove this obstacle for those left behind."

> A leading cause of why people don't grow wealth for themselves is they are slaves to paying off debt.

"Well said."

"Thanks Joyce." I smiled and she smiled back, the fact that our usual banter was returning could only be a good sign.

"So what do you buy?"

"What do you mean James?"

"Is there just life insurance? I know with car insurance there are collision, fire, theft, and comprehensive. Is life insurance the same?"

"Nice segue, thanks for setting this up for me. There are vast arrays of insurance products available. It seems about as many as there are investment options, but for our purposes I'm going to lump them into two basic categories," I had been speaking as I was writing.

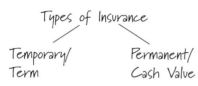

"Temporary insurance?"

"I like the phrase temporary, but most people refer to it as term insurance. Why, you might ask?"

"Why?" In unison. This was a good sign.

"Because the policy is for a fixed term or duration, and these policies share a common feature—no cash value builds up based on the premium that you pay. It is simple life insurance, definitely your best buy for the least amount of outlay. Your premiums are based on the amount of coverage that you purchase, your age and your general health. The premiums rise as you get older. Continue to pay the annual, quarterly or monthly premium and when you die, your beneficiary receives the money. How's that?"

"Ok, but I've heard the term 'whole life,' what is that about? Is there 'half-life' insurance?" I laughed as James finished his statement; his expression showed some signs of being offended.

"I'm sorry James, I'm not laughing at the question. I've just never heard anyone use the phrase 'half-life insurance.' I like that."

"I'll try not to be offended," with a slight smile.

"Ok. Permanent insurance, or cash value insurance, is sometimes referred to as whole life insurance. Earlier I mentioned insurance with a savings component and this is it. You have an insured value amount and part of your premium goes into a savings account at a predetermined amount and investment return. If you needed to at some point in the future, you could borrow against the cash value of the policy. A slightly different form is referred to as 'universal life.' Here, the term and cash portions are split into two accounts, the investment side is more flexible, allowing many different investing options, as such there are no guarantees on the return. The major advantage is that all of your investment growth within your universal life policy is tax free, and the value of that investment account would go to your beneficiaries tax free as well."

"Excellent, Richard would like that."

"Indeed."

"Did he have life insurance?"

"Joyce!"

"I'm just asking a question, I didn't ask how much James."

There are no estate or death taxes in Canada. Instead, the government taxes your income from all sources when you die.

"He wouldn't object to me telling you, he had two policies. One was a basic term policy to cover his basic insurance needs, he started that when he was younger and held the policy ever since. The second was a universal life policy, which he used primarily for the tax free growth component and the insurance aspect of the policy was the basic financial tool for dealing with the taxation aspects at his death."

"Who are you paying taxes to? You're no longer here."

"The government."

"That sucks! You're dead and you still have to pay taxes? No wonder Richard felt the way he did. I'm starting to feel that way myself and I don't pay too many yet."

"You pass away, and you have to pay one last time. After all James it was part of the three guarantees, remember?"

"Don't remind me."

"Yes, but this is an opportune time to do so. There is some good news though, if you are interested."

"Bring on the good news."

"There are no estate or death taxes in Canada. That means there is no tax on the transfer of property or assets from the deceased to those who inherit. Instead, the government simply taxes your income from all sources when you die."

"But what if you aren't working, no job, no income, right?"

"You have no earned income, you might still have income. Remember you might be receiving payment from a RRIF, or you might be receiving interest payments or income distributions from a bond you hold, your investments outside an RRSP or RRIF. There is also one final thing to consider."

"This can't be good Joyce; he saved this until the end."

"Would I do that?"

"Yes!" In unison.

"You're hurting my feelings you know. Just so you don't get away tax free, the government deems everything you own, all your capital assets to be sold at fair market value at the time of your death. The exception is if you are married or in a common-law relationship—then all of your assets can roll over to the spouse with no taxation. Taxation will then occur on the death of the spouse. For tax purposes, arriving at a value for your investment portfolio isn't hard to determine, but for other things it can be, such as the value of a house, cars, furniture, etc. It can leave your estate with a fairly hefty tax bill in its hands, not just from an income perspective, but from a probate perspective as well."

"What's probate?"

"Probate is the act of getting court approval to settle the estate and transfer the ownership of your assets. It ensures that anyone whom the executor of the will—and we'll get to that shortly—deals with knows they have full and complete authority to act on behalf of the estate. But there are fees associated with this. Under current legislation, which varies by province, you could end up paying anywhere from $0 in Quebec to $14,500 in Ontario."

"That is a huge difference."

"It certainly is, and what's worse—the amount payable is due when the will is probated. Does this make that discussion about using insurance as a form of ready cash for dealing with your passing a little more applicable now?"

"Yes. But I still don't like it."

"Understandable Joyce. I don't like it either. You don't have to like it, you just have to accept that it is and deal with it."

"So where does the stuff go once you die?"

"What stuff James?"

"The stuff you had before you died, or the stuff you had when you died, I guess that is what I mean."

"Well, it depends on where your will says it should go."

"You mentioned at Bailey's last week that Richard had a will right?"

"Yes he did, it's right here," I took the copy out of the folder on my desk and tossed it onto the table. As I suspected, neither made a move to pick it up. "It's ok, it won't bite you."

"So Richard's will describes where everything goes, but what if he didn't have a will, then what would happen?"

"Intestate."

"What state?"

"Intestate. To die without a will, or without a valid will, is referred to as dying intestate. It is pretty much as bad as it sounds too."

"So who makes the decisions then."

"Eventually the court will appoint an administrator. Assuming no family member comes forward or applies to act as administrator, a public trustee will be given the task. Your assets get distributed based on the laws of your province, no ifs, ands or buts. These laws may not reflect the wishes of the deceased or the wishes of the family members who are left behind."

"So this is pretty important then?"

"No. Not pretty important. Very important. Extremely important."

"So is it hard?"

"Not at all. Creating a will is not hard; the biggest problem is that creating a will falls under the heading of 'things I'll get to soon' and as such, for many more people than you would suspect, it never gets done at all."

"What do I need to create a will?"

"Two things—desire and a lawyer."

"Wait a minute, I hear ads on the radio all the time for do-it-yourself legal kits. I also see computer software in stores to create your own will. Why do I need a lawyer? I'm seeing big dollar signs here."

"Not really, considering what could be lost if your will is not created properly, declared invalid, or perhaps the computer program makes some assumptions and things get overlooked. In short, it could be considered a case of 'you can pay me now' or 'you can pay me later.' Paying later always costs more."

"So what does it cost?" I wasn't surprised that Joyce would be the first to ask that.

"Typically, and I'm only using an estimate here, somewhere between $100 and $300 per person, depending on the complexity, family situation, amount of assets, desire for trusts to be set up, etc. If a husband and wife do theirs together, as they should, it can be done for less than the cost of two individual wills. This is due to the fact that spousal wills tend to mirror each other in terms of where the assets go. Usually, but not always, everything gets left to the one spouse, then the final disposition occurs after the remaining spouse dies."

"So how do you find a lawyer to do this?"

> **Creating a will is not hard. The biggest problem is that creating a will is on many people's "things I'll get to soon" list.**

"You can start by asking friends or relatives for a referral. This will do two things—first, you'll find someone that other people have had a good experience with, and, second, you'll find out how many of your friends and relatives actually have wills. Most provinces have a legal referral service and good financial planners often have a qualified legal resource that they work with. That can be an advantage as they will have an intimate knowledge of your financial affairs and be able to ask the right questions to ensure coverage of your financial situation is adequate."

"Who did Richard use?"

"Joyce!"

"It's ok James, I would have thought by now you'd have realized that Richard would have said the only stupid question is the one that remains unasked. Richard's will was drafted by Brian Fishman, you might remember him from the funeral service last week. At least Brian wrote the current version. Richard has had a will for close to 25 years and it has gone through various changes as his life changed, and as his requirements changed. But regardless of these changes, the core components of his will, and of all wills, remained fundamentally the same."

"What would those be?" Joyce, pen in hand, seemed eager to take some notes.

"These are just the basics, remember my earlier caveat about my not being an insurance broker? I'm also not a lawyer, but I've read plenty of wills and I have one of my own as well. Any questions beyond the scope of this discussion should be followed-up with a lawyer specializing in this area. Agreed?"

"Agreed," in unison.

I had never been big on acronyms, but for some reason this one stuck with me. I only wish I could remember where I first heard it. It was easy to discuss the issues surrounding wills using it as the base, so it was worth writing on the board.

I R A A D A F A

"So what do you think of that?" I asked the question as I spun around from the board with my best 'ta-da' pose.

"What is that supposed to mean?"

"Yeah, three letter acronyms from months ago were bad enough, now we're using eight letters?"

"Relax, I said I'd explain, so here goes. We'll take it from the start. 'I' is for Identification. The person making the will, states who they are, where they live, declares that this is their will. 'R' is for Revocation, stating this will supersedes any that came before it. 'A' is for Appointment, appointing either an executor or a trustee. Their job is to settle the affairs of the deceased and ensure the will's directions are followed. 'A' is for Authorization, authorizing the payment of any outstanding debts, bills or expenses. This must be done before any other dispositions can be made. This brings us to 'D' for Disposition, where does the stuff you owned go? To which individuals or organizations? How is it disposed of, as property, items or cash? The executor also determines what happens after all the special requests have been taken care of and there is still cash or goods left. The next 'A' is for Appointment once again; this time for guardians of children should you have any. 'F' is for Funeral, as in instructions for it. Not always part of a will because often people are buried or services performed prior to the will being examined. So these are not legally binding. Therefore, make sure those people close to you know your wishes in advance. The final 'A' is for Attestation, stating the will was properly signed based upon the legal requirements of your province and witnessed properly in order to make it legal and binding. For the details on the thousands of ways you can create a will, I'll refer you to a professional in the field."

> **Insurance covers the people we care about, from a financial perspective. A will lets people know what we'd like to happen after we are gone.**

I sat down at the table, I had been rambling on quite a while, and I needed to take some liquid refreshment. I didn't get much of a chance to relax, before I started to get peppered with questions.

"So the executor does all the work?"

"In short, yes."

"Who is Richard's executor?"

"That would be me."

"Do you get paid for this?"

"An executor is entitled to a fee for their time and services involved in settling an estate, but there is no set fee. Trust companies often have published fees and they can be listed as part of the will itself; sometimes the beneficiaries have to approve the fee schedule. It all depends, and every situation is unique."

"So if my understanding of what we've learned today is correct, we need insurance to cover ourselves and the people we care about from a financial perspective and we need a will to let people know what we'd like to happen after we are gone." It seemed obvious, at least to me that Joyce was gearing up for another school term.

"Yes on both accounts, but there are a couple of other things worth considering as well." Since I felt the ideas were board worthy, I added them.

Power of Attorney
Living Will

"Power of Attorney? Sounds very legal."

"It is James. It's also very important. A power of attorney document often gets drafted at the same time a will is created and it designates an individual to take over your affairs should you not be able to for medical or other reasons. For example, if Richard's fall had resulted in a coma and he was unable to act on his own behalf, the power of attorney would have given an individual the legal authority to act on his behalf."

"Was that you as well?"

"In this case yes. But it doesn't have to be me just because I am the executor of the will. It should be a trusted party however, as the PA—sorry, another acronym—gives the person the power and authority to act and you want to be assured they will act in your best interests. Some choose to have a trust company act on their behalf because they want to remove the emotion of family members from the decisions. You can also name more than one person to hold power of attorney status, which can either help or hinder, depending on the situation. As with the executor for a will, you might list a backup or substitute, someone who could step in and act should your first choice decline or be unable to act for some other reason. Any PA you have becomes void when you die, as the directions of your will take over at that time. This is all probably clear as mud—right?" I just wanted to make sure I wasn't losing them with all of the legalese.

"I think we are following you," Joyce cast a curious glance over at James. He hadn't written anything in his notebook since we started, which was unusual. He was not the note taker that Joyce was, but this lack of activity made me wonder if he was completely engaged today.

"Yep. I think we are ok. So what about the living will, sounds like an oxymoron to me. After all, the will comes into effect once you die, not while you are alive."

"Thanks for bringing that up James, I was just going to explain that. Sometimes it can be referred to as a PA for personal care; sometimes it is referred to as a living will; some to be more technical call it an advanced medical directive. Like a PA it has to be created before you become incapacitated so others can act on your behalf if you are incapable."

"So what is the difference between the PA and a living will?"

"PAs generally are for property and financial concerns, while the living will contains instructions about the health care you wish to receive. Some see the PA for personal care and a living will as the same document, or at least as similar documents. The key, as with any of the documents we've talked about today, is to have them in advance of the time you can no longer function on your own behalf. The PA for personal care and a living will are important documents and should be drawn up with the proper care and professionally done. Consult a physician or family doctor for medical advice, and your family should also be involved. The more that is known to the people involved, the easier it will be for those who have to act on your behalf when—or if—that time comes."

> **The Power of Attorney is for property and financial concerns. The Living Will contains instructions about health care.**

"Let me guess, Richard had one of these as well?"

I removed the document from the folder on my desk and added it to the pile on the table, already consisting of his will and the power of attorney for property and finance.

"Yes he did, Richard was certainly prepared. But don't let it fool you, he didn't enjoy creating these documents, nobody does. Richard was quite pragmatic about it; he knew that a time would come when he might need the protection they would afford. The fact that he died suddenly means that he never would have needed the PA or the living will, but life is like that, it doesn't tell you what is coming in advance, it only sets you up to deal with it as it comes."

I snuck a quick peek at my watch, I think perhaps this was the first time out of all our meetings I had ever done that. I was expecting a visitor at 2:30 and we were just about there, but I didn't want to be rude to James and Joyce since they had made the effort to be here.

"So where do we go now?"

"I'm not sure Joyce. I don't have another card for us to follow-up on, and to some extent I think we have completed the basic groundwork that Richard had wanted to cover as part of his blueprint idea from so many months ago. Do you realize that we've been at this almost a year?"

"Eerie actually."

"How so James?"

"The first time we were here at your office was September 14th last year. September 14th is also the date we are going to be at the cabin if memory serves me correctly," I was very impressed with his recollection of dates.

"I hadn't even thought about that. Richard often said there is no such thing as coincidence. Unlike Richard, why don't we just play it by ear, for the next two weeks anyway?"

"Actually, let's not, let's set a date for the next meeting," Joyce was tapping on her BlackBerry®. "Why not Saturday August 18th, we can get together for breakfast here, no agenda. We'll see where we are, what we want to do. It will give us some time to think about it."

"Works for me," James actually wrote the date down.

It was nice to see the enthusiasm return, we had a slow start to today's discussion, but it had picked up as we progressed. We were certainly ending on a high note.

"Ok, I'm game, count me in."

During the pause before my answer, Joyce had cleaned off the table. Richard's documents were sitting in a pile in the middle of the table. We exchanged handshakes as they readied themselves to leave. Before they turned to go, a head popped into the doorway.

"Hey John! Oh, I'm sorry. I didn't know you had visitors."

"Hi Brian," I hadn't told James and Joyce that Brian was coming by today to discuss the very documents that were on the table.

"James and Joyce, hello. Nice to see you again. We met briefly at Richard's funeral. Richard spoke very highly of you both, I hope you know that."

After a polite 'thank you,' James and Joyce looked at me with puzzled expressions. They shook Brian's hand in turn, smiled at me, then made their way down the hall. By the time I turned around, Brian was seated at the table; he had Richard's will, power of attorney and living will spread out in front of him. As I sat down he was surveying the board, full of my writing.

"What do we have here?" Brian was reviewing the board.

"We were just discussing these," I motioned to the documents on the table, tossing today's 5"× 7" card onto the pile. Brian picked up the card, turning it over several times, then he started to chuckle.

"This has Richard written all over it."

The Legacy Lives On

There is a strange charm in the thoughts of a good legacy, or the hopes of an estate, which wondrously removes or at least alleviates the sorrow that men would otherwise feel for the death of their friends.
Miguel De Cervantes

It seems we have now moved full-circle. Fall was here once again, bringing with it my favourite time of year. This year however, it was tempered with sadness about the loss we all felt two months ago. I had spent the past several days cleaning up the great room at Richard's cabin, not just that but around the entire premises. I wanted it to be as inviting as Richard kept it, especially since there were going to be some visitors today who hadn't been here in a long time.

I was tending to a small fire, created more for atmosphere than heat, when I was startled by the arrival of James and Joyce.

"Morning John!"

"Hi guys," slightly startled.

"Did we scare you?"

"No, just caught me off guard, that's all."

"The cabin looks great, you've been busy. We wish you had let us help—at least a little."

"I appreciated the offer Joyce. So what have you two been up to since we had breakfast back in August?"

We had a short rambling discussion about how we had been passing the time. James was in the process of setting up his own bike courier company.

He had also competed in his first cycling road race, finishing a respectable 23rd. Joyce was back in class, the final year underway, and already hitting the books, as was her style.

Me? Business. Staying as busy as I wanted to be, I had taken a week to do some fly-fishing. Great fishing, but it wasn't the same without my fishing partner. In the past two weeks I had spent most of my free time, getting the cabin ship-shape for today. The kids helped me get all of the food arranged on the table.

"So what happens at a will reading?" James broke the silence.

"Well, what you will see and be a part of today really isn't the norm, that's for sure. Hollywood has made some excellent movies containing the reading of the will scenes, all more fiction than reality. Typically, the executor or trust representative simply executes the terms and provisions of the will and if monies are left to people, he ensures the transfer of it to them. If there are physical goods to be distributed, he arranges delivery or to have them picked up. A gathering like this is certainly not the norm."

"Neither was Richard," Joyce said.

"Exactly!"

The three of us laughed, then started to recount the first time we had met, in Fleury Park, just over a year ago—rollerblades, Oreo cookies, and a sunny afternoon. We were all laughing, recalling something Richard had said, when Mary, Daryl, Brad and Samantha appeared at the screen door.

"Hello? Anyone here?"

"Come on in."

Hollywood has made some excellent movies containing the reading of the will scenes, all more fiction than reality.

The four of them entered rather tentatively. I think they may have been surprised to see how comfortable James and Joyce were in these surroundings. "Greetings John, nice to see you again," Brad was coming across the room, his hand extended. It must be his standard greeting.

"Hi Brad, nice to see you too."

Greetings were exchanged among all and everyone settled into a seat, except for Mary. She was standing at the window to the right of the fireplace, staring off into the distance. After several minutes of awkward silence, she joined us around the table. Soon everyone had joined into the conversation; naturally enough, most of it was about Richard. Twenty-five minutes later, we were finally making a decent dent in the available food and I noticed Brad impatiently looking at his watch.

"It's a beautiful place he had here," Mary's gaze was focused on the pine trees just outside the window. "It is Mom; I know that Joyce and I never got tired of coming here. It was a great place for our conversations with Richard and John."

"Conversations?" in unison from Brad and Mary.

"I'm sure we'll talk more about that later," but before I could attempt to move them away from the topic, the doorbell rang. It took me by surprise, I'm not sure I'd ever heard it ring more than once in all the times I'd been here. As the presumed leader of this event, everyone looked at me, so I decided to get up and answer the door.

It was Alan, Alex and Tamara. After a quick greeting at the door, I lead them into the great room where everyone was waiting.

"Hi everyone!" Alan seemed to be the take-charge member of their growing family while Alex was trying to get Tamara to stop fidgeting as she looked around the room.

> **Being punctual is how you honour people you are dealing with.**

"You're late Alan."

"Excuse me?" Alan seemed caught off guard.

"You're late, you should try to be more punctual."

"Where is this coming from?" Alan looked at Joyce as if she had grown a second head.

"It was just a pet peeve of Richard's, that's all. He felt that being punctual was how you honoured people that you were dealing with, and it was important to him."

Brad and Mary looked at each other, then at Joyce and James. I'm certain they weren't sure what to make of the comment, or of the earlier comments about having spent time here. I figured that this would be as good a time as any to take on the role as leader of this gathering. I sat on one of the rocking chairs I had brought in from the porch, opened my folder to the notes I had prepared and began.

"Thank you all for coming, Richard would be happy to know that all of you are here. It was his wish that everyone gather here today in order to be together as a family and to hear about Richard's plans for the future."

"Plans for the future? What future? Whose future?" Brad sat up a bit as he spoke.

"Well, I suspect Richard meant a little about his own, and what will follow from here. As well, the future of everyone here, as we all move forward after today."

"Ok, it sounds strange to me," Brad shrugged his shoulders and settled back into his seat. I'm pretty sure that he wasn't expecting to hear about Richard's future.

"Maybe we should just let John talk, without interrupting, that would be nice," I was getting the distinct impression that Brad and Mary had some discussion following the episode at Bailey's that afternoon two months ago.

> **A simple question spawning many arguments over the years: What is Rich?**

"This is an emotional day for all of us, on many different levels. I think it's important that we realize that the reason we are here was Richard, and if we can put aside any preconceived notion of why Richard asked us to come here for a little while, I think we can move ahead. Agreed?"

"Agreed," from James and Joyce. There were some glances between everyone else in the room, but finally a signal that we should proceed.

"As one of Richard's closest friends, I don't feel the least bit strange in saying that he was as complex, interesting, funny, and unique a person as I have ever met. It is also no surprise to those of us here that in terms of family relationships, Richard felt as if he had missed out on a lot, through the fault of no single person, but perhaps through a series of consequences—some in his control and others not. To the surprise of perhaps everyone here, except James and Joyce, he managed to regain part of what was missing during the last year."

James and Joyce merely smiled at each other, more of a knowing grin than a smile. The rest in attendance looked at them, somewhat puzzled, as people who are privy to an inside joke are looked at by those who don't get it.

"I first met James and Joyce 53 weeks ago today, at Fleury Park. We had a picnic to talk about ideas, share some interesting stories, and mostly because Richard was very impressed with James and Joyce who had made the effort to contact him. Perhaps this would be a good place to explain how that happened. Guys?"

I was pretty sure I had caught them off guard, but it was their story after all, they deserved to tell it. After some initial reluctance, but with some encouragement from Alan, they did. It was exactly as Richard had related the story to me. The meeting, bike race, and our introduction had all been recounted when Joyce had stopped, turned to me and said, "Ok John? Back to you."

"Richard had an idea, something he'd wanted to do for a long time, but the meeting between Richard, James and Joyce finally provided the impetus for it. So that day in the park, Richard had come up with an idea, well, more of a proposal actually, that as a group the four of us create a blueprint about wealth and finance."

"Wealth and finance? Richard?"

"Shut up Brad! Take a look around you. It's obvious he knew something." Samantha certainly knew how to make a point.

"So we began with a simple question, one that has probably spawned many an argument over the years," I reached back into my folder and passed around eight 5"× 7" cards, duplicates of the original from that afternoon in the park.

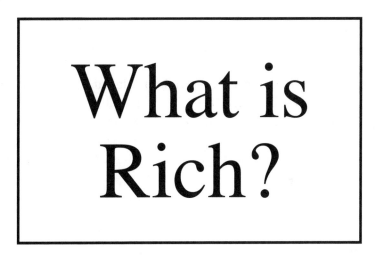

What is Rich?

"What is rich? That was the big question?" Brad asked.

"Not actually the 'big' question, but the first question, followed up by many others, some asked in the form of a question, others asked in the form of a picture or puzzle."

I passed out another one of the 5"× 7" cards, from our discussion about risk. I wasn't surprised to see Mary's eyes light up as she examined the cards. Mary and Richard, like all good teachers, knew that the best way to get people to learn is to interact with them, not just to lecture to them. Brad examined the cards briefly, and then placed his on the table.

"These are pretty interesting. I wish we could have been in on those discussions, we could certainly have

> **The best way to get people to learn is to interact with them, not just to lecture to them.**

used the help," Alex, holding a sleeping Tamara in her arms, seemed intrigued by the cards she was holding.

"Funny you should mention that Alex, you're going to get your chance."

"What are you talking about?"

I actually missed the last part of Alex's comment, as I had gone into Richard's office and rolled the whiteboard out into the room, to its usual position to the left of the fireplace.

"I think the explanation would have more value coming from the source, than from me. Guys, do you mind?"

James certainly didn't, he jumped up to the board quickly enough that it surprised me, not to mention Joyce. He grabbed a pen and started writing.

"We started by talking about 'What is Rich?'—what does money mean, how do you feel about it. Then we talked about goals, why they are the basis for what we choose to accomplish," James was drawing on the board as he spoke, then Joyce joined in.

"Then we talked about compound interest, the 8th wonder of the world, followed by the concept of paying yourself first, creating the habit of saving money," Joyce continued the picture started by James, as he spoke.

"Then we talked about the money factory, otherwise known as the RRSP, but before we got too excited about it all, we were brought back to reality by the three guarantees—death, taxes and inflation. Remember I asked you about that one day mom?

"Once John and Richard had reset our expectations, we looked at the concept of leverage, the ability to move time in a financial sense. After that, we examined where it might make more sense to use leverage as opposed to an RRSP, or at least in conjunction with one.

"In order to temper our enthusiasm once again, Richard and John introduced the concept of risk to us, explaining that risk isn't necessarily where you expect it to be, why some things appear risky and aren't, why others that are don't appear so."

I must admit, I was very impressed with what I saw happening at the whiteboard. They certainly had the attention of their audience, and I'm glad that I hadn't told them I was going to ask them to talk about our meetings—they were putting on quite a show. I know Richard would have approved.

"Part of handling risk is not putting all your eggs in one basket, or the concept of allocating your assets. Once we got to that point it was time to discuss creating a game plan, putting the pieces together, tying all that back to your goals and we'd almost come full circle.

"We would have, until fate intervened. The only topic we didn't discuss as a group, were wills and insurance, which Richard had fortunately taken care of properly. Which is part of the reason we are all here today. John?"

I was standing off to the side of the whiteboard, taking a look at what James and Joyce had drawn for us and it was pretty clear, at least to me, just how much had been taught over the past 12 months. Not just taught, but retained as well.

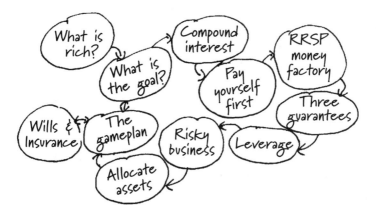

"Now I don't profess to know what each of you is thinking at this moment, but I might be able to speak for Alan and Alex. You might be thinking, 'How do I get all of this knowledge?'"

"That and about 20 other questions!"

"Fair enough, we can talk about that, and I'm sure that James and Joyce would be happy to share their experiences with you as well, but we have some business to attend to before we get to that. As I explained to James and Joyce earlier today, this type of reading of the will is more of a movie cliché, but I can assure you that there are no hidden surprises, no unexpected parties are going to be jumping in to claim some of the estate. Richard's will is pretty straightforward. So with your agreement, I'll proceed." A series of nods indicated agreement.

"As executor, I have taken care of probating the will, filing the terminal or final tax return and setting up the estate to be disbursed, the reason that you are all here today. I must commend Richard on his diligence. Good planning on his part, with some help from me in the past, made this process as smooth as it could possibly be. Here are the particulars. First, a trust account for the value of $25,000 has been set up for each of James, Joyce and Alan with the provision that the funds remain in trust for five years. The investment decisions will be the joint responsibility of John Linden and the trust's beneficiary. Second, the cabin and its contents will be offered to John Linden for the purpose of operating his financial planning practice here. Should John not desire to do that, the cabin and its contents will be sold and the proceeds put into trust for the Canadian Wildlife Federation. Third, the proceeds from Richard's life insurance policies, investment accounts, RRSPs, TFSAs, bank accounts, and any monies owed to the estate are to be pooled together and a foundation be established in honour of Patricia Jarvis for further research into neonatal studies at Hollyoak Regional Health Centre. I'm very pleased to tell you that a cheque was delivered to them yesterday afternoon which will get this project off to a great start."

"That is amazing, way to go Richard!" Joyce cast a casual glance toward the ceiling as she spoke. There certainly was a buzz to the small gathering after I had announced the creation of this new foundation.

"I've known for a long time that this was one of Richard's desires and I'm happy to have played a part in its creation. As you know, or at least figured out, Richard was about giving. He felt that we all had something to give and it didn't have to be just financial. In order to ensure that we carry on that same sense of giving, the inaugural board for the foundation includes everyone here today. Something I feel particularly honoured about."

"What do we know about being on the board of a foundation?" Alex appeared both puzzled and a little afraid of the prospect.

"It's not about what you know or about what you have, it's about what you are willing to learn," James smiled as he pointed a finger toward Alex.

"Well said James, glad to see you were paying attention." I couldn't help but smile.

> **It's not about what you know or about what you have, it's about what you are willing to learn.**

"It's amazing what I've learned in the last 12 months, even though I never liked school. Sorry Mom." James smiled at Mary and she returned it with a slight roll of her eyes.

"Ok, I hate to be a damper on the little 'love-in' as Richard might have called it, but I have to ask, how did he manage to do all of this? How did Richard of all people create this kind of wealth? A cabin in the woods with some property. Money for trusts and foundations. Did he win the lottery at some point?"

"Look at the board Dad, that's how he did it."

"Come on Joyce, there must be more than that."

"No, the keys he kept reinforcing to us were," and she turned to James to get his input, "start early, be patient, let compound interest be your friend, stick to the program, review and relax." James had joined in at compound interest.

"I still don't believe it." Brad was shaking his head in disbelief.

"You don't have to Brad, but from everything I've learned since Richard's accident I don't know if I'll doubt much anymore."

"Well, this might be a good time for the final two requests that I have to carry out as Richard's executor, so I'll continue from where I left off."

"There's more?" I wasn't sure if Brad was expressing surprise or disappointment.

"Yes, patience Brad. Fourth, a trust fund in the amount of $50,000 has been created for the purpose of allowing Mary Thomas to create a scholarship fund to help students of her choosing to further their educational pursuits."

"That will be great mom!"

"Thank you Richard," she closed her eyes as she held Daryl's hand.

"Fifth and final, a trust fund in the amount of $50,000 has been created for the purpose of allowing Bradley Jarvis to complete the successful publication and distribution of a book entitled *Rich is a State of Mind*."

"Rich is what? What book?"

"A book that might help answer some of your skepticism Brad, reinforce some of Mary's beliefs and help with Alan's earlier thoughts about how he can get this knowledge." As with some of the sessions with James and Joyce I decided to pause for dramatic effect, but Alan didn't allow for the pause to build.

"Where's the book? Where do we start John?" Having seen the results, Alan seemed eager to start learning.

"Well, you can start right here." Tucked discreetly beside the fireplace was a cardboard box containing what Richard wanted as his legacy from the project. He had finished 90% of it prior to the accident, completing it was the promise he had asked me to keep that day in the hospital. I was amazed at how much work he had done, the detailed notes he left in 'The Project' folder—all I had to do was supply the last chapter based upon the final meeting I had with James and Joyce. He had created a fill-in-the-blank style template for each chapter, and I only had to follow the format. Cover, title, layout—Richard hadn't left much to chance. While it still needed much work to become an actual book, I took the liberty of copying the material to distribute it today. I pulled a stack of eight cerlox-bound copies from the box and placed them on the table. Everyone reached in to grab their own copy, followed by excited whispering from the group and a couple of side discussions.

"I don't believe it," James was stunned.

"Me either," as was Joyce.

"I'm sorry I had to hold out on you, but you weren't supposed to see these until today. I hope you can accept my apologies."

"Accepted," in unison.

"Hopefully the material in here," I flipped through the pages for effect, "will go a long way to answering some of the questions I'm sure that you have. It may raise others as well; I think that is part of the creation process. James and Joyce certainly understand what this book is about. Any other questions can certainly be asked of me, and I will do my best to answer them. I'm privileged to have been part of this process."

"I think the dedication in the book tells us how Richard felt," Samantha had found the page before anyone else seemed to.

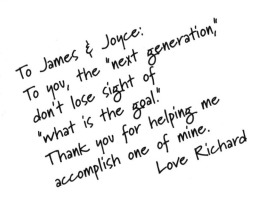

To James & Joyce:
To you, the "next generation,"
don't lose sight of
"what is the goal."
Thank you for helping me
accomplish one of mine.
Love Richard

Brad was flipping through his copy of the book when suddenly all 12 cards that we had used during the project fell onto the floor.

"What are these?" as he picked them up one at a time.

"Those are the 12 cards from the lessons that Richard shared with us through the learning process leading to the creation of the book. You'll find pictures of them in the book, but I thought it might be fun to include them for you to pick up and play with, something to jog your memory while you read. You will be reading this, won't you?"

"Probably before tomorrow," Alan had flipped to the back of the book where I had placed the cards. "Well, assuming that Tamara sleeps through the night." Looking at them, both appeared to need some sleep.

"I don't think Richard would be offended if you don't have it read by tomorrow."

The assembled group launched into a discussion, flipping through the book, playing with the cards, commenting about the picture on the whiteboard. Even Brad seemed to be getting something out of it. I decided to let them stay in this moment for a while; I was in no hurry today. I took the opportunity to reach into my briefcase and remove seven manila envelopes, slightly larger than 5"× 7" in size.

I had found these envelopes while going through Richard's material; they were attached to a note that read: Cards to be distributed after the books have been printed. As such, I decided to do just that. I had taken the liberty of looking into the unsealed envelopes. It felt like a 5"× 7" card, and I was right. Each named envelope contained a different card with an image that Richard created specifically for that person.

"I hate to interrupt, but I have one last thing that I have to do today. It has nothing to do with the will, but it does tie directly to the book." I handed the envelopes out by name.

"Can we open them?" Joyce appeared to be ready to.

"Actually no. Well, you can open them. But not today. The envelopes are Richard's way of carrying on the process that we started a year ago. His first goal was the book and it forms the foundation for building a solid financial base, but these cards are the beginning of the next step for those interested in pursuing it. I'd wait at least two weeks; a month would probably be better. Read the book first, then once you open the envelopes, think about the contents for a bit, and then contact me if you are interested in pursuing it any further. The choice will be yours." With that, I sat back and finally relaxed a little, my 'official' duties for the day were through.

The room was quiet for some time, but soon enough we were all talking again. It started with a story about Richard, naturally. By the end, much laughter had been shared, all the food had been eaten, and everyone had started to make their way back to their respective lives. Hopefully their perspective had been changed a little, and hopefully they felt uplifted by what they heard and saw.

It was no surprise James and Joyce were the last to leave; after all, they had been the closest to Richard over the past 12 months. I'm sure both were holding back emotionally as we shared a Jarvis Hug on the porch, I know I had. It seemed fitting that they bike away today, the same way they had the first day in the park a year ago.

It had been quite a year.

Selecting a Financial **Planner**

Bite off more than you can chew, then chew it.
Plan more than you can do, then do it.
Anonymous

There is a certain stillness to an early autumn morning, seemingly quiet, but filled with small sounds. Birds in the trees, a gentle breeze rustling the leaves, a chipmunk scrambling across the rock garden. I'm sitting in a rocking chair on the porch of what is now my office, still trying to get used to the idea.

I decided to add this final section after two questions were posed by Brad during a phone call last week, when we were discussing the instructions Richard had left.

As with most entrepreneurs who've built their own business, and many other successful people, there is a belief that people should be able to handle their own personal finances, make their own decisions, and implement them by themselves. Given this, Brad's first question seemed logical:

Do I really need a financial planner?

I could provide you with a laundry list of ideas why I think people need one, but I'll use an analogy instead. We go to the doctor for regular medical checkups. We go to the dentist to ensure our dental health. We take our cars in for regular tune-ups. Why? Preventive maintenance. We use the skills of professionals in order to make sure these aspects of our life run smoothly because we don't have the expertise to do it all ourselves.

So when it comes to personal finance, why wouldn't we call an expert? Someone who understands the problems and issues, has seen it before, and can recommend a course of action. Not only that, but they can help you implement it, and if required will follow-up to ensure the solution is working as well as it should. All the best athletes on the planet have coaches. Why? Discipline, encouragement, instruction, feedback, teamwork, dedication, and they help the athlete maintain their focus. A good financial planner does the same for their clients.

While people do not hesitate to hire experts in other areas of their life, hiring someone to help with money and finances can make people feel like failures. The world of personal finance can be complex to navigate—investment options, taxation issues, wills and estate planning, goal setting, dealing with debt—there are no shortage of issues that financial planners help their clients deal with.

Perhaps the key component that a financial planner brings to the table for a client is objectivity—helping a client come to grips with where they are financially. Once that is done, their ability to educate and manage a client's expectations aids in charting a course of action to build a better, more financially secure future.

Brad's second question fit nicely with the first. Once an individual or couple can answer 'yes' to the 'do I need' question, it leads to the next question.

How does one hire a good financial planner?

I don't believe there is a set answer for this, but here are questions I would suggest you ask and feel comfortable with the answers you receive before you consider hiring anyone.

1) What are your qualifications?

Plenty of people offer financial advice, and many call themselves financial planners. These can range from mutual fund salespeople, stockbrokers, insurance agents, tax accountants, or bank and trust company employees. Financial planning requires experience and a technical understanding of topics such as insurance, tax planning, investment options, estate planning, wills, trusts, to name a few. It's very important to be grounded in all these subjects, as decisions in one area will invariably affect another.

Ask what type of training they have taken and which professional designations they hold. Credentials alone don't indicate competence, but the attainment of them should demonstrate a commitment to the profession. Common credentials are: CFP®—Certified Financial Planner, RFP—Registered Financial Planner, CLU—Chartered Life Underwriter, CFA—Certified Financial Analyst, CSC—Canadian Securities Course, IDA—Investment Dealers Association, MFDA—Mutual Fund Dealers Association. For a complete list as well as descriptions of the designations, I will refer you to the Financial Planners Standards Council Web site at: www.fpsccanada.org. Additionally, for a complete list of investment terminology, I will refer you to the Investment Funds Institute of Canada Web site at: www.ific.ca.

2) What experience do you have?

The financial services sector is known for a relatively high attrition rate. As such, experience is an important consideration. How long have they been with their current firm? Do they own their own firm? How long have they been in the industry? Do they have experience with clients in your similar financial position? What industry designations are they pursuing? What continuing education are they receiving? Are they willing to provide references? Can they provide you with a sample client plan?

While seniority alone should not be the deciding factor, working with someone who has experienced the euphoria of bull markets and despair of the bear can help give you the proper perspective in dealing with the psychology of the market. Helping a client manage their expectations through market cycles is perhaps one of the most important roles of a financial planner.

3) How many clients do you have?

While I don't necessarily feel client count should be a determining factor, it can be an issue. If you are one of a thousand clients, how much personal interaction can you expect to receive? A better question might be —what are the demographics of your client base? If they only work with clients in excess of one million dollars in liquid assets, they may not be willing to devote the time to clients who are in the 'building' phase. If their specialty is working with beginning investors, they may not have the experience with financial trusts, tax advantaged investing and comprehensive estate planning.

4) How do you get paid?

Planners can earn compensation from fees billed to you or from commissions from products sold to you (and there are some who work on a salaried basis for particular firms). Some people feel there is an advantage to 'fee only' because there is no pressure to sell you anything, so you get unbiased advice. Fees can range from an hourly rate for work done, a flat fee to create an individual financial plan, or a fee based on the percentage of assets managed. Fee-only planners may not have any direct motivation (i.e.: commissions) to help you implement the plan so your plan might collect dust on your bookshelf. Having a plan and not implementing it is equivalent to having no plan at all.

Many people feel commissions are bad and lead planners to push products. Good planners may recommend a course of action or a product; they don't urge or pressure clients to buy. If you only focus on cost or commissions, rather than focusing on the value of the recommendation you may short-change yourself. A more important measure should be how your plan functions and whether or not you are achieving the benefits/results you set out in the plan.

Good planners are upfront about their fees and all costs associated with any investment you make. If you don't understand the fees, ask for clarification. Ask for full disclosure of the costs and ensure they provide it. If you have questions about any of the costs, ask. If they aren't prepared to fully disclose and explain the costs, that should bother you.

5) How do they handle their non-expert areas?

I don't feel that a planner can be 100% versed in every aspect of the financial arena, so the planner's business relationships are key. As well, planners have a fiduciary responsibility not to provide advice on areas for which they are not certified or hold designations. Ask if the planner has access to tax specialists, lawyers, business accountants, insurance specialists, etc. What is the cost to use these experts? Sometimes if you are dealing with a planner in a large integrated firm, this expertise is all housed in one place and it is part of a blended fee.

There are probably dozens of other questions that you could and will ask, but I think that these are my top five. Before you speak to any prospective financial planners (and I do recommend that you speak to more than one) it will help if you've done your homework as well. Have some idea of what you want to accomplish and be able to articulate your goals. Referrals can be useful. Who do your friends and family use? Are they satisfied with their level of service, quality of the plan that was developed, and the investment advice they receive? If so, that is a great place to start.

Hiring a financial planner can be a scary thought for many people. In order to build a complete and comprehensive plan, a planner will have to become familiar with your entire financial situation. This means that you have to be comfortable with your planner and willing to share personal information with them. They have to understand your dreams and goals. The thought of discussing that much personal information with a 'stranger' can scare people. Please don't be intimidated. Financial planners aren't there to pass judgment, they exist to help you attain the goals you want for yourself and your family. You are responsible for your part in the planning process; nobody will care more about your money than you will.

Lastly, it's not a contract for life. You are free to terminate a relationship with a financial planner whenever you wish. I suggest that you not do that lightly, but if your needs are not being met, if you are unable to attain your goals, if you feel your planner is no longer listening or meeting your expectations—don't hesitate to change. After all, it is your money, your goals and dreams that are important. Peace of mind with the people who are helping you in the process plays a major factor.

I hope that this section has been useful; I hope the entire book preceding it has been useful in answering some questions about wealth, finance, and how to attain your goals and dreams. As Richard was fond of saying, "Rich isn't something you have, it's something that you become in the process, and it has nothing to do with money."

He couldn't have been more right.

Sincerely,

John Linden

Resources for Financial Planning

The following Organizations and Internet resources can provide valuable information in helping you create a well-structured financial plan.

Organizations

Investment Funds Institute of Canada http://www.ific.ca
- The voice of Canada's investment funds industry and has an Investor Centre section

Financial Planners Standards Council http://www.fpsccanada.org
- Not-for-profit organization developing, promoting and enforcing professional standards

Canadian Investor Protection Fund http://www.cipf.ca
- CIPF provides protection of eligible investments for clients of investment dealers

Canadian Association for the Fifty Plus http://www.carp.ca
- Enhancing the quality of life for all Canadians as we age by advocating for social change

Internet Resources

Rich is a State of Mind http://www.richisastateofmind.com
- Articles, reviews, links to resources and more

Canada MSN Money http://money.ca.msn.com
- Personal finance, investing and business news

Globe & Mail—Globeinvestor http://www.globeinvestor.com
- Information on investing, stocks and personal finance

National Post/Financial Post http://www.financialpost.com
- Canadian business news, investing and commentary

Canadian MoneySaver Magazine http://www.canadianmoneysaver.ca
- Investment advisory providing trustworthy and down-to-earth service since 1981

Canadian Business   http://www.canadianbusiness.com/investing
- Financial planning news and articles, guide to personal investing

Canoe Money   http://www.canoe.ca/Canoe/Money/
- Business news, investing articles and financial tools

Globefund   http://www.globefund.com
- Mutual fund news, reviews and research tools

Canada Revenue Agency   http://www.cra-arc.gc.ca
- Everything you want to know about taxes in Canada

The Fund Library   http://www.fundlibrary.com
- Canada's mutual fund resource centre, articles and more

The TFSA–Tax Free Savings Account

Since January 2009 Canadians have another tool at their disposal for helping to manage their finances and create a successful financial future. The TFSA is designed to help Canadians save for important life goals with the benefit of tax-free growth in the account.

The basic concept is that you put after-tax dollars into a TFSA account, and any and all income earned within the account as well as the original contributions can be removed tax-free in the future. TFSAs are still relatively new and may change as they evolve, but the basics of TFSAs are as follows:

Who
- 18 years or older and a Canadian resident

Where
- Any financial institution eligible to open RRSP accounts

Contribution Facts
- Maximum $5,500 per year, government will adjust periodically for inflation in increments of $500
- Unused room can be carried forward to the future, no limit on carry forward
- No upper age restrictions on contributing to TFSA (RRSP limit is 71)
- More than one TFSA account is allowed, but the total limit is $5,500 per year
- The government will determine and advise you of your TFSA contribution limit for the tax year

Withdrawal Facts
- Withdraw funds at any time for any purpose without incurring any tax
- Amounts withdrawn can be re-invested the following year—you don't lose the contribution room
- TFSA withdrawals will not affect federal income-tested benefits
- No upper age restrictions on withdrawals from a TFSA (RRIF withdrawals start at age 71 even if you don't want to withdraw)

Taxation Facts
- No taxation on interest, dividends or capital gains earned in the TFSA when you make a withdrawal
- Unlike RRSPs, contributions are not tax-deductible
- You can borrow to fund a TFSA, but the interest is not tax-deductible
- Contributions over your TFSA limit will be subject to a penalty tax

Allowable Investments
- Mutual funds, Money market funds, Cash deposits, GICs, Publicly traded stocks, Government and corporate bonds

TFSAs are a great topic for discussion and for Canadian investors they will raise a lot of questions. TFSA or RRSP? How can I use both to my advantage? Is an RRSP for retirement and a TFSA for everything else? Where can I open a TFSA and how does it work once opened? Are there any provincial issues to be concerned with?

The integration of the TFSA into your complete financial planning picture is just another reason that you should utilize the services of a financial advisor. This will help ensure that you are taking complete advantage of all the tools at your disposal to create a successful future.

More information on the Tax Free Savings Account can be found on the Canada Revenue Agency website at: www.cra-arc.gc.ca